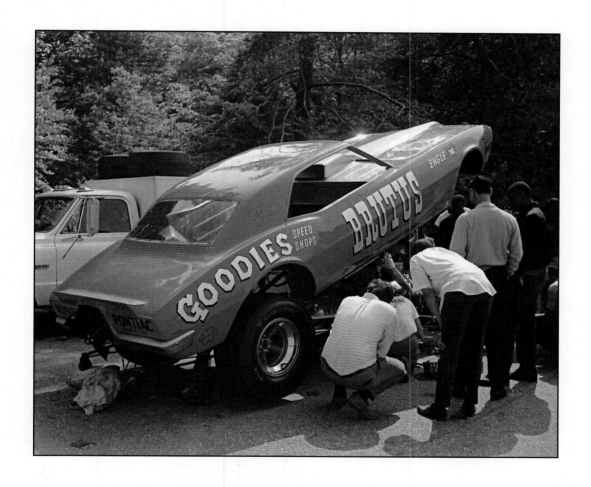

# 1960-1974
# PONTIAC PERFORMANCE

## The Era of Super Duty, H.O., & Ram Air Drag & Muscle Cars

**CarTech®**

**DON KEEFE**

# CarTech®

CarTech®, Inc.
6118 Main Street
North Branch, MN 55056
Phone: 651-277-1200 or 800-551-4754
Fax: 651-277-1203
www.cartechbooks.com

Edit by Wes Eisenschenk
Layout by Connie DeFlorin

ISBN 978-1-61325-777-7
Item No. CT694

Library of Congress Cataloging-in-Publication Data Available

Written, edited, and designed in the U.S.A.
Printed in China
10 9 8 7 6 5 4 3 2 1

**PUBLISHER'S NOTE:** In reporting history, the images required to tell the tale will vary greatly in quality, especially by modern photographic standards. While some images in this volume are not up to those digital standards, we have included them, as we feel they are an important element in telling the story.

Title page photo:
This replica of the original Mickey Thompson/Hayden Proffitt/Lloyd Cox 1962 421 A/FX Tempest was built by Super Duty collector and enthusiast George Knevelbaard in the early 1990s. It is correct—right down to the plug wires. The author currently owns it and has shown it at the 2023 Lake Mirror Concours and the 2023 Muscle Car and Corvette Nationals.

Back cover (bottom photo):
Gary and Charlene Wood earned a class win at the 1976 US Nationals. They are shown here with their trophy and their young daughter Jennifer. (Photo Courtesy Charlene Wood)

Note: Captions for the other photos on the back cover are on the inside pages of this book.

DISTRIBUTION BY:

*Europe*
PGUK
63 Hatton Garden
London EC1N 8LE, England
Phone: 020 7061 1980
Fax: 020 7242 3725
www.pguk.co.uk

*Australia*
Renniks Publications Ltd.
3/37-39 Green Street
Banksmeadow, NSW 2109,
Australia
Phone: 2 9695 7055
Fax: 2 9695 7355
www.renniks.com

*Canada*
Login Canada
300 Saulteaux Crescent
Winnipeg, MB, R3J 3T2 Canada
Phone: 800 665 1148
Fax: 800 665 0103 www.lb.ca

# TABLE OF CONTENTS

**DEDICATION** ................................................................. 6

**ACKNOWLEDGMENTS** ..................................................... 6

**FOREWORD**  by Arnie "the Farmer" Beswick ........................ 7

**PREFACE** ....................................................................... 8

**CHAPTER 1:** Pontiac's Early Years ..................................... 9

**CHAPTER 2:** Semon "Bunkie" Knudsen ............................... 18

**CHAPTER 3:** From Wide Track to Super Duty ........................ 26

**CHAPTER 4:** 1961: 389 and 421 Super Duty Pontiacs Dominate Drag Racing ................. 32

**CHAPTER 5:** 1962: Pontiac Factory-Built Race Cars ................ 40

**CHAPTER 6:** 1963: Pontiac Racing: All in but Then All Done ....... 54

**CHAPTER 7:** 1964: Racing After the Ban and the New GTO ........ 81

**CHAPTER 8:** 1965, 1966, and 1967: The GTO Dominates Muscle Car Sales at Dealerships ............. 92

**CHAPTER 9:** Reaching the Pinnacle: Pontiac's Round-Port Performance Engines ............. 114

**INDEX** ........................................................................... 158

# DEDICATION

This book is dedicated to the memory of my father, Charles A. Keefe, who had a love of cars. This is the first book that I have written since he passed in December 2017, and I think that he would have enjoyed this one the most.

I also dedicate this book to my family: Ann; Rob; Katie; my mother, Shirley; and my brother, Charles.

# ACKNOWLEDGMENTS

Thanks to my long-suffering editor, Wes Eisenschenk, who persevered on my behalf and helped locate hundreds of the photos in this book. He did a wonderful job with this project and pushed me to get this book where it needed to go. I greatly admire his expertise as well as his patience, which I have certainly tested throughout this process. I am proud to call him my friend.

Special thanks to my dear friend, the late Jim Luikens, for opening up his vast collection of photos to me for this project, and thanks to Cyndi Vander Horn and Roger Rosebush for helping to get those photos to me. I appreciate their help with Roger's substantial collection of photos, which he made available for this project.

In addition, very special thanks to Howard Masales, and Mike Huffman who provided me with a wealth of photos of the Packer Pontiac race cars and many other cars from that era. Mike graciously allowed us to photograph his collection of 30 Super Duty Pontiacs at the 2023 Ames Performance Pontiac Nationals. I am grateful for his dedication to preserving those special machines. I included some photos from that historic display.

Clinton Wright is a photographer who was kind enough to provide a huge number of photos from the 1960s. I am grateful for his generosity with his collection.

Thanks to the members of the Pontiac Authors Photo Club, who help each other on book projects with photos and other historical items. The licensing fee is an autographed copy of the book. To Dave Bonaskiewich, Tom DeMauro, Dean Fait, David Newhardt, Rocky Rotella, and Martyn L. Schorr, your signed first editions are coming shortly!

I wish to thank those who helped with information and photos, as well as some very special educators who helped me become an automotive writer and historian: Herb Adams, Matt Adams, Elaine Addington, Gary Atkins, Dr. Donald Bain, Tim Benko, Arnie "the Farmer" Beswick, Dave and Lisa Bisschop, John Bleil, Joe Bortz, Chris and Jodie Brown, David Butler, Jim Butler, Rodney Butler, Imran and Lisa Chaudary, J. B. Clegg, John Clegg, Wade Congdon, Steve Cox, George DeLorean (1932–2022), Steve DeLorean, Jeff Denison, Jim Early Jr., Dean Fait, Ken and Connie Feber, Truman Fields, Ted Fox, Robert Genat, Jack Gifford, the GM Media Archive, Walt Hollifield, Todd Holzknecht, Todd Hoven, Mike and Michael Huffman, Dan Jensen, Dennis Jensen, Don Johnston, Jeff Kauffman, Mark Kauffman, Wayne Kennedy, the Knafel family, Deborah Kritz, William LaDow, Mick Leiferman, Richard Lentinello, Robert Lozins, Jim Luikens (1947–2022), Howard Masales, Ryan Maturski (Dream Giveaways), Jim Mattison, Pete and Jane McCarthy, Lynn and Shiela McCarty, Stacy McCarty, Malcolm R. "Mac" McKellar (1920–2011), Dana Mecum (Mecum Auctions), Jim Mino (1940–2020), Doug Mitchel, David Morton (Mecum Auctions), Ashley Mosher, Jack Mullins, Joel Naprstek, Bob Nelson, Maurice "Moe" Neuburger, Kellen Olshefski (Mecum Auctions), Christopher Phillip (Dream Giveaways), Russ Pflug, Deborah Powless, the Hayden Proffitt family, Dan Purcell, Pat Purcell, Stan Rarden (1951–2023), Jack Ravenna, Andy Rock, the estate of Steve Rollins, Anthony Romano, Nunzi Romano, Rocky Rotella, Rock Running, Ginny Running, Ben Salvador, Martin L. Schorr, Dr. Jim Seward, Lewis Sharp, Fred Simmonds, Geoff Stunkard, Tom and Debbie Stutzman, Larry Swiatek, Scott Tiemann, Mark Tilson, Rick Unterseh, Jim Wangers (1926–2023), Robin Ashley Weatherman, Joe Webber, Eric White (1955–2016), Jean Williams, Randy Williams (1946–2004), Samuel H. Williford, Clinton Wright, Gary Wood (1938–2020), Charlene Wood, Pete and Andrea Woodruff, and Mark Zander.

# FOREWORD BY ARNIE "THE FARMER" BESWICK

What an honor it is to be asked to write the foreword to this book. My most significant qualification may be my age, as I've been around long enough to have seen it all and raced at most of the drag racetracks from the East Coast to the West Coast.

I was a teenager when NASCAR was born, and I *lived* for reading about those race results in the newspapers. If I had lived in the South, I have no doubt that I would have found a way to trade paint on those round southern racetracks. I am still an avid NASCAR fan, and I try to never miss any of its race events. As it turned out for me, my outlet for the need for speed and competition came through drag racing.

In the beginning, I raced various brands of cars and tried to find the best car for the job. Bunkie Knudsen took over Pontiac in 1956, and less than a decade later, I decided to race Pontiacs. I wasn't the only racer who made that decision, as many other drivers switched to Pontiac by 1961 or 1962.

In early 1963, it all came to a crashing end because General Motors pulled the plug on racing and made all of its divisions stop building performance cars.

The success of Ford's Thunderbolt influenced many drivers to switch to that brand. In 1964, Chrysler released its Race Hemi engine, and many of the remaining General Motors drivers went to the Mopar camp. Circle tracks and drag strips were begging for competitive General Motors cars to satisfy that large spectator base. You can be sure that my phone just about rang off the wall because of my competitive Pontiacs.

Being the stubborn German that I am, I found ways to keep my Pontiacs quite competitive for years after that dreaded performance ban. It wasn't until the late 1960s that the skunkworks at Pontiac began to produce better, more competitive parts to help its brand level the playing field. Of course, the tuning skills with Pontiac engines that I previously learned most likely helped my efforts.

I wasn't the only racer who was stubborn and not willing to switch to a different manufacturer. Others kept Pontiac in the limelight, including the Gays from Dickinson as well as Jess Tyree—even if their cars weren't pure Pontiac power. We all began to use aftermarket Pontiac camshafts, filters, and valve springs.

Pure Pontiac power became a thing of the past after 1979, but there were several racers on the circle tracks and drag strips who kept the Pontiac arrow logo in the public eye.

In 2009, the last Pontiac-badged cars were built, and then General Motors took its axe to our beloved division. I'm told that it's a decision the company now regrets, as the Buick sales in China that influenced the decision to keep that brand alive have plummeted. Since Pontiac sales hurt Chevrolet sales, I believe that management was glad to see the axe put to Pontiac, especially after Pontiac reached number three in General Motors sales for a short time.

I still love my Pontiacs and will always be loyal to the brand. In 1960, my Pontiac Ventura put me on the drag-racing map at Daytona Beach. That loyalty was reinforced when I won the first-ever National Hot Rod Association (NHRA)-National Association for Stock Car Auto Racing (NASCAR) nighttime, weeklong Winternationals drag-racing event.

The following year, Wally Parks complained that he didn't make enough money and moved his Winternationals event to Pomona, California, which is in his backyard. I kept going to Florida and had a lot of success during the years that the NASCAR Winternationals took place.

Now, it's time for you to enjoy this special book about the brand that we all love.

# PREFACE

While preparing any historical account, it is necessary to write the relevant facts in a tightly cropped fashion but also to tell the entire story. That seems obvious, but what exactly does it mean? Too often, works that focus on the various topics of automotive history reduce the story of a particular car, developmental program, or generation of vehicles to a bland list of technical facts, dimensions, and other details, such as production numbers and available colors. All details are relevant, but they're only part of the story. If the reader needs to ask why people did what they did or why things happened how they happened, the work is incomplete.

History doesn't take place in a vacuum, and to do the job completely, the author must present those stories within a larger framework that provides context of the times in which they took place. Reading a book that has unanswered questions is not satisfying.

The purpose of this book is to answer the questions above and to present the story of Pontiacs in drag racing so that it covers all of the above. If I am truly successful, this book may even answer a few questions that you may not have thought about.

An example of providing historical context is including information about the Kennedy Administration and the action of then–Attorney General Robert F. Kennedy (RFK). This is likely the first time that RFK has been included in a drag racing history book. In many ways, he had a large hand in the development of the GTO because he set into motion the events that led to the 1963 General Motors ban on racing. Pontiac took the performance message to the street, and the GTO was born. This added context makes the story easier to understand because it completes the picture. It makes no sense that General Motors would suddenly abandon one of the most successful promotional programs and face a possible decline in sales. When a larger picture of the era is presented, the reasoning becomes clearer.

I have chronicled a few different things going on simultaneously: 1) the development story at Pontiac, 2) the lay of the land regarding the larger racing and muscle car market, and 3) the actual racing of those cars. The focus is on cars with the traditional Pontiac V-8 engine, so you won't see anything in this book about cars built after 1981. In addition, there isn't anything more than a sprinkling of the various Pontiac-bodied Funny Cars of the 1960s and 1970s that used powerplants from other manufacturers, such as the Chrysler Hemi. This book focuses on the cars and the people who made the 1955–1981 Pontiac V-8 engine so impactful on the racing world.

As with any book, there will be some omissions. Some items are not covered due to space considerations, a lack of available photography, logistical reasons, or other factors. I apologize in advance if your favorite racer or a racing dealer's story isn't covered. The need for photos and interviewees can make the difference regarding whether a particular car, driver, or group of people are included.

I hope you enjoy reading this book as much as I enjoyed writing it.

Don Keefe
Clearwater, Florida

# CHAPTER 1

# PONTIAC'S EARLY YEARS

To put the story into perspective regarding Pontiac's rise from near cancellation in the early 1950s to its ascension to third place in domestic sales and racing dominance, it is helpful to know its earlier history.

Aside from the short-lived Sheridan nameplate of 1920–1921, the Pontiac brand was the first brand that General Motors created from thin air and stuck. All of the then-current nameplates were independent makes that were purchased as part of the formation of General Motors in 1908 (or soon after). Buick, Cadillac, Chevrolet, Oldsmobile, Rapid Motor Vehicle company and Reliance Motor Car Company (GMC's predecessors), and Oakland (Pontiac's parent company) were all existing marques acquired by William C. "Billy" Durant under the General Motors umbrella.

The marketing plan devised by General Motors President Alfred P. Sloan in the early 1920s was to position these divisions in an order of price point. The buyer began

*This 1926 Pontiac was the first Pontiac that was ever built. Pontiac was billed as the "Chief of the Sixes," and much of its componentry was from the entry-level Chevrolet, which used a 4-cylinder engine. Pontiac and Chevrolet continued to be intertwined for the rest of Pontiac's run. This car is owned by the GM Heritage Collection.*

his career as a young man who needed a lower-priced car, which was a Chevrolet. As he grew older and made more money, he moved up the ladder and purchased Oakland, Oldsmobile, and Buick vehicles until he was in his peak earning years and able to afford a Cadillac. If a person's career or earning potential peaked before they were able to afford a top-of-the-line Cadillac, they'd continue to purchase the brand in their budget and develop loyalty to General Motors. It was a plan that seemed straightforward, but unforeseen issues soon developed.

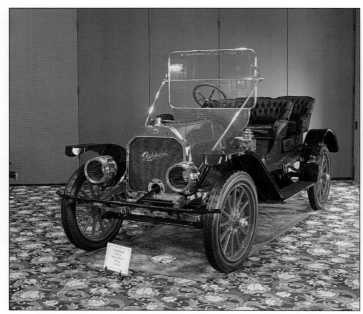

*This 1909 Oakland is part of the GM Heritage Collection. Oakland was an independent, Michigan-based automobile manufacturer that was founded in 1907 and purchased by General Motors in 1909. In 1926, Pontiac was brought to market as a companion to Oakland.*

While the lineup of Chevrolet, Oakland, Oldsmobile, Buick, and Cadillac provided a progression of offerings for a wide range of budgets, by the 1920s, the price differences among the five divisions produced glaring gaps that were being filled by competing manufacturers. Looking at the prices, the differences seem minuscule, but they were actually quite large when accounting for inflation. A single dollar in 1925 is worth $17.85 in 2024, so a seemingly insignificant $200 price difference translates to $3,570 today.

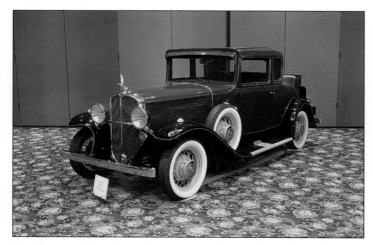

*The last Oakland vehicle was produced in 1931 and featured a V-8 engine that was introduced in 1930. The Model 301 was available in a variety of bodystyles.*

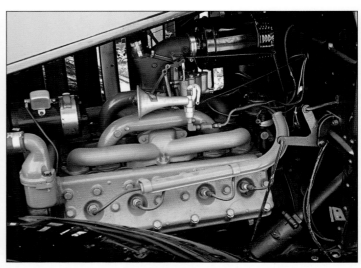

*The first Pontiac V-8 was available only in the 1932 model year. It was inherited from the Oakland and used an unusual horizontal valve-in-block arrangement and a flat-plane, 180-degree crankshaft. Displacing 251 ci, it developed 95 hp with a 5.0:1 compression ratio and a Marvel single-barrel, semi-downdraft carburetor.*

To counter those gaps, new companion divisions were formed. Pontiac was introduced for the 1926 model year as a companion brand priced below Oakland, its parent brand. LaSalle was introduced in 1927 below Cadillac. In 1929, to cover the large gap between Oldsmobile and Buick, Viking was introduced above its parent brand, Oldsmobile. The Marquette nameplate, which was last used by General Motors in 1912, was revived and placed just below its parent brand, Buick.

While the plan was solid, it didn't work as intended. The stock market crash of October 1929 sent the domestic economy into a depression. Marquette was canceled in 1930, and Viking folded in 1931.

Pontiac was successfully placed above Chevrolet and marketed as a 6-cylinder version of the 4-cylinder Chevy. As it offered more value for the price than Oakland, it ultimately killed its host nameplate. In 1932, Pontiac added a V-8-powered Model 302 for one year, which was little more than a rebadged Oakland Model 301. It was a stopgap measure to give Pontiac an 8-cylinder engine, as Chevrolet added a 6-cylinder and needed to have a demonstrable difference in equipment. The V-8 was vibration-prone with its flat crank arrangement and was expensive to produce.

For 1933, Pontiac introduced an all-new straight-8 that was cheaper to produce, much smoother, and offered comparable performance. Combined with all-new Bentley-inspired styling by Franklin Q. Hershey, Pontiac was off and running.

*For the 1940 model year, Pontiacs were available with either an L-head inline 6-cylinder or an 8-cylinder engine. This 1940 Pontiac had the 6-cylinder engine.*

*The 1937 model year featured a new chassis with a redesigned independent front suspension system as well as an all-steel body. This particular model is the rare four-door phaeton.*

In subsequent years, improvements included an independent front suspension, engine upgrades, the addition of an all-new 6-cylinder, and an all-steel top in 1935. In 1937, a new frame with redesigned front suspension and all-steel construction was introduced to replace the rot-prone wood body framing that had been the industry standard since the days of horse-drawn buggies. Sales continued to improve, and by 1941, Pontiac was the only companion brand that remained. LaSalle had been dropped the year before, just in time for the onset of World War II.

For the duration of the war, Pontiac, as with all other carmakers, turned to wartime materiel production and ended the production of automobiles on February 10, 1942. The last of these cars were known as blackout models with painted bumpers and trim to conserve chrome for the war effort. Pontiac's contribution to the war effort included production of Swiss-designed Oerlikon 20-mm anti-aircraft cannons; Swedish-designed Bofors 40-mm automatic field guns; two-stroke General Motors, Detroit Diesel, and GMC 6-cylinder gasoline engine parts; aircraft torpedoes; and M-5 tank axles. In January 1942, Pontiac won the first "E" flag for excellence from Frank Knox, secretary of the Navy. It was the first one presented to any automotive manufacturer.

*While Pontiacs had previously been built as A-Body and B-Body versions, they were also available as a C-Body in the two-door coupe and four-door sedan bodystyles for only the 1940 and 1941 model years. This is a 1940 Torpedo coupe.*

Pontiac soldiered onward with mildly-facelifted versions of its prewar offerings through 1948. This is a 1948 Pontiac Streamliner Eight convertible.

*Pontiac's first postwar redesign came in 1949. This is a 1950 Chieftain Deluxe 8 convertible.*

Under the leadership of General Manager Robert M. Critchfield, who was promoted to the position in 1952, Pontiac expanded its line to include larger, more expensive models to take Pontiac in an upscale direction. Cars such as this 1954 Star Chief Deluxe four-door sedan featured a longer wheelbase and extended rear deck on the A-Body platform. This gave it a size and presence that was similar to the more expensive B-Body offerings from Oldsmobile and Buick. This practice continued on the V-8-powered 1955-1958 Pontiacs.

## The Postwar Market

Pontiac returned to automobile production on September 13, 1945. After nearly four years without a single car being built, demand was overwhelming. The Big Three domestic manufacturers hit the market with mildly-facelifted versions of their last prewar offerings through the end of the 1948 model year while they readied their next-generation offerings. The independents didn't wait, and brands such as Hudson, Studebaker, Kaiser, Frazer, and others introduced all-new cars as a way to get a leg up on the competition.

Pontiac was in a good position after the war, but as time continued, the lack of technical sophistication began to hurt sales. The fully automatic Hydra-matic transmission was not offered in a Pontiac until 1948. A complete restyling came in 1949, but they were pretty much mechanically the same underneath as the earlier version—right down to the L-head inline 6-cylinder and 8-cylinder engines.

Meanwhile in 1949, Oldsmobile and Cadillac had all-new overhead-valve (OHV) V-8 engines. Pontiac was the only General Motors division that offered L-head engines. Buick's Fireball straight-8 and Chevy's Stovebolt 6-cylinder both had an OHV layout. Pontiac was at a distinct disadvantage, and sales began to erode.

## Pontiac V-8 Development

Work on a new V-8 engine began in 1946, and it was originally conceived as an L-Head with horizontal valves, much like the Oakland V-8. The idea increased airflow

*This 1955 Pontiac V-8 display engine shows the compact layout and modern approach to engine design that put it at the front of American production engines of the time. Innovations such as the reverse-flow cooling system and ball-stud rocker-arm system were used in other General Motors engines.*

*Malcolm R. "Mac" McKellar, who lived from August 27, 1920 to April 8, 2011, was one of the chief architects of the 1955 Pontiac V-8. He went on to lead Pontiac's Super Duty racing program and developed competition engines for drag racing and stock-car racing. After his retirement in 1982, McKellar became a regular figure at Pontiac car shows and conventions for the remainder of his life. (Photo Courtesy Malcom R. McKellar)*

*This cutaway image of the 1955 287 Pontiac V-8 engine shows the advances in thin-wall casting technology and the ball-stud rocker-arm system. (Photo Courtesy Malcom R. McKellar)*

over a traditional valve-in-block configuration but wasn't in the same league as a traditional OHV design. The team that developed the Pontiac V-8 included Chief Engineer George Delaney, Roland "Bob" Hutchinson, and Engineers Mark Frank, Clayton B. Leach, Edmund L. Windeler, George Roberts, and the legendary Malcolm R. "Mac" McKellar, who did much of the drawing-board work.

While it was attractive from a cost standpoint, the horizontal-valve flathead was soon deemed to be obsolete, and the idea was discarded. Pontiac engineers worked on a variety of designs. Some used Oldsmobile blocks before efforts were concentrated on a 268-ci OHV V-8 of its own design in 1949. It was an oversquare design that featured many of the technical innovations that were pioneered in the earlier Kettering V-8s, plus several new innovations. News of Chevrolet's new V-8 being 265 ci prompted Pontiac to finalize the bore and stroke at 3.75 x 3.25 inches to provide a displacement of 287 ci,

which was sufficiently larger than the Chevy and added a bit of a gap between the two marques. With a bore center of 4.62 inches, there was ample room for growth. The rods and crankshaft were made of forged steel, the main journal diameter measured 2.5 inches, and the rods featured a 6.625-inch center-to-center length. Valve sizes were 1.78 inches for the intake and 1.5 inches for the exhaust.

The Pontiac V-8 engine design was built with several objectives in mind. Pontiac was a lower mid-priced vehicle line so the production costs were a primary concern, although the budget was not quite as tight as Chevrolet's. As a result, Pontiac V-8s featured some unique innovations, such as reverse-flow cooling, completely machined combustion chambers, and an innovative treatment of the distributor. The block was cast with the right bank slightly ahead of the left which allowed the distributor to be mounted on the right side of the cam gear. This directed thrust upward to give superior lubrication and

*Pontiac built two 1954 Bonneville Special Motorama cars to allow the exciting new design to be shown at two locations at the same time. It gave showgoers a glimpse into Pontiac's new performance-oriented mindset. Both cars are survivors and were shown together for the first time at the 2003 Eyes on Design Classic Car Show in Michigan.*

reduce wear. The distributor itself was mounted on a separate pad at the rear of the block, which allowed the intake manifold to be removed without touching the distributor. This allowed the fuel pump to be mounted on the driver's side of the engine, and the exhaust system exited on the passenger's side to keep the fuel cooler.

Both Chevy and Pontiac V-8s were the recipients of Pontiac's unique ball-stud rocker-arm system, which was developed by Pontiac engineer Clayton B. Leach in 1948. He was a skilled machinist who developed the innovative system in his home shop.

Leach's system eliminated costly rocker-arm shafts and forged rocker arms, which reduced the cost and valvetrain weight. His breakthrough design used stamped rocker arms that were cheap to manufacture and were very durable. A stud placed in the cylinder head for each rocker arm eliminated the rocker-shaft cradles to further reduce cost. It was so brilliant in its simplicity that it was clear that General Motors executives were not going to keep the idea as a Pontiac exclusive. It was shared with Chevrolet and helped to make a huge push forward to give Chevrolet its own V-8 engine.

While some Pontiac engineers bemoaned that their innovation was given to Chevy (General Motors usually gave the division that developed an innovation a one-year exclusive use), the bottom line was that it reduced costs and benefitted both divisions and the larger General Motors corporation. Pontiac saved the day for everyone involved.

In addition to the innovations in the design itself, there were many innovations on the manufacturing end. To cut costs and increase precision, the number of cores required to build a typical V-8 engine was 18. With improvements made at a corporate level about casting technology, Pontiac and Chevy V-8s benefitted from this improvement program because they were the last of the first-generation General Motors OHV V-8s to be released. In the case of Pontiac's V-8, the number of cores needed to cast the engine was reduced to eight. In the process, the accuracy and precision of the finished castings significantly improved and reduced the cost for the castings and the amount of machining needed to make them into functional parts. It was a win-win proposition.

As it turned out, the Pontiac V-8 was brought to market two full model years later than originally intended. Approximately 24 1953 Pontiacs were fitted with V-8 engines for testing purposes. All production 1953 and 1954 Pontiac frames were drilled for V-8 engine mounts in anticipation of an earlier introduction date.

Several issues came into play, including timing delays to prevent watering down the introduction of the 1953 Buick Nailhead V-8 and an economic recession from the summer of 1953 to the spring of 1954, which caused General Motors to delay the release. Perhaps the most significant setback was the sudden death of Pontiac General Manager Arnold B. Lenz and his wife, Amelia, in a tragic car/train collision in LaPeer, Michigan, in 1952. Lenz was skilled in manufacturing, and his loss was a setback for the development of the Pontiac V-8.

Robert M. Critchfield was named as Lenz's replacement, and Pontiac's focus changed somewhat under his direction. He was left to deal with an incomplete engine program and falling sales from the technological advancements of competitive carmakers, so he set out to stabilize the troubled division, release the V-8 engine, and focus on recasting Pontiac as a more upscale choice in the mid-priced field. The introduction of the larger Star Chief line in 1954 and the introduction of air conditioning to the options list are examples to move Pontiac further away from Chevy and to better counter the competition.

> "PRODUCTION OF THE NEW PONTIAC V-8 ENGINE COINCIDED WITH THE RELEASE OF THE NEW-GENERATION 1955 PONTIAC LINE. THE NEW CAR WAS ONLY AVAILABLE WITH A V-8 ENGINE."

### The V-8 Engine Arrives

Production of the new Pontiac V-8 engine coincided with the release of the new-generation 1955 Pontiac line. The new car was only available with a V-8 engine. As with the straight-8, the L-head 6-cylinder was dropped once and for all.

The new 287 was offered in three versions. The first version featured a 7.4:1 compression ratio and a 2-barrel carburetor for manual-transmission applications. At the time, lower compression ratios were used with stick-shift cars to help reduce the chance of detonation while lugging at low RPM. It was rated at 173 hp at 4,400 rpm with 256 ft-lbs of torque at 2,400 rpm. The version used with the Hydra-matic featured an 8.0:1 compression ratio and was otherwise identical. It was rated at 180 hp at

*The all-new 1955 Pontiac featured the new V-8 engine and A-Body platform that it shared with Chevrolet. In addition to the larger V-8 engine, the Pontiac boasted the 4-speed General Motors Hydra-matic transmission as optional equipment. Chevrolet had to make do with the 2-speed Powerglide automatic transmission.*

4,600 rpm with 264 ft-lbs of torque at 2,400 rpm. The third version came to market later in the year and featured the higher compression ratio and a 4-barrel carburetor. It was rated at 200 hp at 4,600 rpm with 264 ft-lbs of torque at 2,400 rpm. It was available with both manual and automatic transmissions.

The engine proved to be trouble-free and reliable. It was a result of more than 1 million miles of testing, which was unheard of at the time and was partially due to the release delays. Pontiac management was very concerned about maintaining its reputation for rock-solid reliability, and the new engine shined in that area. It was very light on warranty claims for a new engine, which was something that the 265 Chevy could not boast right out of the gate. Some manufacturing problems resulted in an uptick in warranty claims, but Chevy was

*Pontiac's first high-performance V-8 engine was the 285-hp, 316-ci Strato-Streak V-8. It featured 10.0:1 compression, a hot hydraulic-lifter camshaft, and a dual-quad induction system. The new engine was met with surprise from the market. At the time, no one expected a hot rod V-8 from Pontiac. Things were certainly changing for the better.*

able to correct the issues quickly.

*MotorTrend* tested a 1955 Star Chief sedan with a 2-barrel carburetor and Hydra-matic for its March 1955 issue. While the performance specifications aren't impressive from a modern standpoint, they were light-years ahead of the car's predecessors. The new Pontiac posted a 0-to-60 time of 13.8 seconds (about 5 seconds quicker than the previous model), a quarter-mile elapsed time of 19.7 seconds, and a top speed of 102 mph. It averaged 16.5 mpg. There was room for improvement, and Pontiac stepped up.

For the 1956 model year, Pontiac enlarged the 287 engine by increasing the bore from 3.75 to 3.94 inches and retained the same 3.25-inch stroke. The resulting displacement checked in at 316.6 ci. With little in the way of other changes beyond a little more compression, power made a significant jump. The base synchromesh version featured an 8.0:1 compression ratio and a 2-barrel carburetor, and it was rated at 202 hp at 4,600 rpm with 294 ft-lbs of torque at 2,600 rpm. The Hydra-matic version featured an 8.9:1 compression ratio and a slightly hotter 273-degree-duration cam and was rated at 205 hp at 4,600 rpm with 294 ft-lbs of torque at 2,600 rpm. The 4-barrel version increased output to 227 hp at 4,800 rpm with 312 ft-lbs of torque at 3,000 rpm. This larger engine increased performance in all aspects, but the big gun soon turned heads toward Pontiac.

## The Strato-Streak V-8 is Released

The February 1956 issue of *Pontiac Service Craftsman News* announced the availability of a new high-performance version of the Pontiac V-8 that was intended for high-performance and competition use. The Strato-Streak V-8 was a significant departure from Pontiac's rather staid persona, and it showed America that the rebirth of Pontiac was well underway. Critchfield's vision was starting to take hold. Although he hasn't received the credit that was due to him for beginning Pontiac's transition from the reliable-but-boring line of lower-to-mid-priced cars to a more upscale position, positive things began to happen.

Motorama show cars, such as the 1954 Bonneville Special, 1954 Strato-Streak, and the 1955 Strato-Star pointed the way to future possibilities and indicated that change was on the horizon. While the new 1955 OHV V-8s finally put them on par with the competition, this new hot rod engine was the first indication that Pontiac was not simply trying to keep up with the crowd.

The Strato-Streak shared the same bore and stroke as the rest of the 1956 Pontiac engines, but several key changes were made. A compression-ratio increase to 10:1 was accomplished by milling the cylinder heads to reduce the combustion-chamber size. To maintain valvetrain geometry, the valves were 3/32-inch longer than normal.

The Strato-Streak V-8 featured a new hydraulic-lifter camshaft that was designed for increased airflow, RPM potential, and horsepower. It featured 289/298 degrees of duration and 0.406-inch lift. It was ground on 111.2-degree lobe centerlines and used special heavy-duty valve springs.

Topping off this formidable engine was an equally formidable induction system that consisted of a special dual-quad intake manifold (casting number 523554) that mounted a pair of Rochester 4-barrel carburetors (casting number 7009820), which used a common Delta Wing oil-bath air cleaner.

The engine featured a substantial jump in performance over the single 4-barrel 316 and was rated at 285 hp at 5,100 rpm with 330 ft-lbs of torque at 3,600 rpm. This was a number that was unheard of from a Pontiac and was 224 percent more powerful than the best 1954 straight-8 ever made. Pontiac had come a long way in a short time, and more was on the horizon.

To capitalize on the newfound performance advantage, Pontiac enlisted the legendary David Abbot "Ab" Jenkins to come out of retirement and help promote the new hot Pontiac. At the age of 73, the *Mormon Meteor* held the all-time record for the most speed records at the time.

In June 1956, Jenkins and his son Marvin took a Strato-Streak-powered Pontiac 860 sedan to the Bonneville Salt Flats for a 24-hour endurance record attempt on the 10-mile round track. Driving more than two-thirds of the 2,841 miles himself, Jenkins and his son averaged 118.337 mph and shattered all the American Unlimited and Class C Stock records. In addition, they set a 100-mile record average of 126.02 mph. Sadly, Jenkins died of a heart attack on August 9, 1956, after attending a baseball game with two Pontiac executives.

Although Pontiac hired veteran IndyCar Mechanic Louie Meyer to prepare two 1956 Strato-Streak-powered Pontiac sedans for NASCAR, no drag-racing efforts had been backed at this point. That soon changed.

*Semon E. "Bunkie" Knudsen was born on October 2, 1912, in Buffalo, New York. As Pontiac's general manager, he was under tremendous pressure to save the ailing division and uphold his family's tradition for excellence. He succeeded in both areas. (Photo Courtesy General Motors Media Archive)*

CHAPTER 2

# SEMON "BUNKIE" KNUDSEN

The appointment of 43-year-old Semon Emil "Bunkie" Knudsen as Pontiac's general manager was impressive. He was the youngest divisional general manager and General Motors vice president in history. The aspect of this situation that is seldom understood is that the new job was full of obstacles.

Knudsen was a car guy from the beginning. As a teenager, he was interested in mechanical items of any kind. When he asked his father for a car, his father bought him a Chevrolet in kit form that was to be assembled locally and used in foreign regions. Dutifully, the enterprising young man assembled it himself.

After high school, Knudsen attended Dartmouth University for two years before transferring to the Massachusetts Institute of Technology (MIT), where he graduated in 1939 with a bachelor's degree in general engineering.

Later in 1939, he began his career at General Motors with Pontiac as a tool engineer. He spent 10 years in that department and rose to the position of general master mechanic. When World War II began, Knudsen was 29 years old. Although he was eligible for the draft, General Motors kept him stateside, where his talents were better suited for the war effort. In 1950, he moved on to the General Motors Process Development Section, and in 1953, he was promoted to manufacturing manager at Allison. In 1955, he became the general manager of the Detroit Diesel engine division.

Knudsen's upward trajectory was a result of his strong drive and a determination to live up to his father's legacy. He was the son of the late General Motors president and three-star US General William "Big Bill" Knudsen, so his success or failure would have a lasting effect on his family's legacy. The elder Knudsen passed away in 1949 and was highly regarded in the automotive industry.

## The Situation

Even though Pontiac received attention from General Motors in the last few years, sales didn't respond as quickly as upper management expected. Although Knudsen's predecessor, Robert M. Critchfield, was seen as a positive influence on the division amidst chaos and unplanned production delays, he was nearing the end of his career. It was obvious that he was not the long-term solution. He was the right man at the right time, but he was up against GM's forced retirement age of 65.

*When Robert M. Critchfield took the helm at Pontiac, there was a great deal of turmoil that was prompted by the sudden death of his predecessor, Arnold B. Lenz. Critchfield did a skillful job of steadying the ship and bringing the Pontiac V-8 into production. In 1954, Critchfield is seen here (left) with Sales Manager Frank Bridge and the 1954 Strato-Streak Motorama car. Critchfield pointed the division in the right direction, but he was close to mandatory retirement. The task of moving the division into a new era went to Bunkie Knudsen. (Photo Courtesy General Motors Media Archive)*

Knudsen understood that his job was to save Pontiac. Significant changes were needed, and if those changes weren't successful, Pontiac would be shut down and the dealership structure would merge with Oldsmobile. Nevertheless, Knudsen took over the troubled division and knew that failure would mean the end of the Pontiac nameplate and, most likely, the end of his career at General Motors. That would be devastating for any young executive, but Bunkie Knudsen was not just *any* young executive. He was Big Bill's son. Expectations were exceptionally high, and he was ready for the challenge.

The situation that Knudsen inherited when he began as Pontiac's general manager was anything but enviable. The 1956-model-year Pontiac sales were down to 358,688 units (compared to 581,860 units in 1955), which reduced the marque's total market share to 6.02 percent. Much of the sales drop was due to the success of Chevrolet's model lineup. Other factors included quality-control issues, which were occurring at other General Motors divisions as well, and the

small-but-significant increase in sales by Ford and Chrysler.

Knudsen understood Pontiac's biggest problem was its image in the market. Pontiac's image was that it was a boring machine chosen by sensible, boring people. That image needed to change.

### The Plan

To implement a new image, the old image needed to be destroyed. Knudsen did so in a dramatic fashion by tearing away one of Pontiac's most enduring design icons: the Silver Streaks. The hood treatment, which was first used in 1935 by designer Franklin Q. Hershey, was removed by Knudsen late in the development stage of the 1957 program.

While it may not seem significant from a contemporary perspective, it is akin to removing the blue oval from Ford or the bowtie from Chevy. It was a symbolic gesture and a very bold move. In a similar vein, he removed the Indian-head hood ornament. From that point moving forward, the only place that an Indian head could be found on a Pontiac was on the high-beam indicator, which was done simply to keep the trademark active. It was no longer business as usual at Pontiac, and it was a hot topic of conversation in Detroit.

Realizing that the postwar Baby Boomer generation would be driving soon, marketers of all types began catering to them. Knudsen redirected Pontiac's focus toward this market.

"You can sell a young man's car to an old man, but you cannot sell an old man's car to a young man," he said.

That mindset did a great job of attracting the current crop of younger buyers and changed the way that the public looked at Pontiac. By the time that the Boomers would be old enough to drive, the groundwork was more than ready to cater to their specific needs.

Knudsen needed the backing of the engineering department to achieve his goals. He quickly acted and

> **" YOU CAN SELL A YOUNG MAN'S CAR TO AN OLD MAN, BUT YOU CANNOT SELL AN OLD MAN'S CAR TO A YOUNG MAN. "**

*Elliott M. "Pete" Estes was recruited by Knudsen and came to Pontiac from the Oldsmobile division, where he was instrumental in the release of the famed J-2 engine that featured a trio of 2-barrel carburetors. (Photo Courtesy General Motors Media Archive)*

*John Z. DeLorean came to Pontiac after working for Packard, where he earned praise for developing an innovative torque converter for the Ultramatic transmission. Knowing that Packard's days as a company were numbered, he accepted an invitation to work for General Motors from Oliver K. Kelley, who was head of the GM transmission group. DeLorean chose to go to Pontiac due to its youthful, performance-oriented mindset. Less than a decade later, he ran the division. (Photo Courtesy General Motors Media Archive)*

formed a new, younger engineering team to develop high-performance engines and drivetrain packages. That team included Elliott M. "Pete" Estes, who became chief engineer and replaced George Delaney, who had been in the position since 1947 and had been with Pontiac since 1934. Like McKellar, Estes graduated from the General Motors Institute and advanced his way through the corporation in the Oldsmobile division. He worked directly with Charles "Boss" Kettering and was part of the team that brought the 1949 Oldsmobile V-8 into production.

Estes had been a key engineer in the development of the J-2 high-performance package for the Rocket V-8, which included a trio of 2-barrel carburetors. As a result, Pontiac was able to quickly develop a similar package and get it into production for the 1957 model year. He also had a lot of experience with high-compression engines. As a result, compression ratios began to climb in the Pontiac V-8s.

The youthful image that Pontiac was developing was also reflected in another of Knudsen's hires. John Z. DeLorean was just 31 years old when he was hired as an engineering assistant who reported to both Estes and Knudsen. Although he was a young man, he was unusually qualified and experienced.

After a short stint at Chrysler, DeLorean moved on to Packard in 1953 and designed a dual-range torque converter for the Ultramatic transmission. The new transmission was named the Twin-Ultramatic. DeLorean's expertise was noticed by Oliver K. Kelley, who was head of the General Motors Transmission Group at the time, and Kelley offered DeLorean a position at General Motors. Seeing the new youth-oriented direction that Pontiac was headed, DeLorean chose to work for Pontiac, and it proved to be a fantastic fit for the new management group. He and Knudsen developed a fast friendship, and,

together with Estes, they began to reinvent the division.

In addition to the newly-hired talent, Knudsen had a long-time engineer who was already engineering the componentry that powered the transformation. Although Malcolm R. "Mac" McKellar was only four years older than DeLorean, he had been with Pontiac since 1937 and started out as a General Motors Institute co-op student assigned to Pontiac. By the late 1940s, he was part of the team that was assigned to design a V-8 engine for Pontiac. McKellar was very loyal to Pontiac and was a performance enthusiast. Although Pontiac was a stodgy type of carmaker in his early years with the division, McKellar made a big impact on the performance potential of the Pontiac V-8 engine's initial design and soon capitalized on that platform.

With the new management team in place and a performance-oriented mission statement, McKellar was positioned to make a massive impact. His expertise in camshaft and cylinder-head technology was used as never before. Fresh from his experience with the 285-hp Strato-Streak V-8, McKellar was ready, willing, and able to begin development work on a new series of high-performance, race-oriented engines. While the upcoming Tri-Power and fuel-injected 1957 V-8 engines were a step in the right direction, those somewhat exotic induction systems sat on top of fairly mild camshaft and cylinder head specifications and were intended for street use. There was much more serious hardware in development for competition.

The Pontiac V-8 became larger in displacement every year since its introduction. Anticipating the inevitable horsepower war, the Pontiac V-8 was built with plenty of room to grow. A generous 4.62-inch bore center and tall 10.24-inch nominal deck height (more than an inch taller than the Chevy small-block) allowed for long rod-to-stroke ratios. This allowed for slower piston speeds, reduced stress on cylinder walls, and room for longer strokes, which would be helpful in years to come. The block itself was a sturdy design and featured generous webbing in the main saddles. The reverse-flow cooling system directed water first to the cylinder heads and then to the block to control heat buildup and detonation. It was a great foundation upon which to build.

In 1955, the initial version was 287 ci, and displacement increased to 316 ci in 1956 as a result of a bore increase to 3.94 inches. In 1957, displacement increased to 347 ci with a stroke increase to 3.56 inches. The longer stroke came with an increase in main journal diameter to maintain proper crank-pin overlap.

The introduction of larger displacements, as well as multiple carburetion and compression ratios, was a clear indication that Knudsen was serious about changing Pontiac's sleepy persona. He made two very bold moves to achieve those goals. First, he purposely ignored the 1957 AMA ban on racing. The ban was a gentleman's agreement made among the Detroit automakers to curb their racing activities. The many reasons ranged from worries about corporate responsibility and cost concerns to spending excessive amounts of money on what was considered by many to be a regional phenomenon.

In 2009, legendary Pontiac Advertising Executive Jim Wangers spoke to Pontiac Talk Podcast host Mark Zander about that era.

"At that time [1956], Bunkie Knudsen made up his mind to go racing," Wangers said. "He quickly picked out members from his engineering group (the guys he knew had a real enthusiasm for performance) and went on to create the Super Duty Group. They created the Super Duty engine, a special version of the Pontiac V-8. In 1957, the Automobile Manufacturers Association (AMA) formed a gentleman's agreement to back out of organized auto racing and motorsports of any kind.

"The AMA was not pleased to be led around by the nose and to throw money at hillbillies [who were] trying to help them beat each other on their own racetracks. Bunkie had other ideas, though.

"'To hell with those guys,' Bunkie said in reference to the AMA agreement. 'I've got a division to save, and we're going racing.'

"The rest of the automakers went to sleep, and Pontiac went racing in full force. The Super Duty group went to work making more horsepower than ever with regular Pontiac engines and began to win on the racetrack. By 1961, Pontiac was dominating absolutely everything."

Knudsen was committed to saving Pontiac and even partially funded the factory racing teams out of his own pocket. Several Pontiac stock cars had the phrase "Sponsored by S.E. Knudsen" painted on their body sides.

## Tri-Power Comes to Pontiac

With his expertise in multi-carburetion, Chief Engineer Elliott "Pete" Estes sped up the introduction of the new optional Tri-Power version of the 347 engine. It was released a few weeks after Oldsmobile's famed J-2 engine, which featured a trio of 2-barrel carburetors. It was rated at 290 hp at 5,000 rpm with 375 ft-lbs of torque at 2,800 rpm. It was optional for all models except the limited-edition Bonneville.

The Tri-Power system was popular with performance fans because it was a relatively inexpensive upgrade that used a progressive linkage that allowed only the center carburetor to operate under normal driving conditions. The end carburetors opened at full throttle to allow additional airflow and power without sacrifices in drivability. The visual appeal of lifting the hood to display a trio of carburetors was an added bonus.

## A New Divisional Flagship

The 1957 model year saw the introduction of Pontiac's new flagship vehicle: the Bonneville. Available only as a two-door convertible, the Bonneville was a bold statement for Pontiac's reinvention as a high-performance, youth-oriented carmaker. It was intended to compete with already-established upscale performance cars, including the Chrysler 300, DeSoto Golden Adventurer, and Dodge D-500. Only 630 production models were built, which were allocated one at a time to the highest-sales-volume dealers. The reports of one Bonneville per dealer is not valid because more than 2,000 dealers existed nationwide in 1957.

The Bonneville featured several design cues that separated it from other 1957 Pontiacs. The front fenders featured "fuel injection" block-letter callouts above the front wheels and seven forward-leaning hashmarks behind the wheel well.

The rear trim was highlighted by a longer, rocket-shaped molding that filled the entire length of the side molding, which eliminated the side stars that were seen on other Star Chiefs. "Bonneville" callouts were placed on the trailing edge of the rear fins. In addition, a ribbed aluminum trim panel (similar to the one on the Transcontinental Safari wagon) was used. In the rear, the dual exhaust exited through the bumpers, and "fuel injection" block letters sat between two small chrome accent spears.

The Bonneville was a showcase for Pontiac's rapidly evolving technical expertise. In addition to offering nearly every luxury and convenience option that was available on lesser models as standard equipment, including leather seating and the Autronic Eye headlamp dimmer, the Bonneville offered exclusive features that included six-way adjustable seats and a special high-compression, fuel-injected version of the 347 engine. Utilizing a Rochester mechanical fuel-injection system that was similar to the one used on Chevy's 283 engine, the Bonneville featured a higher 10.25:1 compression ratio. Although horsepower was not initially reported, Pontiac later rated the engine at 310 hp at 4,800 rpm with 400 ft-lbs of torque at 3,400 rpm.

*Pontiac's first true halo (flagship) car was the 1957 Bonneville convertible. Along with two prototypes, only 630 were built. This car was developed to give the public a glimpse at Pontiac's new high-performance, youth-oriented identity. In addition to innovations that included a six-way adjustable seat and Autronic Eye automatic high-beam dimmer, the Bonneville was powered by an exclusive and technologically sophisticated, fuel-injected V-8, and it had several unique design cues.*

*Although it's difficult to see under the large intake cover and air cleaner, the fuel-injected 347 was a true state-of-the-art engine for the American market in 1957. The engine was only available in the Bonneville, and it was rated at 310 hp at 4,800 rpm with 400 ft-lbs of torque at 3,400 rpm. The fuel-injection system was similar to the unit that was used with the 283 Chevy. These engines were a bit temperamental to tune, but when they were running correctly, they were formidable competitors.*

## Pontiac Gets Serious

Knudsen was aware that even though there was some racing success with the 347 Tri-Power, he knew that the competition wasn't going to sit still. The factory released a camshaft upgrade that increased the output of the Tri-Power 347 to 317 hp. It was good but not enough to keep earning wins for much longer. An additional setback came when NASCAR's Bill France outlawed multiple carburetors and fuel injection during the 1957 season. Things had to change for Pontiac to remain competitive.

Knudsen assigned his team the task of developing higher-output powerplants to set a new standard for Pontiac performance for racing and high-performance street use. The plan of enlarging the bore from 3.94 to 4.06 inches resulted in a new 370-ci displacement. The new larger engine came with additional breathing upgrades, including new cylinder heads that featured 17-percent-larger exhaust ports and matching low-restriction exhaust manifolds. These upgrades, among others, provided a solid base for the high-performance options.

For 1958, the fuel-injection option returned as an option on any model. At

Although factory support for Pontiacs had not entered the drag-racing circles, many racers saw the advantages of the 1957 Pontiac Chieftain's combination, including less weight than the Oldsmobiles and Buicks as well as larger engines than the Chevys. It put Pontiac in a sweet spot for street performance and drag racing. Soon, the factory got in on the action.

nearly $500, it was rarely ordered, and only about 400 were built. The system was a carryover from 1957, except for a new cast-aluminum intake manifold, which replaced the steel tubing unit that was used in 1957. Also carried over was the power rating. As with 1957's 347 engine, the 1958 fuel-injected 370 engine was rated at 310 hp at 4,800 rpm with 400 ft-lbs of torque at 3,400 rpm.

*These two cars are 1958 Bonnevilles. When the Bonneville returned for 1958, a two-door hardtop coupe was added, and the engine lineup was expanded. The base engine was a 4-barrel version of the 370 and Tri-Power versions were available. The fuel-injected version had the same rating as the 1957 fuelie: 310 hp at 4,800 rpm with 400 ft-lbs of torque at 3,400 rpm. Although the Bonneville was considered to be a limited-edition model, production increased to 12,240 units.*

The 1958 Pontiacs were completely redesigned. They had a new cruci-form X-chassis that had no side rails and lowered the floor pan, four-wheel coil-spring suspension, and new Motorama-inspired styling. This styling included an innovative quad headlamp system, a wraparound windshield, and rocket-shaped side spears.

The 1958 370-ci T-395A Tempest V-8 was Pontiac's first serious attempt at a competition-bred engine after Knudsen's appointment as general manager. With a hotter cam, more compression, and a heavy-duty valvetrain, the 370 engine's horsepower level increased to 330 to keep Pontiac competitive in stock drag-racing classes and NASCAR. This is an entry-level Chieftain, which was the smallest and lightest 1958 Pontiac available, which made it the prime choice for racers and performance fans.

The trio of Rochester 2-barrel carburetors were the direct result of having Elliott "Pete" Estes appointed as chief engineer. Estes came to Pontiac from Oldsmobile and had developed Oldsmobile's J-2 system that used three Rochester 2-barrel carburetors. This increase in performance captured the attention of performance enthusiasts. Pontiac's reputation quickly changed from being an old lady's car to engaging the youth market.

The 1958 model year featured the introduction of the new 370-ci Tempest T-395A V-8 engines, which were intended for competition use. In March 1958, 4-barrel and Tri-Power versions were introduced. The 4-barrel version was intended primarily for NASCAR, and the Tri-Power version aimed at drag racing. This was Knudsen's first opportunity to develop and market true competition-bred engines and pick up where the 1956 dual-quad V-8 left off.

The 4-barrel version of the T-395A (code PK) was rated at 315 hp at 5,000 rpm with 400 ft-lbs of torque at 2,800 rpm. The Tri-Power version, which was aimed at drag racing, was rated at 330 hp at 5,000 rpm with 415 ft-lbs of torque at 3,000 rpm. Aside from the induction system, the two engines were identical and used the same

*The rear of the 1958 Pontiac continued the theme of wraparound glass to the rear, and the quad-element taillamps mimicked the headlamps. This was a one-year-only design, as the 1959 Wide Tracks were once again completely redesigned.*

high-performance cylinder heads with heavy-duty valve springs and 10.5:1 compression as well as the same 886 hydraulic camshaft, which featured 283/293 degrees of advertised duration and 0.406-inch lift.

Around this time, drag racers began regarding Pontiac as a viable racing platform. Although there had been some focus in some of the earlier efforts, such as the 285-hp dual-quad engine and the fuelies, most of the interest that Pontiac was generating was with stock-car racing. With teams headed by legendary names, including Louie Meyer, John Zink, Smokey Yunick, and Ray Nichels, making headlines, it was clear to the drag racing community that Pontiac's research and development would pay dividends in their arena. Pontiac was ignoring the 1957 AMA Racing Ban as a means to market its performance. Knudsen had a division to save and wouldn't let that backroom pact destroy Pontiac and his own career.

In the three-and-a-half years since introduction of the Pontiac V-8 for the 1955 model year, the engine had grown by 83 ci, and the top available output increased to 130 hp. With Bunkie Knudsen at the helm, it was the tip of the iceberg. The "Race on Sunday; sell on Monday" philosophy was firmly planted into Pontiac's marketing strategy. Racing and high-performance street cars were changing the way that people felt about Pontiac. Even if not everyone bought a fuel-injected Bonneville or Tri-Power Catalina hardtop, people were influenced to go to dealerships, where they often purchased something a little more in line with their needs and/or budgets.

## The "Farmer" Chooses Pontiac

Midwestern drag racer Arnie Beswick began racing in 1953. He originally raced an Oldsmobile as a privateer but switched to Dodge and competed with a D500-1 Coronet in 1956 and a D-501 in 1957. By that time, he was frustrated with the nose-heavy Dodge, its lack of traction, and its fragile transmission.

Looking to jump ship and not being on the already-full Chevy bandwagon, he admired the 1957 Tri-Power Pontiacs at his local drag strip. When the engine was enlarged for 1958, he purchased a 1958 Pontiac Chieftain with a T-395A powerplant, 3-speed manual transmission, and Safe-T-Track differential. He soon began to accumulate wins. He saw that Pontiac was the way to go with Knudsen at the helm. Not only were its cars performing but its management also aggressively promoted racing. Beswick went on to be the longest-running Pontiac drag racer in history.

*Morrison, Illinois-based drag racer, Arnie "the Farmer" Beswick switched to Pontiac after competing in Dodges for a few seasons. His first Pontiac, a 1958 T395A Chieftain two-door sedan, is seen here in stock form. (Photo Courtesy Dean Fait)*

*This is Arnie Beswick's 1958 Chieftain after it had been converted to a C/Gasser. Beswick continues to be a legendary figure in the Pontiac world, and his ties to the Pontiac nameplate are inseparable. (Photo Courtesy Dean Fait)*

# CHAPTER 3

# FROM WIDE TRACK TO SUPER DUTY

The 1958 General Motors lineup was a one-year-only affair, as increased pressure from Chrysler's upcoming Forward Look styling under Design Chief Virgil Exner proved to be a decisive game-changer. General Motors designers who had a clandestine peek at the new Mopar designs immediately changed course and devised a new, sleeker, more athletically-pleasing design for their models across the company.

Pontiac's product line benefitted from this new body-style lineup. The styling featured an aggressive new split grille with quad headlamps. In the back, V-shaped fins and slotted taillamps ushered in a new design.

Of equal importance was the addition of the new Wide Track stance. The term, coined by Pontiac advertising copywriter Milt Colson, was added to a Pontiac chassis feature that moved the wheels out farther than a comparable Chevrolet. This gave the Pontiac a more pleasing appearance and, as a secondary benefit, improved handling. Soon, Wide Track Pontiacs were seemingly everywhere—most notably, in the winner's circle.

As with each previous year, the displacement of the Pontiac V-8 increased. A 3/16-inch increase in stroke to 3.75 inches resulted in a displacement increase to 389 ci. The main journal diameter increased from 2.5625 to 3.0 inches to allow for generous crank-pin overlap. It also allowed for the use of cast instead of forged crankshafts, which were significantly cheaper to produce.

The 1958 T-395A high-performance-series engine was replaced with the more powerful T-420A V-8s in 4-barrel and Tri-Power versions for NASCAR and NHRA compe-

*A 1958 and a 1960 Pontiac launch from the starting line at the 1964 Presque Isle Timing Association Grad Meet in Erie, Pennsylvania. Regional races such as this were quite common, and the purse for the event was more than $2,500 (nearly $25,000 when adjusted for inflation in 2024). (Photo Courtesy John Bleill)*

tition. It represented a significant step forward in performance and how the division handled its specialized high-performance vehicles.

The Tempest T-420A differed from its lower-output siblings by way of a four-bolt-main version of the regular production engine. The T-420A had freer-flowing exhaust manifolds and a slightly higher 10.5:1 compression ratio. Although it was based on regular production castings and fitted with the same 1.88/1.60 intake and exhaust valves, the heads were fitted with heavy-duty valve springs. They were identified with specific stampings on the center exhaust ports. An "X" was stamped on the left side to identify a 10.5:1 compression ratio, and a "0" was stamped on the right side to denote the heavy-duty valve springs.

Although they came from the factory with the hottest hydraulic cam that was offered, they were given a McKellar #6 flat-tappet mechanical camshaft that featured 283/293 degrees of duration and 0.406-inch lift. They were shipped in the trunk (along with lifters) and intended for dealer installation. This was the beginning of Pontiac's practice of adding the latest and highest-performance equipment with the vehicle for

*The 1959 model year brought a new generation of youth-oriented performance cars with all-new Jet Age styling, split grilles, fins, and the Wide Track chassis. The new cars featured a larger 389-ci V-8, which was the fourth enlargement of the now-familiar Pontiac V-8 in as many years. Although the engines were larger and more powerful, the cars were heavier than before, which offset much of the power increase.*

installation later. It saved time and money and kept the regular production lines moving at full capacity. In addition, it was a way to get the necessary components to the racers in a timely fashion.

The 4-barrel version of the T-420A engine was rated at 330 hp at 4,800 rpm with 425 ft-lbs of torque at 2,800 rpm. The Tri-Power version was rated at 345 hp at 4,800 rpm with 425 ft-lbs of torque at 3,200 rpm. Both versions used the same carburetors as their 300-hp and 315-hp siblings.

Unfortunately, much of the benefit of the larger, more powerful powerplants was minimized by the added weight of the new 1959 bodystyles. The cars were not significantly faster than their 1958 counterparts. In fact, Arnie Beswick had more success in 1959 running his earlier car in the C/Gas class than he did running the 1959 car in the Stock class. Fortunately, Pontiac was working on a remedy.

### The Super Duty Era Begins

The earliest mention of the Super Duty Program arrived in late 1959, when Pontiac released parts for the new 1960 models. The program was implemented through Pontiac's existing parts network and was designed to keep Pontiac racers supplied with the latest and highest-performance parts to remain competitive. The release of new parts superseding older parts was continuous and gave racers the opportunity to stay on the cutting edge of Pontiac's V-8 racing technology.

The first batch of over-the-counter Super Duty parts could be ordered separately, but collectively, they comprised the 389 Super Duty engine package. We now refer to it as a crate engine. It consisted of a four-bolt main block (casting number 535466), big-valve (1.92/1.66 inch) cylinder heads (535461), forged NASCAR connecting rods (535238), a forged crankshaft (533038), an aluminum single 4-barrel intake manifold (535889), and low-restriction exhaust manifolds (passenger's side: 535504; driver's side: 535505). A new solid-lifter camshaft was also part of the package. Known as the McKellar #7 (part number 535480), it featured an advertised 300/304 degrees of duration and 0.445/0.447 inch of lift with 1.65:1-ratio rockers.

*The 1960 model ushered in the Super Duty era with a variety of over-the-counter parts. The Wide Track Division found early success that culminated in Super Duty Sunday, when Pontiac made decisive wins in NASCAR (stock car), NHRA (drag racing) and Pikes Peak (hill climb) events on the same day. This is the actual automatic 1960 Pontiac that Jim Wangers and Dick Jesse drove. Wangers was awarded a red Catalina with a manual transmission (the sister car to the car that is shown) after his win at the 1960 NHRA Nationals. Today, the red Catalina's whereabouts are unknown.*

*Ronnie Sox is most well-known for his association with Mopar; the red, white, and blue race cars that he drove; and his partnership with Buddy Martin. Early in Sox's career, he raced Pontiacs. In 1960, he is shown with his Catalina and a line of trophies. (Photo Courtesy Jim Schild)*

The impact on the competition world was devastating. Pontiacs soon became the cars to beat in NASCAR. Drivers such as Jack Smith, Bobby Johns, and Fireball Roberts carried the flag for the Wide Track Division.

Some racers received preferential treatment from the factory, including the NASCAR teams of Ray Nichels (Nichels Engineering in Highland, Indiana) and Henry "Smokey" Yunick (Smokey's Best Damn Garage in Town in Daytona, Florida). Royal Pontiac in Royal Oak, Michigan, had a direct link to the factory through driver and advertising executive Jim Wangers. Arnie "the Farmer" Beswick from Morrison, Illinois, was on the short list to receive Pontiac's latest cars and equipment. Pete Seaton, a Detroit-based racer and son of General Motors Vice President Louis G. Seaton, was a racer who had early access

to and raced a 1960 Super Duty Catalina that was runner-up to Jim Wangers at the 1960 US Nationals. The 1-2 Pontiac finish was particularly well covered by the magazines and newspapers of the time.

Of course, there was the multipurpose racing team of Mickey Thompson in Long Beach, California, that participated in drag racing, land speed racing, boat racing, the Indy 500, and the Fédération Internationale de l'Automobile (FIA) flying-mile competition.

Nichels and his go-fast factory-built cars were made for a variety of NASCAR racers, including Cotton Owens and Paul Goldsmith. Nichels also competed in United States Auto Club (USAC) racing with Goldsmith, A. J. Foyt, and Len Sutton. Goldsmith won the 1961 and 1962 USAC championships. Joe

> **"THE IMPACT ON THE COMPETITION WORLD WAS DEVASTATING. PONTIACS SOON BECAME THE CARS TO BEAT IN NASCAR."**

Weatherly won the 1962 NASCAR championship in a Nichels-built, Bud Moore–prepped Catalina. Roger Penske had Nichels build his 1963 Catalina.

Yunick's association with Pontiac began with an

*This 1960 Catalina is the earliest known Union Park Pontiac Inc. race car, which is shown in 1962 at US 30 Drag-O-Way in York, Pennsylvania. (Photo Courtesy Clinton Wright)*

Pete Seaton poses with his 1960 389 Super Duty Catalina and some trophies. Pete's father, Louis G. Seaton, was a General Motors vice president and chief labor specialist, which granted him access to Pontiac's latest cars and equipment. Seaton's driver at the time was Jim Howell. (Photo Courtesy Howard Maseles)

invitation by Bunkie Knudsen in 1958 and continued through 1962. It culminated in a series of wins, including victories in the 1961 and 1962 Daytona 500s. The first was with driver Marvin Panch and the second was with driver Glenn "Fireball" Roberts. Roberts won in the Firecracker 250 and the Daytona 500 that year. Yunick was the first team owner to win the Daytona 500 twice, and he did so two years in a row.

## 1960 US Nationals

While the 1960 389 Super Duty was initially aimed at NASCAR competition and did not have specific drag-racing parts and applications, that all changed with the introduction of the first of the race-only aluminum body panels with bumpers for the 1960 models. It was enough for Pontiac Advertising Agency Executive Jim Wangers to win Top Stock

Jim Wangers won Top Stock Eliminator at the 1960 NHRA Nationals in Hot Chief No. 1, the 1960 Super Duty 4-speed Catalina. He beat Jim Howell, who was driving the Pete Seaton 1960 Super Duty Catalina, with a 13.89 ET at 102.67 mph. (Photo Courtesy Howard Masales)

*Dick Jesse is behind the wheel of* Hot Chief No. 2. *Jesse eventually made his way to the finals at the 1960 NHRA Nationals but lost to Al Eckstrand and his 1960 Plymouth.*

Eliminator during the 1960 US Nationals at Detroit Dragway. He drove a 1960 Super Duty Catalina 4-speed for Royal Pontiac, which was in Royal Oak, Michigan. He ran a best quarter-mile elapsed time (ET) of 13.89 seconds at 102.67 mph and beat another Royal Pontiac–sponsored Catalina that was campaigned by Pete Seaton. This performance was remarkable, considering the weight of the car and the available tires at the time.

On Super Duty Sunday, Pontiac made decisive wins in NASCAR (stock car), NHRA (drag racing), and Pikes Peak (hill climb) events on the same day. It was a successful season, and more successful seasons were ahead.

## Royal Pontiac Goes Racing

The phrase "Race on Sunday; sell on Monday," has been overused to the point that it has become a cliché, but it became one because it was true. Racing victories translated into car sales, and Detroit manufacturers were keenly aware of this fact. However, factors such as cost and corporate responsibility often thwarted their efforts.

Car dealerships weren't as tied to the same constraints as the manufacturers, and they were not subject to GM's 1963 racing ban. For Pontiac, the push from the corporation to support dealership racing waned after the racing ban, but it never went away completely.

Racing support for dealerships was essentially nonexistent before Bunkie Knudsen became general manager. In 1956, the introduction of the 285-hp Strato-Streak was the first indication that Pontiac was getting into the racing game. Knudsen's arrival in June of that year quickly changed the division's mindset. Performance and racing victories began to turn Pontiac's fortunes.

The push for dealership support came in response to the Super Duty Program. According to his 1998 book *Glory Days*, Jim Wangers outlined how, as an advertising executive, he presented a plan to Pontiac management to educate the dealers across the nation about the program. The presentation did not go well.

Later, Wangers received a phone call from Knudsen, who apologized for the harsh treatment that had been given to Wangers. While the idea had largely fallen on deaf ears, Knudsen understood what Wangers had in mind. He suggested that it would be better to find one local Detroit dealership that was willing to work with them.

Although the dealership would essentially be a guinea pig to test the idea, that dealership would get an inside line to Pontiac's engineering department and receive preferential treatment regarding new parts availability. From there, it would likely gain traction with the division if it was deemed successful.

*Jim Wangers (in front of the car and on the right) smiles after taking the Top Stock Eliminator crown at the 1960 NHRA Nationals. This win put Pontiac on the map. With Wangers's talent for promotion, he made the most of the opportunity, which helped move Pontiac past Plymouth and Rambler in sales for 1962. (Photo Courtesy Jim Luikens)*

Since Packer Pontiac was the largest volume dealer in Detroit and had stores in Flint, Michigan, and Miami, Florida, Wangers first stopped by to speak with Bill Packer Jr. Packer was interested in the idea and told Wangers that he would consider it and get back to him.

Next, Wangers went to Royal Pontiac in nearby Royal Oak. Dealership Principal Asa "Ace" Wilson Jr. jumped on the idea and accepted the offer on the spot. He knew that it would be a fantastic way to get publicity, which would translate to sales.

The publicity was far more than anyone had imagined. Wangers was a first-class promoter and able to get magazine coverage in all of the major titles of the day, including *Hot Rod*, *Car and Driver*, *Popular Hot Rodding*, *Road & Track*, and *Car Life*. He also received coverage in some smaller but influential East Coast titles, including *Hi-Performance Cars*, *Super Stock & Drag Illustrated*, etc. The publicity sparked the release of special Royal Pontiac editions, which were known as Royal Bobcats. The name gave an aggressive persona to these hopped-up production cars. Best of all, raiding the parts bins gave Royal Pontiac the block letters from Bonneville and Catalina fender callouts to spell out the name.

Royal quickly became known as the go-to dealer to have a car modified, even if wasn't originally purchased there. The Bobcat treatment was available for most Pontiacs— even the Tempest slant four and OHC-6 models. While the pieces varied slightly from model to model, the general formula included thinner head gaskets, a recurved distributor, fattened carburetor jetting, blocked-off heat risers, and adjusting the rocker arms for zero travel to make the camshaft act like it had solid lifters.

Other modifications included a low-pitch fan to free up power and, if so equipped, modified Tri-Power carburetor linkages. The modifications were generally good for 20 to 30 hp. Most importantly, it put those cars ahead of the competition and secured Royal's reputation. Having Royal badges on a car was an instant boost to that car's street credibility. Today, a properly documented Royal Bobcat Pontiac has a substantially higher value than a similar car without the treatment.

### Royal Pontiac's Racing Success

Having a direct line to the factory meant that Royal Pontiac's race cars always had the latest parts and information. Royal Pontiac even tested new parts for the factory as an unofficial research and development arm. The dealership's first race car, a 1959 Catalina that was driven by Bill Sidwell, won the 1960 Daytona Winternationals. It later became the first stocker to run a 13-second ET and exceed 100 mph in the quarter mile at Detroit Dragway.

The wins kept coming. At the 1960 NHRA Nationals, Jim Wangers, who was driving the 4-speed Royal Bobcat, beat Jim Howell, who was driving the Pete Seaton 1960 Catalina, to win Top Stock Eliminator with a 13.89 ET at 102.67 mph. The automatic car narrowly lost in the finals to Al Ekstrand's cross-ram Plymouth.

For 1961, Royal Pontiac fielded a two-car team for stick and automatic classes and won Top Stock Eliminator at the NHRA Regionals in Muncie, Indiana, and Alton, Illinois. This time, the automatic car was more successful, as driver Dick Jesse ran consistent 13.7 ETs at 104 to 105 mph.

For 1962, Royal Pontiac once again ran a two-car team: the 421 Super Duty Catalina sedan and a 421 Super Duty–powered A/FX Tempest. It proved to be the team's most successful year, with Wangers running an unbelievable 12.38 ET at 116.23 mph at Detroit Dragway with the Catalina. The car won eight regional NHRA events but failed to win the Nationals due to a broken differential spider gear. Dick Jesse, driving the A/FX Tempest, lost in the finals at the US Nationals to Lloyd Cox in a similarly-prepared Tempest owned by Mickey Thompson. Interestingly, Thompson had a hand in building the Royal car and is known to have driven it.

For 1963, Royal Pontiac competed with a Swiss cheese Catalina and a Super Duty Tempest wagon. Wangers closed the Super Duty era with a class win in B/FX at the 1963 US Nationals while driving the Catalina.

*Ken Davis's 1960 Catalina is a perfect replica of* Hot Chief #1. *The original car was returned to stock, the lettering was removed, and the car was sold; its whereabouts are unknown.*

# CHAPTER 4

# 1961: 389 AND 421 SUPER DUTY PONTIACS DOMINATE DRAG RACING

For 1961, more focus on Pontiac's drag-racing efforts was achieved through the design of the cars and the effort of the Super Duty engineering team. A significant downsizing of the 1961 Pontiac full-size cars was favorable for Pontiac. The Catalina's wheelbase decreased from 123 to 119 inches, and shipping weights decreased by more than 150 pounds to a more reasonable 3,650 to 3,680 pounds.

In addition to the reduction in overall mass, the 1961 Pontiacs benefitted from a new perimeter frame that was not shared with Chevrolet. Chevrolet still used the X-frame, which was introduced in 1958. The added rigidity and increased side crash protection that the new frame provided resulted in an improved platform for Pontiac's performance intentions.

The styling of the 1961 Pontiacs, particularly the two-door hardtops with their bubble-top rooflines, were regarded as the best in the industry. To this day, they are often included in the list of GM's most beautiful designs. With the return of the iconic split-grille theme, attractive sculpting, and slimmer overall dimensions (when compared to its predecessors), the 1961 full-size Pontiacs, particularly the bucket seat–equipped Venturas, are still top-level collectibles.

*Ralph Hardt of Croydon, Pennsylvania, and his 389-powered 1961 Candy Blue Ventura was the A/Stock Automatic class champion at the 1962 NHRA National Championship. He ran a 14.43 ET and had a trap speed of 98.79 mph. (Photo Courtesy Rocky Rotella)*

The 389 Super Duty was enhanced by the addition of a new aluminum Tri-Power system, a new big-valve cylinder-head design (casting number 306), and an even hotter camshaft. In drag racing, it's all about the power-to-weight ratio. When horsepower is increased and weight is decreased, performance makes a big jump forward. In 1961, that was the precise formula.

The basis for the 1961 389 Super Duty engine was the new version of the 389 engine that was released for high-performance street use. It was known as the 389 425A and was a special version of the 389 that featured four-bolt mains, 10.75:1 compression, an 886 hydraulic cam, and was available in 4-barrel and Tri-Power versions. The 389 425A engine was rated at 333 hp for the 4-barrel version and 348 hp for the Tri-Power version. It was a very flexible, powerful, and responsive engine, especially when it was mated with a 4-speed manual transmission.

Regarding the hardware, the new main items for 1961 included the 540306 heads, which featured 1.92/1.66-inch valves and a 68-cc combustion-chamber volume. It was joined by the McKellar #8 cam, a solid-lifter profile that featured 308/312 degrees of duration and 0.445/0.447-inch lift, and 1.65:1-ratio rocker arms. A new 535489 aluminum 4-barrel intake manifold and a 540510 aluminum Tri-Power intake manifold were released as well as a new free-flowing cast-iron exhaust manifold (part numbers 540297 [right side] and 540298 [left side]). The components combined to make a 363-hp 389 Super Duty 4-barrel engine and a 368-hp Super Duty Tri-Power engine.

The 1961 model year represented a transition in the way that Pontiac distributed its hardware. Previously, all Super Duty parts were marketed as over-the-counter items that could be purchased through Pontiac dealership parts departments and installed by dealership technicians or the customer. The parts were released individually, and as development progressed, new pieces often superseded earlier versions.

The 389 Super Duty was available to be ordered in a new 1961 Pontiac, but one was not technically built on the assembly line. The customer would receive a 425A 389-powered Pontiac with the 306 heads and #8 cam delivered in the trunk for dealer installation. The reasoning was one of convenience for Pontiac, as it did not require a special assembly area for these factory race cars. It also reduced warranty-claim problems, as Pontiac would not warranty an engine with a solid-lifter camshaft. This sleight of hand alleviated both problems and was similar to the delivery of these parts in 1960.

As Pontiac power increased, victories were attained with more regularity. Hayden Proffitt won the OS/S Optional Super Stock class with a 12.55 ET at 110.29 mph. Lloyd Cox won the S/SA class with a 13.80 ET at 105.63 mph, when his wife, Carol, was not allowed to compete.

Arnie Beswick was essentially robbed of the Super Stock crown in Indy with an unwarranted disqualification with his 1961 Catalina. It ran a 13.41 ET at 106.78

*In 1961, it was difficult to find a better-performing full-size car than a Pontiac Ventura with a 389/425A Tri-Power V-8, 4-speed transmission, Saf-T-Track, and 8-lug wheels. This example is Coronado Red. (Photo Courtesy Robert Genat)*

After a short time of driving for Pete Seaton, Howard Maseles raced his own Pontiacs in 1961 under the Packer Pontiac banner. This 1961 Catalina bubble top featured the 389/425A engine, which was upgraded with the 389 Super Duty heads and camshaft that were delivered from the factory to the dealership in the trunk for dealer installation. (Photo Courtesy Howard Maseles)

*Hayden Proffitt is shown at the Thompson Industries shop holding an NHRA-approved steel bellhousing for a Corvette or Chevy passenger car. The engine behind him is a 421 Super Duty with an adapter place to mate the bellhousing to the Pontiac block. The adapter plate also mounted the starter. (Photo Courtesy Hayden Proffitt Family)*

*Mickey Thompson (left) and Hayden Proffitt look up from under the hood of Thompson's 1961 389 Super Duty Catalina. (Photo Courtesy Hayden Proffitt Family)*

mph to beat Proffitt. Beswick narrowly lost the Top Stock Eliminator to "Dyno" Don Nicholson, but it was clear that Pontiacs were a force to be reckoned with.

*Arnie Beswick proudly stands next to his 1961 Passionate Poncho Catalina after earning the win over Hayden Proffitt at the 1961 NHRA Nationals. He was later disqualified in a political move by NHRA Tech Chief Bill "Farmer" Dismuke, who claimed that Beswick's bore size was 0.015 inch too large. It was later proven to be untrue, but the disqualification stood. (Photo Courtesy Arnie Beswick)*

## The 421 Super Duty

Late in the year, the factory released about a dozen 421 Super Duty V-8s, which differed from the 389 engines by virtue of their 0.030-inch overbore and forged-steel crank with 3.25-inch mains and a 4-inch stroke. The 538181 block, which featured a 4.0625-inch bore and a 3-inch main with a 3.75-inch stroke, was machined for the larger bore and main saddles. These early engines were sent to high-profile racers, including Mickey Thompson and Arnie Beswick.

A total of three Super Duty camshaft profiles were released in 1961. In addition to the aforementioned McKellar #8, there was also the McKellar #10 and McKellar #11, the latter of which was included in the short run of late-1961 Super Duty 421s. The #10 (part number 541596) featured 308/320 degrees and 0.445/0.447-inch lift with 1.65:1 rockers. The #11 was assigned part number 542992 and featured a slightly longer duration at 312/324 degrees with the same 0.445/0.447-inch lift as the other grinds.

According to conversations I had with Mac McKellar in the late 1990s, his concern with metallurgy and longevity kept him from going with more radical ramp shapes and higher lift. He preferred to leave the valve open for longer periods to make up for the lack of lift. This was particularly necessitated by the NASCAR applications, which were often 500-mile races, so durability was paramount. In addition, there was a McKellar #9 cam profile that was never released. He experimented with lobe centerlines, and the resulting combination did not make adequate power—hence, the jump from the McKellar #8 to the McKellar #10.

## 3.0-inch vs. 3.25-inch Main Journals

Why did Pontiac enlarge the main journals with the new 421 engine? Certainly, the metallurgy of the forged-steel Super Duty crankshafts more than compensated for the increased stroke and the subsequent reduction of crank-pin overlap. The larger mains increased bearing speeds and put additional strain on the oiling system. There were two reasons for this. First, McKellar was concerned with metallurgy and durability in racing applications, which was reflected in his camshaft profiles. The increased bearing speeds and additional heat could be controlled with proper attention to clearances and high-volume oil pumps.

Relatively speaking, the 421 Pontiac was not a super high-revving engine. It was more than able to run for extended periods in NASCAR in the 6,000-to-6,300 rpm

*Vic Gogola and his 1961 389 Super Duty Ventura were a familiar sight around the Detroit area. Gogola raced the car on the track, where it ran mid-13-second quarter-mile passes, as well as on the street. He is pictured with his car and trophies at his parents' gas station in Dearborn Heights, Michigan. (Photos Courtesy Robert Genat)*

range without significant durability issues. Smokey Yunick was very concerned about the bearing speeds and heat, and he used 389 Super Duty blocks and machined the 421 Super Duty crankshafts down to the smaller 3-inch main size. No other builder was known to have done that, so the durability issues that concerned Yunick were largely unfounded. It is obvious that the smaller mains were beneficial in a racing application like that, as crankshaft strength was not the issue that it would have been with a cast crankshaft.

When the 370 Pontiac engine was enlarged to a 389 in 1959, Pontiac increased the bearing size from 2.625 to an even 3 inches to ensure that there was sufficient crank-pin overlap with the increased stroke and use of new cast crankshafts. Forged crankshafts were out for regular production engines after that. With an eye toward a street version of the 421 coming in 1963, the enlarged mains allowed for the use of a cast-iron crankshaft and room to grow even more.

In terms of power, Pontiac rated the first 1961 421 Super Duty V-8 as having only 5 hp more than the 389 Super Duty, at a nearly ridiculous 373 hp. This was close to a rear-wheel power output figure for these engines. It was clear that Pontiac was sandbagging to get a favorable and competitive position regarding weight breaks.

### The 421 Super Duty's Debut

Just before the 1961 US Nationals on Labor Day weekend, Pontiac's public relations department issued a release that read, "Pontiac is now offering to qualified drivers a 421-ci high-performance engine option. The engine is rated at 373 hp and features dual 4-barrel carburetors, a solid-lifter camshaft, and high-capacity alumi-

num exhaust manifolds. The 421 engine is available only with related heavy-duty driveline components. It can be fitted to any Catalina or Ventura two-door model."

While the 421 Super Duty was a late-season introduction, racers wasted no time putting it on the track. The first car to hit the strip was Mickey Thompson's 1961 Catalina bubble top (#809), which made its debut on August 6 at the Pomona Valley Timing Association meet in Pomona, California. It was placed in the Optional Super Stock (OS/S) class, which was the precursor to the FX class that debuted the following year.

Paired against "Dyno" Don Nicholson in his 1961 409 Impala bubble top, driver Hayden Proffitt narrowly won with a 13.14 ET at 111.11 mph. It was a clear message to the competition that Pontiac was a force to be reckoned with. Later, the same car and driver held on

*Jim Wangers stands next to his original 1961 Royal Pontiac Super Duty Catalina at the 2006 Pontiac-Oakland Club International (POCI) drag race at Auto Club Dragway in Fontana, California.*

Jim Wangers takes his original 1961 Royal Pontiac Catalina down the track for an exhibition run during the 2006 POCI convention drag race at Auto Club Dragway in Fontana, California. Car owner Bob Knudsen is riding in the passenger's seat.

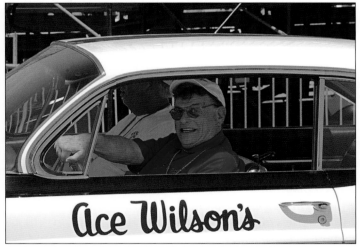

Wangers sits behind the wheel of his old race car at the 2006 POCI drags.

to beat Dave Strickler's 409-powered Biscayne to win his class at the US Nationals with an impressive top speed of 110.29 mph.

### Sizing up the Competition

For most of the Detroit manufacturers, the 1961 model year was a time of transition to remain competitive. The horsepower wars were heating up. With car magazines and newspapers covering victories at racetracks across the country, the philosophy of "Race on Sunday; sell on Monday" had never been more effective than it was at that time. As a result, horsepower took larger and larger steps forward. The 1961 season was the year that things really changed.

Just like Pontiac, Chevrolet came out with a late-season increase in displacement for its existing W-series engine. It rose from 348 to 409 ci by way of a bore increase from 4.125 to 4.3125 inches. The change necessitated a recasting of the block to accommodate the new larger bore size. The stroke was increased from 3.25 to 3.5 inches. Much of the rest of the engine remained the same as the 348, including the cylinder heads and manifolds.

The 1961 version of the 409 was available in limited quantities and featured an 11.25:1 compression ratio, a solid-lifter camshaft, and a single Carter aluminum 4-barrel (AFB) carburetor. It was rated at 360 hp at 5,800 rpm with 409 ft-lbs of torque at 3,600 rpm. The performance was spectacular for the time with a mid-15-second quarter-mile time with 3.36 gearing and the mandatory 4-speed. Only 142 cars were built with this engine, but it would be improved, and production increased for 1962. Racers such as "Dyno" Don Nicholson, Dave Strickler, and more jumped on the new engine option and installed them in their existing race cars before moving on to the 1962 models.

At Ford, the new 390-ci version of its FE (Ford-Edsel)-series engine was released in Ford and Mercury models. It was available in three versions—all with 4-barrel carburetors. The standard version was rated at 300 hp. The police-only, 330-hp version and a high-performance, solid-lifter, 375-hp version were available only with manual transmissions. All three versions developed 427 ft-lbs of torque but at different RPM levels. Later, a dealer-installed triple 2-barrel intake setup was available to increase the 375-hp version to 401 hp. Unfortunately for Ford, it was just beginning to move beyond the 1957 AMA racing ban, and little progress was made for 1961. With the advent of the Total Performance Program in 1962, things were looking better for Blue Oval racers.

Chrysler was at a disadvantage for 1961, but it found a solution. It had a great engine with an exotic induction system: the legendary 413 cross-ram V-8. While the engine produced great power numbers, it was hampered by heavy vehicle weights for drag racing when installed in larger Chrysler and Imperial models. Still, the RB-series 413-ci V-8 was a powerhouse with a 4.18-inch bore and a 3.75-inch stroke. With the cross-ram intake system and a 10.1:1 compression ratio, it developed 375 hp at 5,000 rpm with 495 ft-lbs of torque at 2,800 rpm.

Although the engine was available in the racy Chrysler 300 G, it tipped the scales at about 4,600 pounds and wasn't available in the lighter Plymouth or Dodge models. The largest and most powerful engine available from

*Lloyd Cox holds a trophy after he won the S/SA class with a 13.80 ET at 105.63 mph at the 1961 NHRA Nationals. He did so after his wife Carol was not allowed to compete. (Photo Courtesy Steve Cox)*

the factory was the cross-ram version of the 383, which was rated at 330 hp. Sneakily, the 413 cross-ram engine was included in the AMA specifications for those cars and was legal for NHRA competition in 1961. Dodge's race team, the Ramchargers, installed one of these monsters in a 1961 Dodge Dart hardtop and won the Super Stock class at the 1961 NHRA Nationals.

It wasn't the first time that these sorts of tricks had been used. All of the Detroit manufacturers were playing in the margins of the rules, released new parts on a weekly basis, and worked whatever angle they could to achieve a competitive edge. Something had to give. It was clear to the NHRA that this type of escalation would continue.

Policing the nearly constant release of new parts by all Detroit manufacturers for over-the-counter sales and dealer installation would be next to impossible. Pontiac even assigned a part number to the air to make it legal to cut a hole into a Pontiac hood to mount a scoop. The

*Hole Shot was a 1961 Catalina that was campaigned by the team of Don Royster and Bert Fortier. It was driven by Royster. The car was raced in the Maryland area. (Photo Courtesy Clinton Wright)*

rules were being bent to a breaking point, and it soon came to a head. The solution was fairly simple from the NHRA's perspective. So, it mandated that all Super Stock engines and cars were required to be factory assembled and available to the general public.

## Mickey Thompson's Line of Pontiac Racing Equipment

In the early 1960s, veteran racer Mickey Thompson led one of Pontiac's most favored racing teams. He was immersed in representing the Wide Track Division in multiple race series, including various classes of Stock, Super Stock, dragster classes, and land speed racing.

Thompson competed with a variety of Pontiac powerplants from supercharged slant 4-cylinder engines to production Super Duty V-8s and large-displacement, supercharged V-8s. To comply with FIA rules, Thompson built a 2-71 supercharged twin-cylinder engine that was based on a Pontiac slant four. It developed an impressive 257 hp on a 50-50 blend of nitromethane and methanol. It was estimated to produce 280 hp, but the engine shook so hard that the dynamometer could not withstand the vibration before the engine achieved wide-open throttle.

### Super Duty 4-Cylinder?

An interesting side note to the Super Duty program was the release of special parts for the Pontiac V-8-derived slant four. It was intended for the NASCAR compact racing class and the lower classes of NHRA stock racing.

Pontiac released several crucial pieces, including a high-nickel-content block with four-bolt mains (part number 989825), a forged crankshaft (part number 540341) and an aluminum single 4-barrel intake manifold (part number 544753). These items were built in the 1961–1962 model years.

Mickey Thompson released a variety of parts for the slant four, including a supercharger setup, camshafts, and other specialized parts. This was in addition to the parts that interchanged with the V-8, such as pistons and connecting rods. Thompson's *Attempt* dragster highlighted those engine upgrades for the Pontiac slant four, as did the two-seat 1961 Tempest Monte Carlo concept car.

## Mickey Thompson's Land Speed 1961 Catalina

With the cost of racing being so high today, it's difficult to imagine a single race team campaigning several cars and a boat at the same time. During the 1960–1963 period, Mickey Thompson's team, which was based in

*Powered by a 389 Super Duty engine and a 4-speed transmission, Mickey Thompson and his 1961 Catalina set new records for 1-kilometer and 1-mile averages. The exit speed for the standing mile was more than 167 mph. (Photo Courtesy Jim Luikens)*

*The* White Goddess *1961 Ventura bubble top is seen here with Hurst-Campbell President George Hurst, Jim Wangers (a Pontiac advertising executive and driver), and Dick Jesse (a Royal Pontiac performance car salesman and driver). The car was won by California-based racer Bruce Morgan, who sold his '57 Chevy and set an NHRA record for S/S in November of 1961. (Photo Courtesy Jim Luikens)*

Long Beach, California, competed in drag racing, land speed racing, IndyCar racing, and boat racing. It was a mind-boggling undertaking.

Thompson's land speed racing efforts for 1961 included four Pontiac-powered machines that intended to break 18 land speed class records. One of the vehicles was a bubble-top 1961 Catalina that ran in Stock Car Class B, which allowed engine displacements of 373 to 439.99 ci. The cars ran in July 1961 at the Southern California Timing Association meet at March Air Force Base in Riverside County, California.

The Catalina was powered by a 389 Super Duty V-8 engine that was mated to a 4-speed BorgWarner transmission and a 3.08 Safe-T-Track rear end. The car weighed 3,680 pounds.

The Catalina proved to be very successful and increased the 1-kilometer run from 73.15 mph to 81.497 mph and the 1-mile run from 84.02 mph to 95.571 mph. While that doesn't sound particularly fast to someone with a drag-racing background, keep in mind that the speed records are averages, which means that the exit speed is much higher. The standing-mile speed was more than 167 mph.

Unfortunately, this record-breaking Class B Catalina was lost in a California wildfire that burned Thompson's home to the ground. A replica of that car was constructed in its place.

### The Hurst-Giveaway Catalina

In the late 1990s, former Pontiac Advertising Executive Jim Wangers told me a story that was later included in his autobiography, *Glory Days: When Horsepower*

*and Passion Ruled Detroit.* By the time that the 1961 US Nationals in Indianapolis took place, Pontiac and Hurst (known as Hurst-Campbell at the time) teamed up for a variety of promotions that culminated in Hurst shifters being available on Pontiac production cars directly from the factory. Hurst teamed with other manufacturers at the time and did so for years to come.

For the 1961 US Nationals, George Hurst agreed to give away two new cars to the winners of the points championships. Both cars featured large Hurst decals and callout decals from the manufacturer. The first car was a Ford Thunderbird that was given to Jack Chrisman for winning the Competition class. The Top Stock winner, Bruce Morgan, of San Gabriel, California, won the 1961 Catalina.

At the insistence of Wangers, the Catalina that was chosen for the award was to be a ready-to-run race car that was competitive right out of the gate for whomever won it to help promote Pontiac as a brand with a well-prepped race car and a winning driver to pilot it. Wangers believed that this was a solid plan to garner positive results and extend Pontiac's reach. With Pontiac as the #3 carmaker in the country after Chevy and Ford, it was a well-timed strategy.

The Catalina that was chosen had a factory 425A engine, a 4-speed transmission, a Hurst shifter, and 8-lug wheels. In addition, the car was upgraded to Super Duty specifications and blueprinted by Royal Pontiac. Dubbed the *White Goddess*, this Catalina was the result of a tremendous amount of effort and planning, and that doesn't even consider the large dent in the budget that it made. Finished off with large red "Hurst"

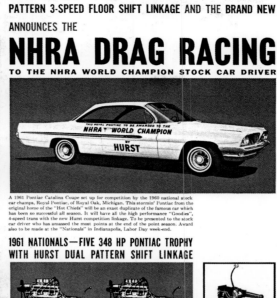

**HURST** ORIGINATORS OF THE FAMOUS DUAL COMPETITION 4-SPEED SHIFT LINKAGE

# HIGHEST AWARDS IN

TO THE NHRA WORLD CHAMPION COMPETITION CAR DRIVER

A 1961 Thunderbird hardtop equipped with Cruise-o-matic transmission and the famous 300 h.p. Thunderbird Special engine. This T-Bird, America's most wanted car, will be presented to the competition car driver who has collected the greatest number of points at the end of the point season. Award will be made at the "Nationals" in Indianapolis, Labor Day week-end.

**PLUS ... SPECIAL "NATIONALS ELIMINATOR" AWARDS ...... TO EACH ELIMINATOR AT THE V-8 ENGINES AND TRANSMISSIONS EQUIPPED**

TOP ELIMINATOR     MIDDLE ELIMINATOR     LITTLE ELIMINATOR

**ALL AWARDS COMPLIMENTS OF HURST-CAMPBELL INC., ORIGINATORS OF**

PATTERN 3-SPEED FLOOR SHIFT LINKAGE AND THE BRAND NEW ANNOUNCES THE

# NHRA DRAG RACING

TO THE NHRA WORLD CHAMPION STOCK CAR DRIVER

A 1961 Pontiac Catalina Coupe set up for competition by the 1960 national stock car champs, Royal Pontiac, of Royal Oak, Michigan. This stormin' Pontiac from the original home of the "Hot Chiefs" will be an exact duplicate of the famous car which has been so successful all season. It will have all the high performance "Goodies", 4-speed trans with the new Hurst competition linkage. To be presented to the stock car driver who has amassed the most points at the end of the point season. Award also to be made at the "Nationals" in Indianapolis, Labor Day week-end.

**1961 NATIONALS—FIVE 348 HP PONTIAC TROPHY WITH HURST DUAL PATTERN SHIFT LINKAGE**

STREET ELIMINATOR     STOCK ELIMINATOR

**HURST DUAL PATTERN FLOOR SHIFT HURST COMPETITION 4-SPEED SHIFTER**

*Hurst DUAL-PATTERN*

*To help promote its presence at the 1961 NHRA Nationals, Hurst produced this advertisement that displayed its prizes for the top points, class, and Nationals eliminator winners. (Photo Courtesy Jim Luikens)*

callouts and identifying the winner as the NHRA Top Stock Champion, the presentation of the *White Goddess* was very impressive.

*George Hurst (left) shows NHRA President Wally Parks the finer points of the fully-prepped 389 Super Duty engine under the hood of the* **White Goddess 1961 Catalina.** *The car was given to the winner of the 1961 NHRA Top Stock competition. (Photo Courtesy Jim Luikens)*

Television commercials always say, "Your results may vary." Wangers's plan didn't work out the way he wanted—or so he thought. The cars were awarded at the end of the event. It seemed to Wangers that Morgan, who was campaigning an A/Stock '57 Chevy, was unimpressed with his prize and acted "arrogantly." He was nonplussed that it was a Pontiac, let alone a fully-prepped race car. According to Wangers, he sold it almost immediately. Wangers was very insulted and felt that Morgan had disrespected Pontiac Motor Division, Royal Pontiac, and Hurst with his behavior. The sidebar in Wangers's book was toned-down in comparison to the conversation that I had with him in the tent at the 1997 Ames Performance Pontiac Nationals. It angered him greatly at the time, and he hadn't cooled down, despite the fact that 36 years had passed.

Some good news for the 1961 Catalina was uncovered regarding how it was received. With some detective work, I learned that Wangers's recollection of the story wasn't correct. While it was certainly possible that Morgan may not have made a good first impression with Wangers, the truth was that he was mightily impressed with the Pontiac. In fact, Morgan towed the Pontiac home behind his '57 Chevy. He hired Don Nicholson to tune the engine, sold the Chevy (which is alive and well to this day), and set an NHRA National record in November 1961 in the Pontiac by running a 14.04 ET at 104.40 mph in Inyokern, California. Wangers's instincts were correct, and the car did go to an appreciative and deserving recipient.

# CHAPTER 5

# 1962: PONTIAC FACTORY-BUILT RACE CARS

Victory at the track resulted in vehicle sales at the dealership. By the time that Bunkie Knudsen had been promoted to be Chevrolet's general manager in late 1961, Pontiac was in third place for domestic production, behind giants Chevrolet and Ford. The formula was working, and Pete Estes, Pontiac's newly-appointed general manager, kept the momentum going.

Estes and new Chief Engineer John Z. DeLorean were in philosophical lockstep with Knudsen. Above all else, they were car guys—engineers who came up through the ranks and had a genuine love for racing and the process of building winning cars. Backed by engineers, such as Mac McKellar, Bill Collins, and Russ Gee, there was still plenty of success to come. It was all built on the foundation that Knudsen had established.

The 1962 model year showed everyone that Pontiac was serious about winning. A separate low-volume assembly line was set up at Pontiac Engineering to build these special Super Duty cars. This assembly-line approach to building race cars created many new lightweight body components designed to keep the relatively heavy B-Body Pontiacs competitive. In addition to hoods, inner and outer front fenders, the radiator core support, and bumpers, the selection of aluminum parts included doors for the hardtop and two-door sedan models as

*Howard Maseles competes with his 1962 Packer Pontiac 421 Super Duty Catalina. It was built on March 30, 1962, and was an NHRA record holder. It continued to be a competitive class racer long after the racing ban, and Maseles raced it for the rest of the decade. (Photo Courtesy Howard Masales)*

well as decklids and rear bumpers. Aluminum doors and decklids were especially rare. In another effort to reduce weight, some items were not installed, including insulation, sound-deadening material, radios, and heaters.

The amount of weight reduction that a full complement of aluminum body panels provided was substantial and decreased the stripped-down Catalina's weight to just under 3,500 pounds. Cars that were ordered with the full complement of aluminum panels were rare due to the cost. NASCAR Super Duty Catalinas didn't use them, and steel-bodied cars that were intended for drag duty often added those panels as parts-department replacements when the need to stay competitive necessitated the need to reduce weight.

The 421 engine received some updates for 1962. The original 389 Super Duty 306 heads, which were carried over to the late-1961 and early-1962 421 Super Duty engines, were superseded by a new head (casting number

*George DeLorean is behind the wheel of the 421 Super Duty Kimosabi SS/S Catalina two-door sedan. The Grand Prix grille was used to reduce weight. (Photo Courtesy Robert Genat)*

*This is the original Packer Pontiac 1962 Catalina. It was recovered and restored by Bill Blair, a collector and racing historian. It featured the dual-quad 421 Super Duty V-8, 4-speed transmission, 4.30 gears, and an aluminum front end. It is seen here at the 1994 Tri-Power Sunday in Norwalk, Ohio, and is now part of the Brothers Car Collection in Salem, Oregon.*

544127). This new head featured recontoured ports and larger 2.02/1.76-inch valves. The combustion-chamber volume remained 68 cc.

The 421 Super Duty differed from the 389 Super Duty in several ways. The most prominent was the use of two Carter AFBs instead of the trio of Rochester 2-barrel carburetors. Both were available with single 4-barrel carburetors for NASCAR use.

The larger engine could make use of the additional airflow without bogging problems, although the NASCAR 421 Super Duty engines continued to use a single 4-barrel carburetor. The 389 Super Duty was held over into 1962 and was now rated at 385 hp due to cylinder-head and camshaft upgrades.

A total of seven engines were installed in cars and another seven were built for over-the-counter sales.

The 1962 389 Super Duty was presumably intended for NASCAR use. Factory records indicate that only one 1962 389 Super Duty Catalina two-door hardtop featured aluminum body panels and 3.42 gears without limited slip. This car was ordered for a private individual in Las Vegas and not for a race team. It still exists and is part of the Mike and Michael Huffman Collection. It is the only factory-built 1962 389 Super Duty Catalina that is known to exist with its original powertrain.

Interestingly, the 1962 *MotorTrend* Catalina test car that was recovered and restored by the late Eugene Riotte was factory-built as a 389 Super Duty Car and was later converted to a Code 13U 421 Super Duty car, allegedly by Royal Pontiac. It is also part of the Huffman Collection.

The new 421 Super Duty dual-quad intake manifold carried part number 542991 (54299 for the Thompson version of the same casting). A later version of the dual-quad intake was installed with the 127 heads (casting

*The original Gay Pontiac 1962 Catalina is on display at the 2010 Ames Performance Pontiac Nationals in Norwalk, Ohio. At the time, it was owned by collector Herb Patton. It is now owned by Mike Huffman, who owns more than 30 Super Duty cars.*

*The original Royal Pontiac 1962 421 Super Duty Catalina is on display at the 2011 Pontiac-Oakland Club International (POCI) convention in Bowling Green, Kentucky. This particular car has the only known set of aluminum doors for the pillared bodystyle as well as an aluminum decklid, which only appeared on three cars from the factory. It is now owned by Idaho-based collector Bob Knudsen.*

*Bill Abraham is sitting behind the wheel of his 1962 Golden Arrow II Super Duty Catalina that was sponsored by Knafel Pontiac and ran in the A/Stock class. Tragically, Abraham was killed in a non-racing traffic accident in Indianapolis in 1972. Bill was employed by Firestone's racing division. He was only 30 years old when he died. (Photo Courtesy Knafel Family Archives)*

number 9770319). As with the 991, the 319 had an exhaust heat crossover. However, another version (casting number 9770859) did not have the heat crossover. There is evidence to suggest that this no-heat intake was an over-the-counter part and was not installed on factory-built cars, although it hasn't been confirmed.

An unusual twist to the Super Duty story was that the race engine was also installed in at least 16 cars that were not intended for professional racing. That's how many dual-quad, 405-hp 421 Super Duty V-8s were installed in luxury-oriented Pontiac

*This race took place at the 2008 POCI drag race event in Sturgis, South Dakota. Ken Davis's 1960 Royal Pontiac Catalina replica takes on the original 1962 Gay Pontiac Super Duty 421 Catalina with Herb Patton behind the wheel.*

Grand Prixs in 1962. Interestingly, 4 of the 16 were delivered to one dealer: Jernigan Pontiac in Eastchester, New York. The first one of the 16 was built with air conditioning, which was not normally available in a car with a factory-installed race engine. There must have been some VIP intervention for that combination to be approved to go down the assembly line.

As of now, I only know of the existence of 3 of those 16 cars, although it's likely that 1 or more are still in hiding. There are rumors that one undiscovered example is in north central Pennsylvania and possibly one is somewhere in the Midwest. It's anyone's guess, but I certainly hope there are more.

*The original Lane-Moak Pontiac* Big Chief *Super Duty Catalina is seen at the 2011 POCI Convention in Bowling Green, Kentucky. It was expertly restored by the late Eugene Riotte.*

## The Competition Raises the Stakes

It was good that Pontiac didn't rest on its laurels after a successful 1961 season, as the competition had similarly elevated its game. Chevrolet added a new cylinder-head design with larger ports and 2.08/1.734-inch valves, which were increased in size from the 1961's 2.06/1.72-inch valves. It also added a new dual-quad intake with a pair of 500-cfm Carter AFB D-series carburetors. The horsepower increased from 360 to 380 hp for the single-4-barrel version and to 409 hp for the dual-quad version. Added to a lightweight Biscayne two-door sedan or a Bel-Air bubble top with lightweight aluminum front-end pieces, it made for a potent combination. Racers such as "Dyno" Don Nicholson, Bill "Grumpy" Jenkins (and his driver Dave Strickler), Frank Sanders, and Buddy Martin piloted 409-powered full-size Chevys. Later in the year, Hayden Proffitt joined them.

Later in 1961, Chevrolet released a 425-hp version of the 409 engine and featured new 2.203-inch intake valves. A late-season introduction of the Z-11 package was released and was rated at 430 hp. It consisted of 12.5:1-compression pistons, a wilder cam, improved heads, and a new dual-quad intake.

Chevrolet's effort paid off. Dave Strickler won the SS/S class at the 1962 US Nationals. At the same meet, Hayden Proffitt left Pontiac to race a Chevy and won Stock Eliminator. This happened after Proffitt won Stock Eliminator and $3,000 at Detroit Dragway the previous week. Moreover, "Dyno" Don Nicholson won Stock Eliminator at the Winternationals for the second year in a row. All in all, it was a very respectable showing for Chevrolet.

| 1962 421 Super Duty Grand Prix Production Information | | |
|---|---|---|
| **VIN** | **Dealer Code and Name** | **Note/Current Status** |
| 962P4901 | 17-283 Stewart Pontiac, West Palm Beach, Florida | Only Super Duty with A/C; Unknown |
| 962P5979 | 35-997 Pontiac Retail Store, Pontiac, Michigan | Unknown |
| 962P7416 | 02-698 Wides Motor Sales, Far Rockaway, New York | Unknown |
| 962P7455 | 02-263 Jernigan Pontiac, Eastchester, New York | Unknown |
| 962P7464 | 02-263 Jernigan Pontiac, Eastchester, New York | Unknown |
| 962P7492 | 02-263. Jernigan Pontiac, Eastchester, New York | Black/Parchment Mike Huffman |
| 962P7503 | 02-263 Jernigan Pontiac, Eastchester, New York | Unknown |
| 962P8232 | 02-637 Triangle Pontiac, Astoria, Queens, New York | Recovered by Allan Gartzman; now in private collection |
| 962P8273 | 29-219 Don Owen, Inc. Endwell, New York | Unknown |
| 962P8356 | 02-415 Myrtle Motors, Maspeth, New York | Unknown |
| 962P8404 | 03-459 Paul S. Spaar Pontiac, Palm, Pennsylvania | Unknown |
| 962P8833 | 10-227 Heights Motors, Chicago Heights, Illinois | Unknown |
| 962P10457 | 17-167 Holman Motors, Vero Beach, Florida | Burgundy/Black; Mike Huffman |
| 962P10646 | 14-629 Jerry Spady Pontiac-Cadillac, Hastings, Nebraska | Unknown |
| 962P11271 | 02-011 Don Allen Pontiac, Manhattan, New York | Special Paint; Unknown |
| 962P11329 | 20-097 Oklahoma City, Oklahoma Zone/Unknown Dealer | Unknown |

*The Street Eliminator competition at the 1962 Winternationals in Pomona had A/FX champion Hayden Proffitt face the Grassman-Osterman-Nicholson 1961 Corvette. The Corvette won with a 14.02 ET at 101.80 mph. The eventual winner of the Street Eliminator was Earl Wade in a Corvette. (Photo Courtesy Robert Genat)*

*In a classic Pontiac-versus-Pontiac finish, Lloyd Cox won the A/FX class with the Mickey Thompson 1962 421 Super Duty Tempest at the NHRA Nationals. He is shown in the last round defeating Dick Jesse in the Royal Pontiac version of the same car. (Photo Courtesy Jim Luikens)*

Ford worked hard to play catch-up for the 1962 season. The Total Performance program, which sought world dominance in all forms of auto racing, was going in the right direction, although it was not up to the same level as the competition. Its new 406-ci version of the FE series V-8 was available in two versions.

The first version was the B-Code, which was a single 4-barrel-equipped engine that was rated at 385 hp at 5,800 rpm and was aimed at NASCAR. The second version, the G-Code, was intended for drag racing and featured three 2-barrel carburetors that developed 405

hp at 5,800 rpm. They were both now available with a floor-shifted BorgWarner 4-speed transmission, which added to the Ford powertrain's competitiveness.

In addition to the increased horsepower, Ford reduced the weight of its full-size vehicles with fiberglass hoods, fenders, doors, and decklids as well as aluminum front and rear bumpers. The result reduced the curb weight of the Ford race cars by 164 pounds. While it was helpful, it was not enough. Part of the problem was that the 406's 405-hp rating was fairly accurate, while Pontiac's 405-hp rating was more than 60 hp shy of the actual output. The other problem was that the NHRA didn't classify the Galaxie lightweights in the Super Stock class. It put them in the same A/FX class as the 421-powered Tempests, the 413-powered Lancers, and the 327-powered Chevy IIs.

The 406 Galaxies weren't terribly competitive. However, racers including Dick Brannan, Gas Ronda, Phil Bonner, and Tasca Ford raced them, often with the late-year addition of a new aluminum intake manifold and a pair of Holley carburetors. It was a way to make the Fords more competitive in the FX class. Although it was a slow start, it was the beginning of a successful program for Ford.

Mopar posed the biggest threat to Pontiac race teams in 1962. Not only was its 413 engine upgraded from the engine that came from the 1961 Chrysler 300, it was classified with a new generation of smaller and lighter unibody cars that featured simple suspensions and reacted well to tuning and traction aids.

The Max Wedge 413 boasted a substantial increase in power. It featured a new cross-ram system with shorter runners that boosted top-end power. The 413 featured two different compression ratios: 11.0:1 for 410 hp and a whopping 13.5:1-compression version that made 420 hp. New heads featured 25-percent-larger ports, bigger valves, and heavy-duty valve springs that worked with a new 300-degree duration.

The other portion of the equation was the all-new, smaller, and lighter B-Body platform. The Plymouth Savoy and Dodge 330 were 400 pounds lighter than the models they replaced, which translated into at least an advantage of 3/10 of a second without the engine improvements. With them, the gap between Mopar and Pontiac closed significantly.

### Giveaways

Hurst-Campbell once again gave away a new Pontiac for 1962. This time, a Hurst-shifted Tri-Power 389 Grand Prix was presented to eventual NHRA World Champion Jess Van Deventer, who drove a Chevy-powered B/MR roadster. The Grand Prix was handed over to Van Deventer by none other than Mrs. George Hurst. She presented an identical car to Tom Sturm, who won the championship in the Stock class with a 1962 Bel Air.

### NHRA Announces the FX Classes

For the 1962 season, the NHRA introduced a new class called Factory Experimental (FX). It was for cars that no longer fit in the Super Stock classes, which now required factory-built cars (as opposed to cars that were later fitted with factory-special equipment). The new Factory Experimental (FX) class was an expansion of the previous season's Optional Super Stock class that allowed for the constant stream of factory-built upgrades to be used on existing cars. The result was a class that turned the world of drag racing upside down and changed the course of history. The FX classes were determined by weight per cubic inch: A/FX (0 to 8.99 pounds per ci), B/FX (9.00 to 12.99 pounds per ci), and C/FX (13.0 or more pounds per ci).

The big news for the FX classes was that non-factory-built 409 Impalas, 406 Ford Galaxies, 421 Super Duty–powered Catalinas, and 413 Max Wedge Mopars were allowed. The class also allowed cars to be built by racers with any engine or driveline from a specific manufacturer to be mated in any model that was made by that manufacturer, regardless of whether it was available from the factory in that configuration.

No interdivisional mixing and matching were allowed, but the rules were remarkably open, which made for some fascinating interpretations of the rules. Soon, racers installed fuel-injected 327s into Chevy IIs, 413 Mopars into Dodge Lancers, and at least two 421 Super Dutys into Pontiac Tempests.

The key to whether a part was legal in the FX class was whether it could be obtained from a dealer with a factory part number. Chevrolet offered a swap kit with factory part numbers for a small-block installation in a Chevy II, and they were

CLEAN SWEEP AT DAYTONA!

WHEN PERFORMANCE REALLY COUNTS THE TOP DRIVERS-MECHANICS DEPEND ON **HURST**

GRAND NATIONAL 500 WINNER—A 1962 Pontiac averaged 152.529 m.p.h. to set a new international record for the 500 miles. The field was full of great cars and great drivers. The record breaking pace was terrific. It took determination and endurance on part of both man and machine to win this one.

**MR. STOCK ELIMINATOR**
Bob Harrop of Camden, N.J. turned the back stretch quarter mile consistently in the low 13's at speeds over 107 m.p.h. . . . as he pulled his big 368 h.p. A-Stock "Pony" to a real surprise win in this hotly contested meet. In seven straight nights of drag racing, Bob eliminated all other cars and drivers, never missing an important shift in his 4-speed trans.

**PURE OIL SAFETY AND PERFORMANCE TRIALS**
A 1962 Pontiac Catalina Sedan equipped with a new 421 cu. in. engine and a 4-speed stick out-started, out-shifted and out-stopped all other cars in this grueling test of machinery and skill. Accurate, quick and positive shifting of gears made the difference here. Pontiac surpassed the field, adding points to its total, to win the Pure Oil Grand Prix Award.

All these Pontiacs were equipped with Hurst floor shift linkage, standard equipment with Pontiac's new "421" package. Once again in actual competition here's proof that when it takes performance and perfection, the nation's top drivers, mechanics and automobile manufacturers make Hurst their choice.

**WORLD'S FINEST FLOOR SHIFT CONVERSIONS**

## HURST-CAMPBELL, INC., GLENSIDE, PA.

**THE GREATEST NAME IN FLOORSHIFTS**

*Hurst-Campbell had a great relationship with Pontiac and celebrated its role in the Wide Track Division's racing success with advertisements like this. All 1962 Pontiac 421 Super Duty cars came with Hurst shifters as standard equipment. That OEM status was part of the GTO package for 1964.*

*Dick Jesse is behind the wheel of the* Royal Pontiac A/FX 421 Super Duty Tempest. *It is debated that this car was built by Nichels Engineering and later repurposed for drag racing use by Mickey Thompson on behalf of Royal Pontiac. Jesse lost to Hayden Proffitt at the Nationals, and this particular car slipped into obscurity. (Photo Courtesy Jim Luikens)*

soon available from the factory as a regular production option. Mickey Thompson developed and manufactured a wide variety of Pontiac speed equipment with factory part numbers that could be ordered from any Pontiac dealership, including aluminum connecting rods, pistons, cams, stroker kits, and other items that could be raced legally in FX. Other items, such as lightweight fiberglass or aluminum body panels, were not allowed, simply because no such items were developed. Hood scoops were not allowed without a factory part number.

## The Original A/FX Tempests

Dual-quad 421 Super Duty engines found their way into at least two 1962 Pontiac Tempests. One was built by Mickey Thompson and Hayden Proffitt and the other was built by Royal Pontiac in Royal Oak, Michigan, and was driven by Dick Jesse. The Thompson/Proffitt car was originally a Yorktown Blue Tempest LeMans with a blue bucket seat interior. It was delivered to Mike Salta Pontiac in Long Beach, California. It was built with the 110-hp, 195-ci Pontiac 4-cylinder engine with a single-barrel carburetor, a 3-speed manual transaxle, and a 3.31 axle ratio. As you may expect, it didn't stay that way for long.

The Thompson entry was built by Hayden Proffitt and Lloyd Cox, and it used the complete drivetrain from one of Thompson's 1962 421 Super Duty Catalina sedans. The original 4-cylinder and rope-drive transaxle system were removed. It received a dual-quad 421 Super Duty; a BorgWarner T-85 3-speed manual transmission with an unsynchronized first gear; and a 4.30-geared, 9.3-inch,

Safe-T-Track rear end with full-size-car rear brake drums. The firewall and transmission tunnel were modified to fit the conventional drivetrain, and the rear end was located on custom-built ladder bars and used the stock rear coil springs. A feature on the build appeared in the September 1962 issue of *Hot Rod* magazine.

The Tempest, known as #672 for its NHRA number, was initially lettered with the incorrect class identifier (FX/A) instead of the correct identifier (A/FX). That error was later fixed.

With Hayden Proffitt at the wheel, the little Tempest was a terror. It won the A/FX class at the NHRA Winternationals in Pomona, California, running a best ET of 12.20 at 117 mph to beat Marvin Ford in a 413-powered 1962 Dodge Dart. Proffitt left the Thompson team in the spring of 1962, opened his own shop, and got a factory deal with Chevrolet. With Lloyd Cox driving later in the season, the Tempest (now numbered #972) continued to win and took its class at the US Nationals that year, beating Dick Jesse in the Royal Pontiac 421 Super Duty 1962 Tempest.

After the 1962 season ended, the original Thompson 421 Super Duty Tempest was rendered obsolete by the introduction of the factory-built 1963 421 Super Duty LeMans coupes and Tempest wagons. It was sold and later converted to an altered-wheelbase Funny Car that was raced by Bob Porter. It passed through an unknown number of owners before being rediscovered in Southern California in the 1980s. It has since been moved to Idaho with the current owner. It is now a rolling shell with a straight front axle and an altered wheelbase.

An exact replica of #672 was built in the early 1990s by George Knevelbaard, a prominent Super Duty collector and historian who was living in California at the time. As a teenager in the early 1960s, he hung around at Mickey Thompson's shop in Long Beach and had firsthand experiences with Thompson, his employees (including the legendary Fritz Voight), and the cars. The Tempest had a profound influence on him. After decades of collecting parts, he found the perfect car to base his re-creation on and began construction in the late 1980s. As of 2024, I currently own this car.

Interestingly, little is known about the Royal Pontiac 1962 Tempest. According to Pontiac Historic Services President Jim Mattison, it was alleged to have been built

## Carol Cox: Drag Racing Pioneer

After finally being allowed to race at a national event, Carol Cox delivered with a class win at her first possible opportunity: the 1962 Winternationals in Pomona. She won the Stock Automatic (S/SA) class with a 13.06 ET at 107.65 mph. She is regarded as a pioneer in the sport as well as a pioneer for women's rights. (Photo Courtesy Steve Cox)

Carol Cox and her 1961 Ventura runs a 13.69 ET at 106.25 mph to defeat Roy Christian and his 1960 Plymouth. (Photo Courtesy Steve Cox)

Although Carol Cox was a pioneering woman drag racer, her name is not as well-known as other female racers, such as Shirley Muldowney and Shirley Shahan or modern racers Brittany Force and Leah Pruett. Nevertheless, Carol was someone who made it possible for other female drag racers to gain entry and earn the respect of their peers and fans. As is often the case in history, the actual barrier-breakers are not the ones who reach the highest levels of success, although their contributions are no less significant.

Female drag racers have been around nearly as long as male drag racers, although they weren't as plentiful and they were not treated with the respect that they deserved. They were often relegated to powder-puff classes and competed against each other, rather than against men. It was an era when women were often marginalized. Although white women were allowed to vote throughout the US in 1920, they weren't allowed to serve on juries in many areas of the country. Well into the 1970s, unmarried women were often denied loans or credit. It seems crazy today, but social norms were different during that time period than they are now. Barriers needed to come down, and for woman racers, Carol Cox held the sledgehammer.

For Carol, the idea of competing at a national event was something that she was willing to fight for—and she did. After racing at Lions Drag Strip, which Mickey Thompson managed, she caught Thompson's eye. As a result, he hired her husband, Lloyd, to work at his shop. In turn, Lloyd purchased a 1961 Pontiac Ventura with a 389/425A engine and automatic transmission. It featured Doug Thorley headers and prototype Lakewood 90/10 shocks in the front. Carol was pressed into driving duties.

They drove the Ventura from Southern California to Indianapolis for the US Nationals. Although Carol normally drove the car and her husband served as crewchief, Lloyd had to drive the car at the US Nationals in 1961 because Carol was denied entry to race. Lloyd proved to be successful and won the S/SA class that year.

Although her husband won the race in which she should've competed, it was of little comfort to her. After being barred from participation in NHRA competition, she used the power of the press to achieve her goal. Both of her parents had previously worked for the *Los Angeles Herald Examiner*, so she was familiar with the players in the local media. She contacted the *Examiner*, the *Los Angeles Times*, and her congressman to put pressure on the NHRA to let her and other women racers compete alongside their male counterparts. She increased the pressure by gaining the support of Peggy Hart, the wife of Santa Ana Drags owner C. J. "Pappy" Hart, Mickey Thompson (with Pontiac's factory backing), and fellow female racers Shirley Shahan and Roberta Leighton to garner support and force the NHRA to let women race at its national events (not just in a powder-puff setting).

Eventually, the NHRA relented and allowed women to race. Carol's first event was the 1962 NHRA Winternationals in Pomona, California. She took the crown in the Super Stock/Stock Automatic class, which was a very competitive segment. She and her 389 Super Duty–powered Ventura ran a 13.06 ET at 107.65 mph. Despite her significant win, *National Dragster* played it down and called her a "powder-puff handler." At the same time, it completely disregarded the fact that not only was she the first woman ever to earn a class win at an NHRA event but she also did it at the first possible opportunity that was given to her. Whether or not this was intentionally done has been the topic of debate, but there's no doubt that she opened the door for other women racers to compete at the same level as their male counterparts. She later repeated her performance at the 1962 NHRA Nationals in Indy, running a 13.69 ET at 106.25 mph and defeating the 1960 Plymouth of Roy Christian.

*The legendary Jess Tyree is shown behind the wheel of the Bill Barry Pontiac 1962 421 Super Duty Catalina at Lions Drag Strip. (Photo Courtesy Clinton Wright)*

by Nichels Engineering using parts supplied by Pontiac Engineering. It was said to be one of the four cars that were used at Daytona Speedweeks that year. Four cars were entered into the Daytona three-hour endurance race, which is also known as the NASCAR Daytona Continental race. Only one of the four finished the race.

What we do know is that it was prepped by Mickey Thompson for Royal Pontiac, who is also known to have driven it. It was painted in the normal Royal livery and was driven by Dick Jesse in competition. Its whereabouts are unknown and the fact that it disappeared immediately after the 1962 season adds credence to the idea that it was a Pontiac Engineering prototype. If that is the case, it was almost certainly destroyed per corporate policy.

## Pontiacs Possess Greatness at the Track

The 1962 season was wildly successful for Pontiac, with wins for the 1961 and 1962 models. In addition to the Mickey Thompson team, independent racer Ralph Hardt, "Akron" Arlen Vanke, Jess Tyree, Midwesterner Don Bennett, Bill Sasse (driving for Anderson Pontiac in Akron, Ohio), and Larry Leonard (driving for California-based Bell-Leonard Pontiac) earned wins at NHRA national events.

*The Big Bear Anderson Pontiac A/Stock 421 Super Duty Catalina sedan was originally purchased by George DeLorean, who sold it to Arlen Vanke, who raced it through Anderson Pontiac in Akron, Ohio. The Catalina was a successful mount for Vanke and set an NHRA national record in the A/Stock class and won the 1962 A/S points championship in York, Pennsylvania. From there, the car was sold to local racer Jim Shultheis, who had a good deal of success with the Catalina (as the trophies suggest). Shultheis ran the car in NHRA A/Stock. (Photo Courtesy Thomas A. DeMauro)*

*Jim Shultheis (right), wipes down the fender of his car as Paul Whipkey looks on. Note the tow bar on the Catalina. (Photo Courtesy Thomas A. DeMauro)*

Pontiac cleaned house with the 389 and 421 Super Duty V-8s in national and regional competitions. At the NHRA Regional Meet in Orange, Massachusetts, Bob Harrop of Camden, New Jersey, took a class win with his C/Stock 1961 *Batwing* Catalina 389 Super Duty with a 13.69 ET over Pat Castagna's 1961 Catalina bubbletop. Harrop won for a second time a week later in Vineland, New Jersey. Hayden Proffitt won the Stock Eliminator title at the NHRA California State Championship in Half Moon Bay, California, in the *#670* 1962 421 Super Duty Catalina two-door sedan. Proffitt absolutely dominated in his Mickey Thompson–team cars until he left the organization during the 1962 season because he opened his own shop and got a factory deal with Chevrolet.

Regionally, 1962 421 Super Duty Catalinas driven by Jess Tyree, Howard Masales, Harold Ramsey, Jim Wangers, Arnie Beswick, Lewis Sharp, Fred Davisson, Don Gay, and others found success at tracks across the country. Whether they were regional or national wins,

*A lesser-known but competitive Super Duty Catalina was Hairy Canary Too, which was driven by Skip Stegenga for Goodwin Pontiac in Grand Rapids, Michigan. (Photo Courtesy Jim Luikens)*

> "PONTIAC CLEANED HOUSE WITH THE 389 AND 421 SUPER DUTY V-8s IN NATIONAL AND REGIONAL COMPETITIONS."

*Capitalizing on its use of aluminum sheet metal, Alcoa sponsored a 1962 421 Super Duty Catalina that was raced by driver Kenny Alcoa. It was a frequent competitor at York US 30 Drag-O-Way. Alcoa Presents: One Step Beyond was a TV series that was similar to the Twilight Zone. (Photo Courtesy Jim Luikens)*

*Howard Masales continued to run his 1962 421 Super Duty Packer Pontiac Catalina for the rest of the decade. It is seen here on the back of a Chevy ramp truck in 1969. (Photo Courtesy Howard Masales)*

*Lewis Sharp ran the car in the A/Stock class, where it eventually ran ETs as quick as 11.87 and produced top speeds as fast as 122 mph. (Photo Courtesy Samuel H. Williford)*

*Lewis Sharp is seen here with his 1962 Catalina shortly after he took ownership of it in 1964. It was delivered to Lane-Moak Pontiac in Jackson, Mississippi. The car featured the 421 Super Duty engine, a T-10 4-speed transmission, and a 4.30:1 rear end. The car was shipped to Nichels Engineering for blueprinting. It had an aluminum hood, inner fenders, and bumpers, but the fenders were steel. Sharp later purchased aluminum fenders from a different Mandalay Red Catalina that was raced in Louisiana. They matched perfectly after buffing the whole car. Sharp drove the car for the dealership before he purchased it from Lane-Moak. (Photo Courtesy Samuel H. Williford)*

*The Lane-Moak Super Duty Catalina initially ran in the NHRA's B/Stock category under ownership by the dealership and later with Lewis Sharp. The 405 number was chosen due to the 421 Super Duty's power output rating. (Photo Courtesy Samuel H. Williford)*

*The Lane-Moak 421 Super Duty Catalina is shown at the Jackson Sports Arena drag strip in Jackson, Mississippi. Note the nose-up attitude, which greatly aided traction. (Photo Courtesy Samuel H. Williford)*

*Lewis Sharp is reunited with his original 1962 Catalina 421 Super Duty race car at a show in Mississippi in 2023. (Photo Courtesy Samuel H. Williford)*

*In late 1964, the Lane-Moak Catalina is seen at the dealership. Lewis Sharp owned the car at this point in its history. (Photo Courtesy Samuel H. Williford)*

the result was fantastic for Pontiac in terms of publicity, sales, and headlines, which translated to sales records for the now-number-three manufacturer in Detroit.

In a recent interview with Lewis Sharp, who raced a 1962 Super Duty Catalina in Mississippi in the 1960s, his success with the car lasted long after the General Motors racing ban took effect. He ran the car through the 1969 season and was very successful at tracks in the South.

Sharp posted a best ET of 11.87 in Biloxi, Mississippi. It eventually ran up against a 409 Chevy that was quicker in every round and was running in the 12s. Each car worked its way through eliminations to meet in the finals. Sharp edged him by a nose for the win.

Lewis told the story of meeting up with Sox & Martin and their Plymouth GTX.

"They had a meet at Hub City Dragway in Hattiesburg, Mississippi, and we drew names to see who was running against who," he said. "The competition was tough. One of my friends said, 'I just drew an altered-wheelbase Dodge!' I said to him, 'I just drew Sox & Martin!'"

The race was a bit of an upset for many fans. Although Ronnie Sox got the jump on him, Lewis caught up and won.

"By the time I hit fourth gear, I passed him on the top end," Lewis said. "My motto always was 'drive it like someone else owns it!'"

### The Crown Jewel Races

Ultimately, while Ford, General Motors, and Mopar played catch up, Pontiac ran away with the most prestigious titles in drag racing. Its steadfast performance from February (Winternationals) through September (US Nationals) encapsulated a tremendous year that few other manufacturers were ever able to duplicate.

| Pontiac Wins at the 1962 NHRA Winternationals in Pomona, California | | | | |
|---|---|---|---|---|
| **Class** | **Driver** | **Hometown** | **Car** | **Other Details** |
| A/FX | Hayden Proffitt | Westminster, California | 1962 421 Super Duty Tempest | Ran a 12.37 ET at 117.27 mph to defeat Marvin Ford in the Glen E. Thomas Dodge |
| SS/S | Hayden Proffitt | Westminster, California | 1962 421 Super Duty Catalina | 12.75 ET at 111.94 mph |
| S/S | Jess Tyree | Santa Ana, California | 1962 421 Super Duty Catalina | 13.11 ET at 108.85 mph |
| S/SA | Carol Cox | Whittier, California | 1961 Ventura 389 Super Duty | 13.06 ET at 107.65 mph |
| SS/SA | Lloyd Cox | Whittier, California | 1962 Catalina #671 | Ran a 13.00 ET at 107.65 mph to defeat Gary Nichols in the *Hot Rod Magazine Special* 1962 Chrysler 300 |
| A/SA | Don Bennett | Clinton, Iowa | 1962 Catalina | 14.21 ET at 96.98 mph |
| D/Stock | Allen and Pat Hart | Temple City, California | 1960 Catalina | Ran a 14.20 ET at 96.15 mph in D/Stock to defeat the *Bill's Service* 1958 Chevy Impala |

*Lloyd Cox was busy at the 1962 Winternationals. In addition to tuning Carol's Ventura, he prepared and raced his Mickey Thompson 421 Super Duty Catalina sedan. He took home the SS/SA trophy, running a 13.00 ET at 107.65 mph, beating Gary Nichols in the* Hot Rod Magazine Special *1962 Chrysler 300. (Photo Courtesy Steve Cox)*

*Lloyd Cox shows off the trophy for his A/FX win at the 1962 NHRA Nationals at Indy. The car was renumbered from 672 to 972 to signify Cox taking over driving duties from Hayden Proffitt. Proffitt left the Thompson camp and took a factory deal with Chevy at his own shop. (Photo Courtesy Steve Cox)*

| Class | Driver | Hometown | Car | Other Details |
|---|---|---|---|---|
| Pontiac Wins at the 1962 NHRA Nationals, Indianapolis, Indiana | | | | |
| A/FX | Lloyd Cox | Whittier California | 1962 421 Super Duty Tempest | 12.66 ET at 115.68 mph |
| S/S | Bill Sasse/ Arlen Vanke | Akron, Ohio | 1961 Catalina | Ran a 13.40 ET at 108.43 mph to defeat Bob Harrop's 1961 Catalina |
| S/SA | Carol Cox | Whittier, California | 1961 Ventura | 13.69 ET at 106.25 mph |
| A/SA | Ralph Hardt | Croydon, Pennsylvania | 1961 Ventura | 14.43 ET at 98.79 mph |
| B/SA | Larry Leonard | Bell-Leonard Pontiac, Garden Grove, California | 1961 Catalina | 14.77 ET at 96.77 mph |
| G/SA | Dan Roberts | Horsepower Engineering, Pasadena, California | 1956 Pontiac two-door sedan | 16.04 ET at 84.90 mph |

## Beswick Wins in Albany, Georgia

Arnie Beswick had a rough start for the 1962 season. There were delays in the build of his 1962 Catalina race car, and he was stripped of his wins at Daytona due to some political actions on the part of NASCAR, which sanctioned the drag-racing program. Nevertheless, the season smoothed out with a brisk match-racing schedule, and the wins continued to pile up.

His 1962 Catalina was prepped by Ray Nichels, who bored it out and balanced and blueprinted the short-block.

> "ARNIE AND HIS NEW CAR DOMINATED AT HIS HOME TRACK (CORDOVA DRAGWAY IN CORDOVA, ILLINOIS) SO MUCH SO THAT TRACK OWNER BOB BARTEL OFFERED TO PAY BESWICK'S ENTRY FEE AT ANY OTHER TRACK TO GIVE OTHERS A CHANCE TO WIN AT HIS TRACK."

The car was delivered to Beswick in June 1962, and the results were significant. It quickly proved to be a much quicker car than his 1961 model. Arnie and his new car dominated at his home track (Cordova Dragway in Cordova, Illinois) so much so that track owner Bob Bartel offered to pay Beswick's entry fee at any other track to give others a chance to win at his track. Beswick won a highly-publicized best-of-three match race against popular Ford racer Dick Brannon. Beswick won with a sweep.

Beswick and his hard-charging *Passionate Poncho* 1962 Catalina closed out the 1962 season with a gigantic feather in his cap: a world record for low ET at the famed US 19 Dragway in Albany, Georgia. There, he set a record low ET of 12.11 and backed it up with a 12.12. It was one of the highlights of his racing career at that point.

### Looking Forward

The 1963 model year brought a lot of new and exotic cars and parts for Pontiac racers, although the 1961s and 1962s continued and found their own successful niches in various Stock and Super Stock classes.

# CHAPTER 6

# 1963: PONTIAC RACING: ALL IN BUT THEN ALL DONE

Although the Super Duty 421 engines helped Pontiac amass victories across the country, the competition began to catch up by 1963. Chrysler, whose unibody cars were 200 to 300 pounds lighter than the Catalinas, posed the greatest threat. Combined with the cross-ram Max Wedge V-8s that increased in displacement from 413 to 426 ci, Dodge and Plymouth quickly emerged as the cars to beat. They weren't alone.

Chevrolet elevated its game with the Z-11 package that featured a new 427-ci version of the W-series V-8 and lightened body panels. Ford was also busy and released a hotter version of its Galaxie Lightweight, featuring a new 427 side-oiler V-8 and a wide array of lightweight body panels. The engine was available as the R-Code in standard Galaxies.

Pontiac had no time to rest on its laurels. It released a new version of the 421 Super Duty and two new versions of its factory-built race cars. In addition, three Grand Prix Super Duty 421 cars were built in 1963, although none are known to have survived.

## Super Duty Engine Updates

The 389 Super Duty engine was discontinued for 1963, but the 421 Super Duty was available in NASCAR and drag-racing versions. While the basic short-block remained essentially unchanged, it received essentially

*These cars show two different approaches to competing with a factory race car in 1963. The conventional full-size* Old Reliable IV *Chevy B-Body (left) features a host of lightweight componentry and a 427-ci W-series V-8. The Pontiac Y-Body features a 421 Super Duty engine, an exotic rear-mounted 4-speed transaxle, and a lightweight aluminum front end. Unfortunately, both were caught up in the aftermath of the General Motors ban on racing. Neither car was homologated for competition in the NHRA's Stock or Super Stock classes, which put them both in the FX class. (Photo Courtesy Jim Luikens)*

an all-new top end for 1963 with redesigned cylinder heads (part number 9711980) and a wider variety of intake manifolds. In addition to the familiar single 4-barrel NASCAR intake (part number 544128), a new 3-barrel intake manifold (part number 9772390) was designed to accept a Carter 3636S trap-door 3-barrel carburetor.

For the drag racers, a variety of dual-quad intakes were available in factory-built cars and over the counter through the parts network. In addition to the standard dual-quad unit (part number 9770859) that was used on factory-built Catalinas and Grand Prixs, there was a tunnel-ram design, known as the bathtub intake (part number 9772128). It was revised during its production, and several versions were made.

"Little Joe" Weatherly (left) and Glenn "Fireball" Roberts are seen here with Roberts's #22 1963 Catalina at the inaugural Winston Western 500 at Riverside. Both racers drove for Pontiac before they headed over to Ford for 1964. Weatherly was the 1962 Winston Cup champion, and he repeated the feat in 1963. Sadly, both drivers were killed during the 1964 NASCAR season. (Photo Courtesy LaDow Publishing Company)

*A. J. Foyt sits on a moped next to his 1963 Catalina stock car at Riverside Raceway. Although Pontiac built NASCAR-specification Super Duty cars, not all of the cars that competed were factory-built Super Duty cars, as the number of cars that raced was more than the number of suspected NASCAR Super Duty builds. Many builders either bought a car off the lot or rebuilt a wrecked car and fitted it with the latest Super Duty engine and driveline parts and crafted their own suspension. (Photo Courtesy LaDow Publishing Company)*

*Miami-based racer Bobby Johns stands next to his Allison Pontiac 1963 Catalina stock car. He competed in 12 races that year and finished in the top 5 three times and top 10 six times. Johns raced from 1956 through 1969. (Photo Courtesy LaDow Publishing Company)*

The bathtub intake came with a provision to use an optional Corvair YH side-draft carburetor for idling purposes that was located between the AFBs. If the system wasn't used, the opening was closed with a block-off plate. A later version did away with the Corvair carburetor idling system, which added weight and complexity.

While the heads still featured the same 2.02/1.76-inch valve sizes, the distance between the exhaust ports was widened to increase airflow. The change necessitated the use of redesigned exhaust manifolds. Tuliped valves were used for additional flow. In addition to an updated version of the familiar cast-iron headers used on the 1962 engines, the same design was cast in aluminum to reduce weight. The cast-iron versions weighed about 70 pounds per pair, while the aluminum versions dropped

*Oregon-based Len Sutton poses next to his 1963 Catalina stocker. Along with stock car racing, Sutton raced Indy cars and finished second in the 1962 Daytona 500. He retired from racing in 1965 and had a successful career as a radio broadcaster. (Photo Courtesy LaDow Publishing Company)*

*The only known example of a 1963 421 Super Duty Pontiac that used the 9772128 dual-quad bathtub intake manifold with the Corvair side-draft idling carburetor was displayed at the 2014 Pontiac-Oakland Club International (POCI) convention in Wichita, Kansas. Owner Jim Allen, of Davenport, Iowa, has this special engine installed in a 1953 Studebaker Starliner coupe.*

the weight to about 25 pounds per pair. They were not intended for extended-time use because the aluminum would heat up and melt. A third design was a stamped sheet-metal header design that was used in the 1963 Y-Body cars.

It was true that the Pontiacs were 200 to 300 pounds heavier than the unitized B-Body Mopars, but they made up the difference with the weight-reducing aluminum body panels. However, Chrysler also began to use aluminum body parts, so that same 300-pound weight difference returned, despite Pontiac's best efforts. With the level competition being so high, something had to be done, and it was.

## Advertised Power versus Reality

How much power did the 421 Super Duty engine make? With a factory rating of 405 hp in 1962 for dual-quad engines with 11:1 compression, the same 405 hp in 1963 for 12:1 compression, and 410 hp for 13:1 compression engines, it is clearly evident that the factory played games with ratings to make them more attractive for weight breaks and other factors in NHRA Super Stock racing. While the legendary journalist Roger Huntington experimented with homemade accelerometers to measure acceleration and arrive at an estimate of 460 to 465 gross hp at the flywheel, modern methods have put a real number on the 421 Super Duty's true output.

*American Muscle Car*, a cable TV show that aired on Speedvision and Fox Speed, was produced by the late veteran muscle-car and racing enthusiast Stan Rarden. The show set out to discover exactly how much power the engines had. The episode pitted a stock dual-quad 409/409 Chevy engine against a stock 1963 421 Super Duty engine with the 980 heads and the low-profile dual-quad intake.

The 421 Super Duty engine registered a maximum of 488 hp and 470 ft-lbs of torque, and the 409 produced 406.5 hp and 430 ft-lbs of torque. Huntington's estimations were in the ballpark—if not a bit conservative. Even Chevrolet's oppositional research determined that the 1963 421 Super Duty made an additional 40 hp compared to the previous year, which bolstered the case for the late-1962 release of the Z-11 and the NASCAR-inspired 427 Chevrolet Mystery Motor. At that time, the divisions had no idea that the racing ban was looming. At the time, the competition between Pontiac and Chevy was fierce.

## The Competition

The culmination of competition on the drag strip for the Big Three manufacturers was in 1963. All three manufacturers offered displacement above 420 ci and created what many believe to be the zenith of the golden era of doorslammers. Unfortunately, the war never saw itself through, but here's what the competition brought to the table.

### The Chevy Z-11

The Chevy Z-11 engine was the ultimate version of the W-Series Chevy big-block, which was introduced as a 348-ci engine for passenger cars and trucks. Higher-performance versions of the 348 included a Tri-Power engine that made 350 hp as well as a limited-production, 360-hp, 4-barrel 409 engine that was released in late 1961.

The 409 engine returned in 1962 in single and dual 4-barrel versions with power ratings up to 425 hp. With the larger power numbers and lightweight Biscayne and Bel Air bodies sporting aluminum sheet metal, Chevrolet was justifiably anxious about what the competition had in store. It already knew that Pontiac was increasing the power and going on a diet for 1963, and it was a sure bet that Ford and Mopar were working to go faster as well.

The RPO Z-11 Chevy was a complete package that put Chevy back at the top level of competition. Sharing the same bore size as the 409 engine, the familiar W-block was stroked from 3.5 to 3.65 inches. New cylinder heads were designed, and while they retained

*Bill Clay is behind the wheel of the Silver Blue A/FX 1963 Chevrolet Z-11 Impala at the 1963 NHRA Nationals in Indianapolis. The Z-11 was sponsored by Hattan Chevrolet of Wichita, Kansas. The fragility of the lightweight aluminum body parts is evident here. (Photo Courtesy Martyn L. Schorr)*

the quirky combustion-chamber design and the 409's 2.19/1.72-inch valve sizes, the castings were taller, allowing for straighter ports.

The valves were operated by a new solid-lifter cam design that featured 325 degrees of advertised duration and 556 inches of lift. The new heads required a new two-piece dual-quad intake system. The bottom piece contained the water jackets and served as a valley cover. A pair of Carter AFBs topped the engine and were fed by a large cowl-induction air cleaner. Exhaust gases flowed through cast-iron headers.

With a whopping 13.5:1 compression, the Z-11 427 engine was rated at 430 hp at 6,000 rpm. However, modern estimates put the actual output closer to 500 hp. All Z-11 engines were backed by a BorgWarner T-10 4-speed transmission and 4.11 gears. Other features included a full array of aluminum sheet metal, the deletion of all sound-deadening material and insulation, and the use of a front sway bar. The weight reduction resulted in 300 pounds of weight being shed for the Impalas and racers, such as Dave Strickler and Don Nicholson. These cars were extremely competitive. Only 57 were built in 1963 before the axe came down on all of GM's racing activities.

### Max Wedge Mopars Get Bigger

Across town in Highland Park, Michigan, the Mopar engineers worked diligently to maintain the competitive

edge of their Max Wedge cars. As with their rivals, they maintained a competitive edge with more displacement and less weight. A bore increase from 4.19 to 4.25 inches combined with the 3.75-inch stroke added 13 ci and provided 426 ci of displacement. Plymouths were called the 426 Super Stock, while the Dodge version was known as the Ramcharger 426. They were actually the same engine.

In addition to the bore increase, the 426 Max Wedge engines benefitted from a new cylinder-head design with 25-percent-larger ports and 2.08/1.880-inch valves, which greatly increased airflow from the year before, and the manifold heat risers were also eliminated. Streamlined cast-iron headers were once again used. On top of the engine was an aluminum cross-ram dual-quad intake that was fed by two Carter 4-barrel carburetors.

Two versions were available. The first had a street-friendly 11.0:1 compression ratio, and the all-out racing version had a high 13.5:1 compression ratio. The lower-compression version was rated at 415 hp at 5,200 rpm with 470 ft-lbs of torque at 4,400 rpm. The higher-compression engine increased those ratings to 425 hp and 480 ft-lbs of torque. The mechanical-lifter camshaft featured 300 degrees of duration and a 0.509-inch lift.

Later, a Stage II version was introduced with true square-bore intake flanges for 700 cfm from each

*Hayden Proffit's carousel of cars landed him at Plymouth in the second half of 1963. Proffitt went from Pontiac (1962) to Chevrolet (1963) to Plymouth (1963 and 1964) to Mercury (1965) and back to Chevrolet (1966). In 1967, he drove an AMC. (Photo Courtesy Tom Bettencourt)*

carburetor as well as modifications to the combustion-chamber design. It had a new camshaft with 300/308 degrees of duration and 0.520-inch lift. The Stage II engine's rating remained the same as before, but horsepower did actually increase.

As with Ford and Chevy, Chrysler stamped out aluminum sheet metal for its cars to maintain the 300-pound weight advantage that it had over the Chevys and Pontiacs. The combination of more power and less weight helped keep racers such as Roger Lindamood, the Ramchargers, and others in the mix during the 1963 season.

In many respects, the 426 Max Wedge was a placeholder that was designed to keep the competition at bay for the 1963 season and early into 1964. Although a Stage III engine came out in 1964, it was a precursor to the release of the new-generation 426 Hemi.

### Ford Releases the 427

Meanwhile, in Dearborn, Michigan, the Ford Total Performance program hit its stride with a wealth of new parts and cars for racers. The new R-Code Galaxie lightweight offered new styling, a 427-ci powerplant, lightweight body panels, and a substantial power increase.

The big news for 1963 was the engine. It featured a 4.232-inch bore and a 3.784-inch stroke, which was shared with the 390 and 406 engines.

The actual displacement was 425.81 ci but was referred to as a 427 for marketing reasons. The R-Code engines used a special high-nickel block with cross-bolted mains for added durability. Forged pistons and rods as well as wedge-type heads with 2.09/1.66-inch valves provided 11.5:1 compression. A solid-lifter cam with 306 degrees of duration and 0.500-inch lift was used, and a transistorized ignition fired off the mixture. Streamlined cast-iron headers routed out the spent gases.

On top of the Q-Code engine was a single 780 Holley carburetor, while the R-Code engine featured a pair of 540-cfm 4160-series Holley carburetors—each on its own low-rise aluminum intake. The Q-Code engine was rated at 410 hp at 5,600 rpm with 476 ft-lbs of torque at 3,400 rpm. The R-Code produced an additional 15 hp (425 hp) at 6,000 rpm to go with 480 ft-lbs of torque at 3,700 rpm. Both ratings are significantly undervalued, with the R-code engine making 480 to 500 hp.

The big Fords shed weight starting with a frame that used a lighter gauge of steel tubing that was similar to the units that were used in the 300-series 6-cylinder full-size cars (but not exactly the same). The bodies featured all the standard weight-saving techniques, such as deleted insulation and sound-deadening material. They also had a full complement of fiberglass body parts and aluminum bumpers. Approximately 212 were built. Each of the cars featured Wimbledon White paint, a red interior, a Dearborn Toploader 4-speed, and a 4.11-geared 9-inch rear end.

As it turned out, the big white Fords were not in the winner's circle as much as the manufacturer had hoped during the 1963 season. However it motivated Lee Iacocca to put the Blue Oval in the winner's circle in 1964. Several of the factory lightweight 1963 cars found success in later years in the hands of privateer racers.

### The "Swiss Cheese" Catalinas

For 1963, Pontiac released the "Swiss cheese" Catalinas that were so aptly named by legendary journalist Roger

*Dick Brannan's 1963 Galaxie lightweight is shown at Howard Masales's house in suburban Detroit in the summer of 1963. Brannan was friends with Masales and was staying at his house when the photo was taken. (Photo Courtesy Mike Huffman)*

*Arlen Vanke's Anderson Pontiac* Tin Indian III *1963 Swiss cheese Catalina is shown at the 1963 Winternationals but did not compete at that event. (Photo Courtesy Joe Webber Archives)*

*The 421 Super Duty engine in the* Packer Pontiac *Swiss cheese car made use of the latest technology that Pontiac offered. It had the 980 heads with the wide exhaust-port spacing, an improved dual-quad intake, and aluminum exhaust headers. Although the low production number didn't qualify the heads for use in the NHRA's Stock or Super Stock classes, they fit nicely into the FX category. (Photo Courtesy Mike Huffman)*

Huntington. He commented that the holes drilled in the frame for weight reduction reminded him of Swiss cheese. The holes reduced weight by about 70 pounds but caused some structural issues.

The weight-loss program was as ambitious as any previous attempt by an American manufacturer on an existing car. Pontiac engineers were able to eliminate more than 800 pounds from the Catalinas and employed such tricks as Plexiglas windows, a single windshield wiper, single exhaust, and aluminum differential center sections. This is in addition to the full complement of aluminum body panels, the deletion of sound-deadening material and insulation, and the omitted equipment, including the radio, heater, and front sway bar. Fourteen of these cars were built: 12 in Frost Silver, 1 in a Cadillac color, and 2 in Silvermist. Of those 14, 9 are known to survive. One is known to have been wrecked and dismantled early on.

The efforts produced mixed results. While the weight was reduced, there were some negative side effects. The frames were substantially weakened by the hole drilling. Every unit that went down the track experienced frame twisting, cracking, or outright breaking. Gusseting was needed to repair the frames to make them race-worthy. The track record of the Swiss cheese Catalinas was not as sweeping as it was in 1962, as the competition elevated its game. However, the Pontiacs continued to be a force to be reckoned with. In addition, they took longer to sort out and perform at their best due to the fragility of the chassis.

Royal Pontiac could not match the winning record of its 1962 Super Duty Catalina two-door sedan with its Swiss cheese lightweight car. Although, on paper, the

*The Hodges Pontiac* Swiss cheese Catalina *was driven by Clyde "Red" Snell and Bill Fletcher for dealership/team owner Al Hodges. Its ultimate fate is unknown, but it may have been the base for a Super Gas race car built in the 1980s for East Coast racer Ed Alessi. (Photo Courtesy Jim Luikens)*

## Howard Masales's 1963 Swiss Cheese Catalina

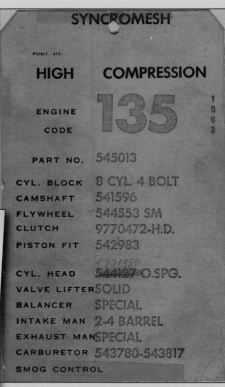

The original Packer Pontiac *Swiss cheese* Catalina is shown in 2006 at the home of then-owner Randy Williams. The Swiss cheese cars had more than 800 pounds removed for competition use. The weight-loss program was extensive and included Plexiglas windows, aluminum parts (sheet metal, steering box, differential center section, intake manifold, and exhaust manifold), and holes drilled in the frame. This car was restored by Scott Tiemann at Supercar Specialties in Portland, Michigan, and is now owned by Mike Huffman.

The 421 Super Duty engine is shown just before it was removed from the chassis. The 980 heads with the wider exhaust ports, cast-aluminum headers, and 9770859 dual-quad intake are visible. (Photo Courtesy Mike Huffman)

This delivery tag provides the specifications for the engine that was used in the Packer Pontiac *Swiss cheese* car, including the camshaft, flywheel, clutch, and carburetor part numbers. Note that the 544127 head listing is crossed out, and "9771980" is handwritten in its place to indicate that there was a running change. It is amazing that this tag still exists. (Photo Courtesy Mike Huffman)

Howard Masales took delivery of his 1963 Swiss cheese Catalina in February 1963. The car is fresh from the factory in these photos. The plastic coverings on the seats are still present. The Plexiglas side windows were provided but had to be installed by the owner. (Photo Courtesy Mike Huffman)

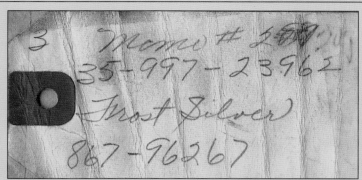

Another delivery tag shows the memo number that was used as a guide for the building of the Packer Pontiac Swiss cheese car. Information includes the zone, delivering dealer, and color. The overspray on the tag was used by Scott Tiemann to match the paint during the car's restoration. (Photo Courtesy Mike Huffman)

This photo of the factory exhaust system for the Swiss cheese Catalinas shows a single-outlet design with cutouts to allow the headers to be run wide open. The choice of a single exhaust was to keep the weight down. The added weight of a second muffler and the related pipe was seen as unnecessary. (Photo Courtesy Mike Huffman)

The Packer Pontiac Swiss cheese Catalina is being lettered by Mr. Burns of Burns Sign Studio in Detroit. Burns handled all of the custom sign painting for Packer Pontiac, and he lettered the shop trucks and other equipment. Here, he is using a stick brush to letter the "M" in Miami, which was one of the dealership's locations. (Photo Courtesy Mike Huffman)

A young Howard Maseles stands next to his freshly lettered Swiss cheese Catalina race car. Masales's car was built in January 1963, just before the racing ban was issued. (Photo Courtesy Mike Huffman)

## Howard Masales's 1963 Swiss Cheese Catalina

The Packer Pontiac *Swiss cheese* Catalina is shown shortly after the lettering was completed. These photos were critical in the restoration of this car in the late 1990s. (Photo Courtesy Mike Huffman)

Although the racing ban was in effect at the time that these cars were raced in competition, Pontiac agreed to pay for the repair of the frames when they were damaged while racing. Masales sent his car to Nichels Engineering in Highland, Indiana. It is seen there on lifts to repair the cracks that developed. (Photo Courtesy Mike Huffman)

Maseles raced the Swiss cheese Cata lina north of the border. Here, the car is shown with trophies that were won at St. Thomas Dragway in St. Thomas, Ontario, Canada. St. Thomas is only a two-hour drive from Detroit. (Photo Courtesy Mike Huffman)

The Packer Pontiac *Swiss cheese* Catalina is shown with the 1962 Packer Pontiac Catalina. According to Howard Masales, the 7-11 was a reference to Mr. Packer Jr.'s interest in games of chance. If you look closely, the "P" in Packer Pontiac is not there on the white car. Masales was in the process of removing the name from the quarter panel. Packer Pontiac only sponsored one car at a time, so he was making space for a new sponsor. (Photo Courtesy Mike Huffman)

Maseles was always careful to make sure that the relatively fragile chassis was properly supported when it was jacked up. It was easy to damage the frame, as about 70 pounds of metal had been removed from it at the factory. (Photo Courtesy Mike Huffman)

A shot of the Packer Pontiac *Swiss cheese* Catalina soon after preparation for racing in the spring of 1963. (Photo Courtesy Mike Huffman)

The frame of the Packer Pontiac shows the meaning of the term "Swiss cheese." The nickname was coined by the late automotive journalist Roger Huntington. More than 100 holes removed about 70 pounds of metal from the frame, which had the unwanted effect of weakening it in the process. All the Swiss cheese cars that raced needed some sort of reinforcement. (Photo Courtesy Howard Maseles)

*Howard Masales (center) poses with crew members Charlie Ferlotte (left) and Gary Maten, who assisted him at the home shop and the track. Here, they are seen with the Swiss cheese Catalina's engine sitting in a Radio Flyer wagon just after removal. (Photo Courtesy Mike Huffman)*

Howard Maseles and the Packer Pontiac *Swiss cheese* Catalina make a run in the A/FX class at St. Thomas Dragway. Due to the low production numbers caused by the General Motors racing ban and no prospect for more being built, there was no way that it would be homologated for NHRA Stock or Super Stock. As a result, those cars were sent to the FX classes. While the Packer Pontiac car competed in A/FX, Royal Pontiac added some weight in the Swiss cheese Catalina and won the D/FX class at the NHRA Nationals. Note the customized grille. (Photo Courtesy Howard Maseles)

The 1963 421 Super Duty bathtub intake was an early version of what became the tunnel-ram intake manifold. The intake runners were designed to generate a high degree of velocity. Combined with the cam timing, it could achieve approximately 100-percent volumetric efficiency. Two Carter 4-barrel carburetors were mounted on the intake manifold, and the car featured a removable top. (Photo Courtesy Howard Maseles)

*While the Royal Pontiac Swiss cheese Catalina was not as successful of a race car as the 1962 sedan, it still made its mark. The car won the B/FX class at the 1963 NHRA Nationals with a 12.59 ET at 110.83 mph but lost to Dave Strickler's 1963 Z-11 Chevy in the Little Eliminator finals. (Photo Courtesy Jim Luikens)*

> "THE NHRA INTERVENED AND DISALLOWED THE SWISS CHEESE CARS FROM SUPER STOCK AFTER THE RACING BAN."

*Jim Wangers makes an exhibition run with his original Royal Pontiac 1963 Swiss cheese Catalina at the 2009 Ames Performance Pontiac Nationals. Owner Bob Knudsen is in the passenger's seat.*

1963 model was clearly superior with its lighter weight and engine upgrades.

The NHRA intervened and disallowed the Swiss cheese cars from Super Stock after the racing ban, as the minimum homologation number of 50 units built had not been met. Knowing that no more would be made, they were sent to Factory Experimental, where they fit quite nicely in B/FX.

| Swiss Cheese Catalina Information | | |
|---|---|---|
| VIN | Original Dealer and/or Racer | Current Owner (2023) |
| 363P100338 | Pete Seaton | Unknown- Hidden in Chicago area |
| 363P104314 | Packer Pontiac/Howard Masales | Mike Huffman, Ohio |
| 363P165870 | Cub Collingwood | Mike Huffman, Ohio |
| 363P096968 | Mike Salta Pontiac/Mickey Thompson | Mike Huffman, Ohio |
| 363P097384 | Royal Pontiac/Jim Wangers | Bob Knudsen, Idaho |
| 363P097386 | Mike Salta Pontiac/Mickey Thompson #2 | Bob Knudsen, Idaho |
| 363P097500 | Anderson Pontiac/Arlen Vanke | Unknown |
| 363P097733 | Van Winkle Pontiac/Monk King | Irwin Kroiz, Pennsylvania |
| 363P097991 | Seltzer Pontiac/Arnie Beswick | Jerry Kelley, Georgia |
| 363P099198 | Union Park Pontiac/ Harold Ramsey | Mike Huffman, Ohio |
| 363P097766 | Unknown | Unknown |
| 363P104307 | Unknown | Unknown |
| 363P106262 | Unknown | Unknown |
| 363P167168 (Silvermist Gray) | Milner Pontiac | Don Snyder, Ohio |

Notes: The information about which car is which among the missing cars has not been verified at this time. This includes the Bobby Watson/Miller Pontiac car that was destroyed early on, the George DeLorean car, and the Hodges Pontiac car. The Hodges Pontiac car's remains may have been used to build the Super Gas race car that is owned by Ed Alessi.

*Pete Seaton's 1963 Swiss cheese Catalina was customized with Nocturne Blue bodysides and was originally tuned by George DeLorean's Wynn Engineering Company. It was planned to run in the Super Stock class, but those plans changed after the racing ban. (Photo Courtesy Howard Maseles)*

*Pete Seaton was sponsored by Royal Pontiac and competed in the B/FX class, although it wasn't a Royal Pontiac car. Seaton is shown standing on the left, and he handled the tuning in-house by Seaton. (Photo Courtesy Jim Luikens)*

*Arnie "the Farmer" Beswick's 1963 Passionate Poncho Swiss cheese Catalina is seen here in the pits at the Drag News Stock Car Invitational during the 1963 Fourth of July weekend at Dragway 42 in West Salem, Ohio. (Photo Courtesy Mike Huffman)*

### The Super Duty Tempest/LeMans Program

To remain competitive, Pontiac's approach to winning was multi-faceted when it came to drag racing. The Super Duty Catalinas that were equipped with lightweight sheet metal were the most popular version of the car. In addition, there were the Swiss cheese cars and the Super Duty Tempest/LeMans race cars.

The idea of shoehorning a 421 Super Duty V-8 into the compact Tempest came the year before, as Mickey Thompson, Royal Pontiac, and Pontiac Engineering crafted their own versions of the big-engine/little-car engine swap. The results were successful, essentially dominating the new A/FX class. The race cars used conventional drivetrain layouts and pirated transmissions and differentials from full-size Pontiac models. Pontiac Engineering's cars for 1963 were a bit different, though.

Pontiac engineers had a significantly different approach to achieving their goals. While the 421

Arnie Beswick's **Mrs. B's Grocery Getter** *Super Duty Tempest wagon is being serviced at Doug Thorley's header shop in East Los Angeles, California. (Photo Courtesy Arnie Beswick)*

Super Duty engine was going to be part of the plan, they rejected the idea of a conventional driveline, as the 1962 cars experienced traction problems that were associated

*In July 1963, Beswick's Super Duty wagon features a graphics package on the tailgate at the Drag News Stock Car Invitational. The event was held at Dragway 42 in West Salem, Ohio. (Photo Courtesy Mike Huffman)*

*Arnie Beswick poses for a photo with the Mrs. B's Grocery Getter. Although Pontiac was officially out of racing by this time, Beswick made the most of the combination and went after the factory-backed teams with this exotic race car. (Photo Courtesy Mike Huffman)*

*The* Mrs. B's Grocery Getter *is shown in action. The car has disappeared but some say that it is mostly intact somewhere in the Midwest. (Photo Courtesy Jim Luikens)*

*The* Mrs. B's Grocery Getter *launches against a Max Wedge Plymouth at Dragway 42. The fact that the wagon is nearly lifting the front wheels off the ground on those skinny 7-inch slicks proves that the rear-mounted transaxle, despite the complexity and rarity of parts, did what it was designed to do. (Photo Courtesy Jim Luikens)*

with their nose-heavy nature. Adding to the problem was the fact that tire technology was nowhere near what it is today. The 7-inch slicks were the best available tires for the A/FX racers. Experience gained during the 1962 season showed Pontiac's Super Duty program engineers that there was significant room for improvement. Most drag races are won or lost at the starting line. If your tires go up in smoke, the chances of catching up for the win are slim.

Pontiac Engineer Bill Collins was intrigued by the idea of retaining a rear-mounted transaxle to put more

*Bill Jarrett drove this 1963 421 Super Duty LeMans coupe (VIN 263P076861) for Superior Pontiac in San Antonio, Texas. After the whereabouts*

*of this car had been unknown for decades, it was located in 2014 in western New York and purchased by collector Andrew Rock. He is having it restored by Scott Tiemann of Supercar Specialties in Portland, Michigan. (Photo Courtesy Jim Luikens)*

The 1963 Union Park Pontiac 421 Super Duty Tempest wagon was originally raced by Joe DeNick, who named it Instant (after the Fels Naphtha soap of the same name). To date, it is the only one of the six 421 Super Duty Tempest wagons that are known to exist. Rumors of the possible existence of the Royal Pontiac car and the original Mrs. B's Grocery Getter being hidden in the Midwest persist.

This is a vintage photo of the Union Park Wagon after DeNick owned it (circa 1964–1965). At this time, it was owned by Buzz Hoge and Bill Blair and sponsored by Hoge's employer, Doug Willey Pontiac in Birmingham, Alabama. After moving around for several years with a variety of other owners, including Mike Garfinkel and Dave Johnson, the car was eventually purchased by Randy Williams in 1980. It was largely intact but was in need of restoration. (Photo Courtesy Todd Holzknecht)

The 755 A/FX 1963 421 Super Duty Tempest was campaigned by Mickey Thompson. It is seen here at the 1963 NHRA Winternationals in Pomona. This car was Yorktown Blue and was the first of two 421 Super Duty/Power-Shift transaxle prototypes built about a month before the six production LeMans coupes and Tempest wagons. This car is in a private collection in Florida. (Photo Courtesy Jim Luikens)

The Ray Nichels prototype 421 Super Duty Tempest is probably the last factory Super Duty car currently competing. It is seen here with then-owner Bill Blair racing against a 409 Chevy in a nostalgia race in Farmington, North Carolina, in the late 1980s. Current owner Ken Freeman raced it at the 2023 Ames Performance Pontiac Nationals. (Photo Courtesy Jim Luikens)

The **Royal** Pontiac 421 Super Duty Tempest wagon was driven in the A/FX class by Dick Jesse for the 1963 season. Like the 1962 Tempest, it quietly slipped from the public eye. Some claim that it is hidden in a collection in the Midwest, but little else is known. (Photo Courtesy Jim Luikens)

Jess Tyree drives one of his 1963 LeMans race cars. This car is known as the "Mystery Coupe" because it can't be conclusively confirmed which of the three cars it is. Although, it is likely the original Thompson 749, which was driven to victory at the 1963 Winternationals. (Photo Courtesy Jim Luikens)

Dick Jesse in the **Royal** Pontiac *Super Duty* Tempest wagon lines up against Dave Strickler in the **Old Reliable IV** 1963 Z-11 427 Chevy, which was tuned by Bill "Grumpy" Jenkins from Jenkins Performance in Malvern, Pennsylvania. (Photo Courtesy Jim Luikens)

weight over the drive wheels to preserve 50-50 weight distribution of the regular production Tempests. The added traction was a substantial bonus to racers who were dealing with the challenge getting the 421 Super Duty's power to the ground. Unfortunately, the Corvair-based production 3- and 4-speed manual transaxles and the Powerglide-based TempestTorque 2-speed were not able to handle the output of a 421 Super Duty.

Collins's solution was ingenious and made use of existing production technology. The result was a special race-only PowerShift transaxle. The PowerShift was unique, even in the rarified air of the Detroit factory race car. To oversimplify, he designed a new transmission case that held the internal components from two Corvair Powerglide transaxles. More than 200 new parts had to be designed and built to facilitate the conversion. The transaxle ratios were 2.44, 1.76, 1.38, and 1.00. Reverse was 2.44, and the final-drive ratio was 3.90:1. No other final-drive gearset ratios were offered, and the differential was locked for additional traction.

The added traction provided four forward speeds and enough torque capacity to harness the power of the 421 Super Duty V-8, which made about 500 hp. It made a big difference, and the PowerShift Tempests had a traction advantage compared to their competitors. They did need to be rebuilt after 10 runs or so. This innovative transmission used either a clutch or a torque converter, which made it quite versatile from a performance standpoint. Most racers used a clutch for its simplicity and to minimize driveline power losses. The clutch was engaged off the line and didn't need to be used to shift gears during the run. Unfortunately, the lack of parts availability after the racing ban caused many of the original PowerShift-equipped cars to be converted to conventional drivetrains, as wear and breakage inevitably took their toll.

*Tim Benko, the owner and restorer of the original* Running Bear *Tempest, is behind the wheel as original owner and driver Arlen Vanke is in the passenger's seat at the 2010 Ames Performance Pontiac Nationals.*

The 421 Super Duty Tempest/LeMans program produced a total of 14 cars. In addition to the six production LeMans coupes and six Tempest wagons (the latter was included for the added traction provided by the station-wagon bodystyle) that were built in December 1962, there were two earlier prototypes. Both were Tempest coupes with the larger rear window and small round taillamps. One was Silvermist Gray and was sent to Ray Nichels in Indiana for testing. The second car, a Yorktown Blue color, was sent to Mickey Thompson in California, where it was raced.

Although the Y-bodies were much lighter than their Catalina and Grand Prix counterparts, Pontiac equipped them with aluminum front ends (minus the fender trim) and lightened steel doors with the crash beams removed. They were built without any radios, heaters, insulation, or sound-deadening material. The total weight was about 3,160 pounds for the coupes and about 3,300 pounds for the wagon.

Perhaps to obscure their actual origin, Pontiac made it look as if the Super Duty Tempests were used cars. They were fitted with used front tires and delivered with about 2,000 miles on the odometer.

*This full-page advertisement for Bill Knafel's Anderson Pontiac appeared in the program for the 1963 Drag News Invitational. In the advertisement, Arlen Vanke stands between his* Running Bear *car, a 1963 Tempest that was upgraded to Super Duty specifications, and the Anderson Pontiac Swiss cheese Catalina. The Tempest was found and restored in the 1990s by Tim Benko. The ultimate fate of the Catalina remains a mystery. (Photo Courtesy Knafel Family Archives)*

*Arnie Beswick's 1963 421 Super Duty LeMans was originally campaigned by Mickey Thompson as the 756 race car, which was driven by Jess Tyree. This car was raced with the PowerShift transaxle and eventually converted into the orange and tiger-striped* Tameless Tiger *Funny Car that Beswick campaigned until it was destroyed in a crash in 1967. (Photo Courtesy Arnie Beswick)*

*The Gay Pontiac 1963 421 Tempest wagon was originally delivered to Van Winkle Pontiac in Dallas, Texas, before Gay Pontiac picked it up late in the year. It is seen here in 1964. (Photos Courtesy Clinton Wright)*

*Don Gay stands next to the Super Duty Tempest, circa 1964. (Photo Courtesy Clinton Wright)*

"FOR 1963, THE SUPER DUTY 421 ENGINES WERE AVAILABLE IN THE GRAND PRIX SERIES."

*An autographed photo from Paul Goldsmith shows the legendary 50 LeMans before the 1963 Daytona 250 Challenge Cup. (Photo Courtesy Roger Rosebush)*

| Super Duty Tempest/LeMans Information Prototype Tempest Coupes | | |
| --- | --- | --- |
| VIN | Original Dealer and/or Racer | Current Owner (2024) |
| 163P55754 | Yorktown Blue/Mickey Thompson | Private owner, Florida |
| 163P55781 | Ray Nichels | Ken Freeman, Oklahoma |

| Production LeMans Coupes | | |
| --- | --- | --- |
| VIN | Original Dealer and/or Racer | Current Owner (2024) |
| 263P076227 | George DeLorean | Louis J. Mascaro Automotive Museum |
| 263P076237 | Unknown | Thompson 756/Beswick |
| 263P076752 | Stan Long Pontiac/Stan Antlocer | Private owner |
| 263P076861 | Superior Pontiac | Andy Rock, Florida |
| 263P076881 | Unknown | Unknown |
| 263P076971 | Unknown | Unknown |

Notes: The information about which car is which among the missing cars has not been verified. The VINs of the Ray Nichels/Paul Goldsmith #50 LeMans and the Mickey Thompson #749 have not been verified (I do not yet know which is which).

| Production Tempest Wagons | | |
| --- | --- | --- |
| VIN | Original Dealer and/or Racer | Current Owner (2024) |
| 163P095462 | unknown | unknown |
| 163P095476 | unknown | unknown |
| 163P098420 | unknown | unknown |
| 163P098422 | unknown | unknown |
| 163P099224 | Union Park Pontiac | Nick Smith, Florida |
| 163P100134 | unknown | unknown |

Notes: The only VIN that is positively matched to the car at this time is the Union Park Wagon. No other wagons are known to exist, although there are unverified rumors that the Royal Pontiac and Arnie Beswick wagons are in the Midwest. The Van Winkle/Gay Pontiac wagon was reportedly destroyed somewhere between 2008 and 2010 after spending decades in a junkyard. The whereabouts of the Anderson/Knafel and Hodges Pontiac Super Duty wagons are unknown.

For 1963, the Super Duty 421 engines were available in the Grand Prix series. This time around, only three cars were built and were optioned quite differently than the 1962 cars, which were all steel-bodied cars with the 405-hp dual-quad engine and a 4-speed transmission. None of the dealers that ordered 1962 models repeated their order for the second and final year of availability. They were probably difficult to sell with their high price and temperamental engines.

The first car was delivered to Peter Epsteen Pontiac in Skokie, Illinois, for racer Larry Swiatek. This Cameo White Grand Prix was built on October 24, 1962, and ordered with the single 4-barrel, 390-hp 421 Super Duty

engine. As the car was an early build, it came with the 544127 heads and a 544128 intake manifold. They were replaced with the later 908 heads and 390 4-barrel intake, which were legal for that car and had better performance.

Each of the other two 1963 Super Duty Grand Prixs were ordered with the dual-quad 421 Super Duty engine, 4-speed transmission, and aluminum front end. One was Silvermist Gray with 3.42 gears (963P19219), and the other was Nocturne Blue (963P88796) with 4.30 gears. Unfortunately, none of these three cars are known to exist.

| VIN | Original Dealer and/or Racer | Current Owner (2024) |
| --- | --- | --- |
| 963P19219 | Ramey Motor Company, Abbesville, South Carolina | Unknown |
| 963P35067 | Peter Epsteen Pontiac, Skokie, Illinois/Larry Swiatek | Unknown |
| 963P88796 | Stevens Pontiac, Rochelle, Illinois | Unknown |

*American Muscle Car*, a cable TV show that aired on Speedvision (rebranded as Speed) and Fox Speed, was produced by veteran muscle car and racing enthusiast Stan Rarden. The show set out to find out exactly how much power the engines had. One episode pitted a stock dual-quad 409/409 Chevy engine against a stock 1963 421 Super Duty engine that had 980 heads and the low-profile dual-quad intake. The 421 Super Duty registered a maximum of 488 hp and 470 ft-lbs of torque against the 409's 406.5 hp and 430 ft-lbs of torque. Huntington's estimations were in the ballpark—if not a bit conservative.

As amazing and collectible as the 1963 limited-production factory drag cars were, they faced an uphill battle with the competition. Favorable classes still existed for older Pontiacs, and they were able to capitalize at the two biggest cards on the schedule: the Winternationals and the US Nationals.

*Arlen Vanke and the Anderson Pontiac Papoose 1 421 Super Duty Tempest wagon takes on Bob Spar, who is driving for Mickey Thompson in the 749 A/FX 421 Super Duty LeMans at the 1963 Winternationals. Spar waded through the field of competitors to win the A/FX class with a 12.04 ET at 116.27 mph. (Photo Courtesy Jim Luikens)*

Fred Davisson was an Ohio-based racer who successfully campaigned his 235-hp 389 "economy" engine in the I/Stock class, where it ran a best ET of 14.92 at 92.78 mph for a class win at the 1963 NHRA Winternationals. It also held the national record. He was on his honeymoon when he competed at that event. (Photo Courtesy Joe Webber Archives)

| Pontiac Wins at the 1963 NHRA Winternationals in Pomona, California | | | | |
|---|---|---|---|---|
| Class | Driver | Hometown | Car | Elapsed Time and Top Speed |
| A/FX | Bob Spar/ Bill Shrewsberry | Long Beach, California | #749 1963 Super Duty 421 LeMans | 12.04 ET at 116.27 mph |
| C/Stock | Bob Lambeck | Los Angeles, California | 1962 Catalina 389/348 | 13.85 ET at 100.67 mph |
| I/Stock | Fred Davisson | Akron, Ohio | 1961 Catalina | 14.92 ET at 92.78 mph |
| B/SA | Lloyd Cox | Whittier, California | 1961 Ventura | 12.84 ET at 108.17 mph |
| D/SA | Larry Leonard | Anaheim | 1961 Catalina | 13.81 ET at 100.44 mph |
| E/SA | Ken Dixon | Bellflower, California | 1958 Pontiac | 13.93 ET at 99.66 mph |
| F/SA | Ramon Lowe | Long Beach, California | 1962 Grand Prix | 14.16 ET at 97.29 mph |

Lloyd and Carol Cox's 1961 Ventura was a serious contender at the time. Lloyd took the B/SA crown at the 1963 Winternationals with a 12.84 ET at 108.17 mph. (Photo Courtesy Joe Webber Archives)

" INTERESTINGLY, NOT ALL OF THE CLASS WINNERS USED THE SUPER DUTY ENGINES. "

| Pontiac Wins at the 1963 NHRA Nationals, Indianapolis, Indiana | | | | |
|---|---|---|---|---|
| Class | Driver | Hometown | Car | Elapsed Time and Top Speed |
| B/FX | Jim Wangers | Royal Oak, Michigan | 1963 Swiss cheese Catalina | 12.59 ET at 110.83 mph |
| A/Stock | Don Gay | Dickinson, Texas | 1962 Catalina 421 Super Duty | 12.81 ET at 111.52 mph |
| C/Stock | Ron Broadhead | Porterfield, California | 1960 Pontiac | 13.54 ET at 103.00 mph |
| A/SA | Bill Abraham | Akron, Ohio | Anderson Pontiac *Golden Arrow II* 421 Super Duty Catalina, beating Ron Mandella in the *Reynolds Auto Supply* 1963 Plymouth wagon | 13.28 ET at 109.48 mph |
| D/SA | Lowe and Easley | Long Beach, California | 1958 Pontiac | 14.10 ET at 99.33 mph |
| F/SA | Ray Pace | Dayton, Ohio | 1958 Pontiac | 14.66 ET at 93.84 mph |

Arlen Vanke was able to hold on to the A/FX record for 1963 with his *Running Bear* homebuilt 1963 421 Super Duty Tempest. It used a conventional drivetrain with an added-on aluminum front end. His 11.89 ET at 123.11 mph was the best of the season, although Dave Strickler won the A/FX trophy at Indy.

As a sidenote to the wins in the 1963 season, there were many near-misses for Pontiac, including the Bell-Leonard team's narrow loss in the C/SA class finals to Plymouth racer Dave Kempton at the Winternationals as well as Phil Chisolm's win over Dan Roberts and his 1956 Pontiac at the same meet. One of the more frustrating losses of the season was Jim Wangers and his *Royal Pontiac* Swiss cheese Catalina in the Little Eliminator finals to A/FX champ Dave Strickler and his Z-11 Chevy at the NHRA Nationals in Indy. Although Wangers had won a hard-contested victory in the B/FX category, he wasn't able to bring home a second title.

Interestingly, not all of the class winners used the Super Duty engines. Pontiacs fit into a variety of classes, which were strategically exploited by the more experienced racers for maximum effectiveness. For example, Ramon Lowe and his 303-hp, base-engine 1962 Grand Prix was a brutal competitor and set national records in the F/Stock class. Tom Bell's 1961 389/348 Ventura ran competitively in the D/SA category and was regarded to be the fastest non–Super Duty Pontiac at the time.

Ohio-based racer Fred Davisson was very successful with his 389/235 economy-engine Ventura. Export engines with low compression and 4-barrel carburetors were chosen for their low horsepower ratings and ability to make competitive horsepower in a relatively soft class.

### The Last Super Duty

The last factory-built Super Duty car was a red Catalina for driver Johnny Mauro, who drove it in that year's Pikes Peak Hill Climb. He had driven a total of 14 times at Pikes Peak and competed in the 1948 Indianapolis 500 in an Alfa Romeo and finished in eighth place. Mauro was a Ferrari importer and started the United States Truck Driving School, which is still run by his family.

*Johnny Mauro's 1963* Pikes Peak *Catalina Super Duty was a one-off combination of NASCAR and drag racing versions of the factory racer that used the single 4-barrel 421 Super Duty and aluminum sheet metal. It was built in May 1963, long after the racing ban. It was constructed in secret at General Motors Engineering—away from GM's upper management's view. It was the only Super Duty car ordered after the ban and was the last Super Duty car that was ever constructed.*

The Grenadier Red Catalina was built on May 16, 1963, and was the only Super Duty car built with an order that came in after January 24. It was built without the knowledge or consent of GM's upper management.

Beginning as a production 421 H.O. 4-speed car, it was whisked off the production line and sent directly to Pontiac's engineering garage. Under the direction of Memo 1075, the car was transformed into a Super Duty Catalina. Although Memo 1075 was destroyed as soon as the car was built to avoid a paper trail, we know how this Catalina was outfitted.

For a Super Duty car, the Mauro Catalina was oddly optioned. It used a NASCAR powertrain, including the 390-hp single-4-barrel 421 Super Duty engine, 4-speed transmission, and 4.30 gears, and it featured aluminum front sheet metal. Unfortunately, the big Catalina did not finish at Pikes Peak. The engine blew up during qualifying.

Since the Super Duty program ended, replacement parts were not readily available. All of that clandestine effort and career-ending risk to defy GM's corporate policy was for naught. The car slipped into obscurity before it was rediscovered in the late 1980s. After passing through a few hands, including those of former North Dakota Governor Ed Schafer, the last Super Duty Pontiac is now part of the Mike and Michael Huffman Collection.

### Pontiac: Turning off the Lights

For Pontiac, the 1962 model year built upon the successes of the Super Duty program, and its performance reputation was in spectacular shape. In NASCAR, Pontiac won 22 of 53 races that season. This included the Daytona 500 with Glenn "Fireball" Roberts as well as the series championship with driver Joe Weatherly, who won nine of those races. Pontiacs were feared competitors in NASCAR. When they didn't win, it was often due to a crash or some other misfortune. They were always in the hunt, and the impression that they made resulted in the public flocking into dealership showrooms.

In drag racing, Pontiac's factory-built Super Duty Catalinas were cleaning house in the NHRA's Stock and Super Stock classes. That year, the NHRA opened up the new Factory Experimental class, which allowed a manufacturer's best racing drivetrains to be installed in any of the same manufacturer's models (regardless of whether they were

*Joe Weatherly poses with his 1963 Catalina stocker at Riverside. (Photo Courtesy Jim Luikens)*

1962 A/FX Tempests prompted Pontiac to build its own versions in coupe and wagon bodystyles using the famed PowerShift transaxles that were described in chapter 3. That, along with the dramatic weight-reduction program that was used in the famed Swiss cheese Catalinas, had Pontiac's fortunes looking very bright in the latter weeks of 1962. Then, it all came to a crashing halt.

## The Precursor to the Racing Ban

The story of the racing ban goes back to June 1957, when the Automotive Manufacturers Association (AMA) ban on racing was instituted. It was a gentleman's agreement, as the Big Three manufacturers agreed to not support racing on a factory level to reduce negative public relations and development costs. To this day, many insiders and historians look back at it as a deception intended to derail Ford's successful racing programs.

According to author Alex Gabbard in his book *Ford Total Performance*, General Motors President Harlow "Red" Curtice made a seemingly off-handed remark at the end of an AMA board meeting and stated that manufacturers shouldn't compete against their own customers. This caught Ford President Robert S. McNamara by surprise. He was never a proponent of racing and thought that it was a waste of resources that would never translate into profits for Ford.

McNamara was subsequently lured into signing the resolution that came from the discussion on June 6, 1957. The document laid out the terms of the racing discontinuation and stated that the undersigned would "end factory involvement in racing, eliminate all high-performance and racing equipment out of their catalogs, remove personnel from racing, and delete any mention of competition or engine outputs from advertisements."

offered that way from the factory). The car had to run on gasoline, and, at first, supercharging was not allowed. This prompted a flurry of activity with fuel-injected 327 engines being installed into Chevy IIs, 413 engines being installed into Dodge Lancers, and 406 Ford engines being installed into Fairlanes.

For 1963, it shaped up to be an even better year, as advances in engine and drivetrain technology moved the Super Duty Pontiacs even further. Engine updates for 1963 included freer-flowing cylinder heads, the innovative bathtub intake manifold, cast-aluminum exhaust manifolds, aluminum rear-end center sections, and other lightweight componentry. The successes of the converted

*Under the hood of the Union Park Pontiac 1963 421 Super Duty Tempest Wagon is a rare bathtub intake manifold, which was an early version of the tunnel ram. Note the special Harrison radiator, which was also used on the Grand Sport Corvettes. Randy Williams had to order a new run of these manifolds to get one for his restoration.*

With that, Ford pulled out of racing in the middle of a very successful season in NASCAR that featured NASCAR powerhouses Holman and Moody as well as Smokey Yunick, who was essentially stolen from Chevy. Ford paid off Yunick for the rest of the year, and he committed to running with Ford for the rest of the 1957 season.

According to Gabbard, General Motors had no real intention of remaining true to the agreement. Chevrolet initially hid its racing activities in the marine engine development programs. Pontiac General Manager Bunkie Knudsen essentially ignored this agreement altogether and saw the opportunity for Pontiac to make headlines for racing success. "Race on Sunday; sell on Monday" was his philosophy, and he was very serious about saving Pontiac. He even went so far as to hire Yunick for the 1958 season, and Yunick stayed until 1962.

*Robert S. McNamara was the general manager of the Ford Division of the Ford Motor Company in 1957 when he signed the AMA 1957 ban on racing, which sidelined Ford's successful 1957 season mid-stream. He later became president of the Ford Motor Company and was tapped by the Kennedy Administration to become Secretary of Defense. (Photo By Oscar Porter/Department of Defense/US Army, Courtesy Library of Congress)*

*In 1961, at the age of 35, Robert F. Kennedy became the US attorney general. He set his sights on a variety of issues, such as civil rights, price fixing, and breaking up potential monopolies. At the time, General Motors had more than 55 percent of the domestic auto market and inched toward 60 percent, which triggered litigation to break up the giant automaker. (Photo Courtesy Library of Congress)*

At some point, Henry Ford II realized that the company had been duped. When Ford Motor Company purchased Autolite in 1961, it promoted racing in its advertising and stated that since Autolite was a supplier, not a manufacturer, the AMA agreement didn't apply to them. It was the first step in regaining the ground that it had lost, which culminated in the beginning of the Ford Total Performance program that launched in 1962. Ford officially withdrew from the AMA agreement in June 1962.

Although Ford was back in drag racing, it faced tough competition from Pontiac, Chevy, and Mopar. Clearly Curtice's sleight of hand cost the Blue Oval dearly.

By that time, McNamara had left Ford to be John F. Kennedy's Secretary of Defense and was replaced by Henry Ford II. McNamara was close friends with Robert F. Kennedy, and many speculated that he had an influence on pushing an antitrust case against his former competitors. However, no hard evidence of this has surfaced.

As was previously mentioned, Knudsen's efforts in the rebranding of Pontiac, in which racing played a major part, put the division into the #3 position for domestic sales after Chevrolet and Ford. For his efforts, he was promoted to the general manager position at Chevrolet in 1961. He was succeeded by Pete Estes, and John DeLorean assumed Estes's previous position as chief engineer.

As with Knudsen, Estes and DeLorean were committed to bringing performance cars to market and planned to keep the momentum going. This included continued development of the Super Duty program, which, by 1962, was building complete race-ready cars in a limited-production capacity.

### Changing Political Climate

In January 1961, President John F. Kennedy was elected to office, narrowly defeating Vice President Richard M. Nixon in the 1960 presidential election. As part of building his cabinet, he appointed his younger brother Robert F. Kennedy (RFK) as the 64th attorney general of the United States. Just 35 years old at the time, he was seen by his supporters as a breath of fresh air. His critics, which included the editorial boards of the *New York Times* and the *New Republic*, accused him of not having enough experience or the qualifications that were needed for the position.

However, the younger Kennedy had quite a bit of practical experience for the position. Right after he was admitted to the Massachusetts Bar in 1951, he was hired at the US Justice Department, where he worked his way up to chief counsel of the senate permanent investigative subcommittee, and he was later the head of his brother's presidential campaign. Although he didn't have trial experience, he was skilled at questioning witnesses in a committee setting and was seen as aggressive and effective at his job.

In response to this criticism, he embarked on an ambitious, multi-pronged program that championed civil rights, went after organized crime and the Teamster's Union, and investigated large corporations that had unfair monopolies. In many ways, as attorney general, RFK continued and expanded the investigations that he conducted as chief counsel in the 1950s. In modern terms, it was an attempt to drain the swamp.

In actuality, the justice department had looked closely at General Motors as far back as the 1950s. Although, the efforts were squashed by top-level officials at the Justice Department. That changed in 1961.

Kennedy set his sights on US Steel for price fixing and large corporations, such as General Electric, General Mills, and General Motors, for their large market share. The case against US Steel was dropped after the anticipated price increases didn't occur. Critics saw this as a case of judicial overreach on the part of the Kennedy justice department.

In the case of General Motors, the corporation had ample reason to be concerned. Today, in this age of import dominance and the rise of independent electric vehicle manufacturers, the thought of any single corporation having a hold on the market as strong as the hold that General Motors had on the market in the 1960s is inconceivable. At the time, General Motors had approximately 55 percent of the US domestic market. Chevrolet alone made up 30 percent. General Motors was wildly successful at the time and inched closer to a 60-percent market share. This would have triggered legal action to break up the automaker—with the most likely scenario to split Chevrolet into a separate corporation.

Adding to the claims of a monopoly, General Motors was involved in several non-automotive areas, such as Frigidaire, and financial areas, such as General Motors Acceptance Corporation (GMAC). General Motors was one of the nation's dominant corporations, and the justice department dropped significant hints that it was in its crosshairs. Understandably, the

GM's board of directors took heed.

In response, General Motors greatly reduced its promotional activities regarding racing as well as in other areas. It reverted to the 1957 AMA racing ban to justify its actions. The fact that the original ban was a ploy to defeat Ford at the track was irrelevant at that point because the rest of the world was unaware of its true purpose at the time.

To the world at large, General Motors was being more responsible on a corporate level, and those sorts of indulgences (racing) were deemed unnecessary. Of course, it was a means to an end, and it worked in both 1957 and 1963. As additional insurance for the future, General Motors made significant internal structural changes, such as centralizing operations to make a breakup far more difficult. While it did accomplish its goals, it also consolidated a lot of processes and platforms that internally ate away at the autonomy of the divisions.

## The Ban

On January 24, 1963, which was a bitterly cold Thursday morning in Detroit, General Motors issued a press release that announced all support for competition was suspended. No additional orders would be accepted for factory race cars, but previously ordered-but-unbuilt

*Within hours of the General Motors racing-ban announcement, Pontiac sent this memo to its zone offices. It outlined the cancellation of 389 and 421 Super Duty engines and instructed them to inform affected dealers verbally. (Photo Courtesy Rocky Rotella)*

cars would be completed and delivered. Established teams that were already factory-backed would receive the unused inventory of parts so that they could continue for the 1963 season. No other support (financial or otherwise) would be supplied. Pontiac issued its own version of the bulletin to zone offices later that day. The notice advised zone managers to personally contact dealerships that would be affected.

## The Wide Track Response

Pontiac was immediately forced out of racing, the Super Duty program was shut down, and production of all race cars and parts was immediately halted. Existing parts inventories were distributed among factory-backed teams. All attention returned to regular production cars.

Other programs, including development of the experimental overhead cam V-8, were halted. Energy and resources were reallocated to other more sedate production cars and engines. General Motors enforced a zero-tolerance program, where any employees who were found to be in violation of the racing ban in any capacity would be immediately terminated. Keeping the corporation intact was by far the most important objective. If heads had to roll, so be it.

In early 1963, Pontiac was in a precarious position regarding its image in the marketplace. The division had built a solid reputation that was so centered on performance and racing success that it easily could have been kneecapped by the racing programs being canceled.

Despite the racing ban, Pontiac found success on the track during the 1963 racing season. Huge victories included Paul Goldsmith's win while driving a Ray Nichels–prepped 421 Super Duty LeMans at the Daytona 250 Challenge Cup and NHRA wins by Bill Shrewsberry in a Super Duty LeMans and Jim Wangers's B/FX win in a Swiss cheese Catalina. Although the wins were big, their draw in the showrooms was fleeting. Something had to be done to keep the momentum going.

Fortunately, Pontiac had a very talented group of engineers, product planners, and marketers. This seemingly insurmountable obstacle was overcome far more easily than many industry insiders thought. Pontiac was able to distinguish between racing and high performance. One does not need to race to market high-performance cars, although it certainly helps. By taking its performance message to the street, Pontiac retained the brand equity that it had worked so hard to develop over the past seven years and still be compliant with the new anti-racing mandate.

**Speed Sport News's Chris Economaki interviews Paul Goldsmith (left) and Ray Nichels after the record-setting performance of the Nichels Engineering Pontiac LeMans at the 1963 Daytona 250 Challenge Cup. The LeMans had a lead of more than 5 miles over second-place finisher A. J. Foyt, who drove a Nickey Corvette. (Photo Courtesy LaDow Publishing Company)**

*Paul Goldsmith poses with the 50 LeMans at Daytona during the 1963 Speed Week. (Photo Courtesy LaDow Publishing Company)*

To put things into perspective, in 1962, Chevrolet sold more than two-and-a-half times more full-size vehicles than Pontiac sold with its entire product line. This didn't even count the Chevy II, Corvair, Corvette, or truck sales. Things were about to change radically for Pontiac. The product planners and marketers were put to the test to keep sales numbers moving forward.

## Epilogue

As it turned out, Robert F. Kennedy never filed suit against General Motors. By the summer of 1961, critics chastised him for not pushing forward. The truth of the matter was that GM's corporate structure was so complex that it would have been a nightmare to split up. How can Chevrolet be split off if it has no assembly plants? The cars were built by GM's assembly division.

Another reason that the suit never happened was because General Motors never hit that 60-percent market share, which made such a suit meritless. In addition, other factors came into play. The assassination of President Kennedy in November 1963 forever changed the course of history. The newly-installed Johnson administration had larger issues to handle. Inflation, the escalation of the war in Vietnam, and the Civil Rights Movement had the administration altering its priorities. With the economy in a less-than-ideal condition at the time, it made little sense to go after the country's largest taxpayer and the employer of more than a half million people. The will to proceed against the corporate giant was lost in the political shuffle. RFK left the Johnson administration, became a senator in 1965, and ran for president before he was assassinated on June 6, 1968, at the age of 42.

Although the heat seemed to be off by January 1963, General Motors executives weren't taking any chances. They knew that the winds of change could blow back in their faces at any time. For that reason, the ban on racing was not lifted. General Motors had many other run-ins with the federal government on the topics of safety, the environment, and corporate responsibility before the decade was over.

The plan that Pontiac enacted changed automotive history and created a completely new market segment: the muscle car.

At a casual glance, it seemed counterintuitive—even ridiculous or foolhardy—to pull the plug on such a successful program. Just like Pontiac, Chevrolet enjoyed the benefits of racing victories that generated foot traffic at dealerships. While Oldsmobile, Buick, and Cadillac plugged along without missing a beat, Pontiac was in a particularly vulnerable position.

Although Pontiac was in third place in sales (behind Chevrolet and Ford), it was a distant third. While Chevrolet's lower price points and broad brand line extended into areas that Pontiac didn't go, such as trucks and high-volume fleet sales, it availed it to the performance market. However, all of Pontiac's marketing strategies were not necessarily dependent on a performance message.

For the General Motors racers with factory deals, most migrated to greener pastures with Ford and Chrysler. Thompson moved on to the Blue Oval almost immediately after getting the word from Pontiac. He received a 1963½ R-code Galaxie lightweight and drove nearly everything that Ford built, including a 1964 Thunderbolt.

Stock car builder Ray Nichels, whose expertise in the field was legendary at that point, landed at Chrysler, which gave him the contract to build its 1964 team stock cars. This arrangement lasted several years. Others, such as Arnie "the Farmer" Beswick, Dick "Mr. Unswitchable" Jesse, and others, soldiered onward in the match-race and Funny-Car ranks, which really took hold in 1964 and 1965. The need for track promoters to keep General Motors fans happy resulted in a profitable niche for some Pontiac and Chevy racers.

For the cars themselves, many of the Super Duty Pontiacs went on to live long and successful careers, often in the hands of smaller, privateer racers. Some continued to be campaigned by their original owners. Howard Masales held onto his 1962 Catalina for nearly six years after he sold his Swiss cheese Catalina.

"The 1962 was my moneymaker," Masales said in a January 2024 phone interview. "I held onto that car long after my other ones, and that was the one I won the most races with."

On the East Coast, Brooklyn-based Nunzi Romano made a name for himself with his 1962 Catalina. His shop was the hot spot in the metro NYC area for Pontiac racers and performance enthusiasts. With extensive magazine coverage from *Hi-Performance Cars* and *High Performance Pontiac*, Nunzi became a nationally-recognized authority on Pontiacs. His reputation endures to this day.

Down south, Mississippi-native Lewis Sharp raced his

> **"FOR THE CARS THEMSELVES, MANY OF THE SUPER DUTY PONTIACS WENT ON TO LIVE LONG AND SUCCESSFUL CAREERS, OFTEN IN THE HANDS OF SMALLER, PRIVATEER RACERS."**

red 1962 Catalina for the rest of the decade and remained competitive after the parts dried up at the factory and dealership level.

"By 1969, I didn't have the time or money to continue running it," Sharp recalled. "I also didn't have a crew to help at that point, so I sold the Catalina and bought a GTO."

Other famous Pontiac race cars went on have to successful careers with other owners. The *Gay Pontiac* Catalina was campaigned as the *Rainmaker* by Don Visovatti, and the *Royal Pontiac* Swiss cheese Catalina was raced for many years by Ohio-based Phil and Vance Heck. The 1962 Catalina 421 Super Duty sedan was repainted and raced by Tex Smith.

North Carolina–based racer Bill Blair raced and restored several Super Duty cars over the years, including the Beswick Swiss cheese Catalina and the prototype 1963 Super Duty Tempest that was originally delivered to Ray Nichels. Of course, we must not forget the exploits of Arnie Beswick's original 1963 Super Duty LeMans, which evolved into the wildly famous *Tameless Tiger* altered-wheelbase Funny Car that astonished crowds until its untimely demise during the 1967 season.

On the East Coast, Nunzi Romano raced his 1962 421 Super Duty Catalina and worked out of his thriving Brooklyn shop called Nunzi's Automotive. (Photo Courtesy Tony Romano)

# CHAPTER 7

# 1964: RACING AFTER THE BAN AND THE NEW GTO

While this book takes an in-depth look at the events that led to the 1963 General Motors racing ban, it wasn't quite the end for Pontiac's racing exploits that many insiders expected. Even though there was no more factory backing, quite a few Pontiac racers remained loyal to the brand—most notably Arnie "the Farmer" Beswick, Jess Tyree, and Dick Jesse.

Tyree ran a slogan on his race cars that was a play on the popular Tareyton cigarette advertisement of the day that proclaimed, "Us GM owners would rather fight than switch!" Detroit-based racer Dick Jesse adopted the nickname "Mr. Unswitchable." Others proclaimed their loyalty to Pontiac with nicknames or simply by not switching to another manufacturer. Relying on a rather finite supply of factory Super Duty parts and whatever aftermarket parts that could be adapted to their engines, these Pontiac racing loyalists pushed forward.

In an interview with Arnie Beswick at the 2023 Ames Performance Pontiac Nationals, he said that the lack of General Motors race cars in the 1960s created a profitable niche market for independent racers such as himself. In fact, he ditched a short-lived deal with Mercury to concentrate on his Pontiac race cars.

*Arnie Beswick's first GTO race car was this fire-breathing 1964 Sport Coupe, which was known as the Mystery Tornado. It was powered by a blown and injected 421 Super Duty engine and competed in the FX class. Even though General Motors was out of racing, Beswick built up such an association with Pontiac that he decided to keep campaigning its cars. (Photo Courtesy Arnie Beswick)*

"Race promoters wanted more variety in their programs, as it was for the most part Mopar versus Ford," Beswick recalled. "There were still a lot of Pontiac and Chevy fans out there, and they still wanted to see their favorite [brands] out there. We were booked all over the country, and more often than not, we won."

As a business decision, many other racers secured factory deals with Ford and Chrysler. Those manufacturers did not have the problems with the federal government that General Motors did. Many racers who ran Pontiacs in the 1959–1963 period found themselves in a position where it was either financially impossible to continue with Chevy or Pontiac, or they found better deals with the manufacturers from across town. General Motors–backed racers, such as Mickey Thompson, Arlen Vanke,

*Arnie Beswick (left) and "Dyno" Don Nicholson converse in front of the* Mystery Tornado. *By this time, Nicholson had moved on from Chevy as a result of the General Motors racing ban and was competing with a Mercury. (Photo Courtesy Arnie Beswick)*

Ronnie Sox, Bob Harrop, and "Dyno" Don Nicholson soon found greener pastures and developed strong brand ties to those new manufacturers.

Those who remained loyal to Pontiac would fight an uphill battle for several years to come. Although Pontiacs remained competitive in several classes of Stock and Super Stock, the little factory backing that was available was done through the back door and would have resulted in termination for the employees

*This rare photo from January 1964 shows the fleet of Arnie Beswick's cars, including the* Passionate Poncho III *Swiss cheese Catalina, the* Mrs. B's Grocery Getter *421 Super Duty Tempest wagon, the* Little B's Runabout *421 Super Duty LeMans coupe (originally the 756 Thompson coupe), and his new 1964 GTO with Anderson Pontiac livery. This car became the wild, supercharged, and injected* Mystery Tornado. *(Photo Courtesy Bob Nelson)*

*After selling his 1963 Swiss cheese Catalina, Howard Maseles moved on to a 1964 GTO that was competitive in the B/Stock class. (Photo Courtesy Howard Masales)*

In 1964, Gay Pontiac moved on to race a GTO in the B/Stock class and kept running its A/Stock 1962 421 Super Duty Catalina two-door sedan and its 1963 421 Super Duty Tempest wagon, which was now running in Modified Production (A/MP). (Photo Courtesy Jim Luikens)

*For racing and promotional purposes, dealerships across the country latched onto the 1964 GTO, which had fallen competitively into the NHRA's B/Stock category. This 1964 hardtop was driven by Dan Ruzewski and sponsored by Ed Reilly Pontiac in Depew, New York. (Photo Courtesy John Bleil)*

that were found responsible. Nevertheless, many dealerships picked up where the factory left off and soldiered onward, promoting Pontiac drag racing to help sell new models in the showroom.

### Taking It to the Street

The trajectory of Pontiac's path to success and racing victory was undoubtedly altered by the 1963 racing ban. Although it was the race victories in NASCAR, NHRA and AHRA drag racing, and elsewhere that cemented Pontiac's performance reputation, the momentum could have been lost without proper direction and management.

As Pontiac's marketing strategy and reputation was based on racing and performance, the division was in a particularly vulnerable position. So, its next move was especially important. While Chevrolet was in a similar

position with its marketing strategies, Buick, Oldsmobile, and Cadillac were not affected, as they weren't racing on any significant level at that time.

Even though Bunkie Knudsen had already moved on to be the head of Chevrolet, Pontiac was still in very capable hands with Pete Estes as general manager and John Z. DeLorean as chief engineer. Pontiac's pivot was simple and effective: take the performance message and turn it loose on the street.

In hindsight, the loss of the racing program came at a very strategic time for Pontiac. In a conversation that I had in the early 2000s, retired Pontiac Chief Motor Engineer Mac McKellar said that the end had already come for Pontiac as a dominant force in motorsports in many ways.

"We just didn't have the engineering budget to compete with the SOHC Fords and the Chrysler race Hemis," he said. "While we had built some experimental SOHC and DOHC V-8s, they were not evolved to a level that could keep up without a lot more development. The money just wasn't there for us.

"From my perspective, it was a relief, as we could get back to producing top-performing production cars without the same level of pressure that racing put on us."

### General Motors Helps Out

A General Motors corporate program that had been already in the works helped make the transition as seamless as possible. It came in the form of a new General Motors A-Body platform, which was set to replace the complex and trouble-prone Y-body platform that included the 1961–1963 transaxle Tempests. Essentially a 7/8-scale version of the existing B-Body, the new platform was thoroughly conventional and featured a full perimeter frame with a separate body and an engine connected directly to the transmission. With a beam axle in the rear, it represented an opportunity for General Motors to produce a versatile, inexpensive platform and create a new generation of entry-level vehicles for Buick, Oldsmobile, and Pontiac. It was a step up from Chevrolet's Chevy II/Nova.

Pontiac continued the Tempest and LeMans nameplates on the new A-Body platform. From a styling standpoint, they were a logical evolution from the 1961–1963

> **"WHILE WE HAD BUILT SOME EXPERIMENTAL SOHC AND DOHC V-8s, THEY WERE NOT EVOLVED TO A LEVEL THAT COULD KEEP UP WITHOUT A LOT MORE DEVELOPMENT."**

Y-Body models. The basic design elements were similar. While the new Pontiac A-Body cars were a bit larger (an additional 3 inches of wheelbase and just under 9 additional inches of overall length), they didn't look radically different from their predecessors. However, they were completely different cars.

The other factor for Pontiac was the 421 H.O. V-8 engine. A new set of high-flowing cylinder heads that were based on the 1961–1962 421 Super Duty units were identified by casting number 716 on the center exhaust ports. They featured revised ports as well as pushrod oiling and re-routed cooling passages. Valve sizes were 1.92 inches for the intake and 1.66 for the exhaust.

The camshaft (initially referred to as the "009" or "C" and later as the "067" or "P") featured 273/289 degrees of advertised duration and a 0.406-inch lift. It followed McKellar's conservative approach to cam design. He preferred longer durations with shorter lift to promote valvetrain durability and longevity.

*When the GTO hit dealership showrooms in the fall of 1963, the public's reaction was far more positive than Pontiac anticipated. It built 32,450 that year and began a revolution in the industry and a new market segment: the muscle car.*

## The GTO

Numerous books and magazine articles have told the story of the release of the 1964 GTO, so I will focus on a few key details of interest to racers and performance enthusiasts.

First, conventional wisdom tends to oversimplify the development of the powertrain, stating that the 389 engine was plucked out of a Bonneville and simply dropped into the GTO. That notion is an oversimplification that understates the time and effort that went into the project. While it's true that the first prototypes came together that way, it was clear that revisions had to be made.

It was quickly observed that the power band of the Bonneville-sourced 389 was not ideal for the GTO. It had far too much low-end torque and not enough top-end horsepower to get the job done. Seeing how the GTO could be as much as 1,000 pounds lighter than a loaded B-Body car, the car would spin the tires and stop making usable power above about 4,500 rpm. While it would have been a fun prospect from a short stoplight-to-stoplight perspective, the production version required a higher level of refinement. Fortunately, Chief Motor Engineer Mac McKellar had a solution.

McKellar's plan was to take the heads and camshaft from the 4-barrel version of the 421 H.O. engine and install them on the 389 engine. This swap accomplished two objectives. First, the camshaft and heads softened the bottom end enough to give the red-line tires a chance while the engine continued to make power past the effective limit of the big-car version. Second, the new version developed superior top-end performance and provided the all-around response that the engineering and marketing departments wanted.

The results were impressive. With a 10.75:1 compression ratio, the base 389 4-barrel engine that was used in the GTO produced 325 hp at 4,800 rpm with 428 ft-lbs of torque at 3,200 rpm. The optional Tri-Power increased the rating to 348 hp at 4,900 rpm with 428 ft-lbs of torque at 3,600 rpm.

When compared to the 389 engines that were used in the full-size cars, the differences were clear. The 4-barrel version used heads with smaller 1.88-inch intake valves and 1.60-inch exhaust valves, 10.5:1

The base engine for the 1964 GTO was a 325-hp version of the 389 that featured the heads and camshaft from the 421 H.O. Note the chrome air cleaner and valve covers.

The optional powerplant for the 1964 GTO featured Tri-Power carburetion and was rated at 348 hp at 4,900 rpm with 428 ft-lbs of torque at 3,600 rpm. The system utilized three small air cleaners.

*This 1964 GTO two-door hardtop is painted in the rare Sunfire Red Iridescent color, which was a one-year-only option.*

compression, and the mild 472 (D) cam, which was essentially the same grind as the later 273/282-degree, 0.406-inch-lift 066 (N) cam.

This version developed 303 hp at 4,600 rpm with 430 ft-lbs of torque at 2,900 rpm. The difference in cam, compression, and heads made a 22-hp advantage with an extra 200 rpm of usable power, which is not an insignificant number.

The 330-hp Tri-Power version used the good 716 heads with the milder 472 cam and developed 330 hp at 4,600 rpm and 430 ft-lbs of torque at 2,800 rpm. While this version had 18 fewer horsepower than the GTO Tri-Power, it had 2 more ft-lbs of torque coming in at 800 rpm lower, which accounted for the difference in breathing. The verdict was that McKellar's plan did exactly what it aimed to do. It tamed the torquey V-8 low in the RPM range while increasing high-RPM power.

## No 421 Engine for the GTO

Why didn't Pontiac just install a 421 engine in the GTO? There were numerous reasons. Adding the 389 to the A-Body lineup seriously pushed the envelope from a corporate standpoint. At the time, the General Motors corporate limit for intermediate cars was 330 ci. In 1963, Pontiac had been caught with an engine that was perceived to be larger than was allowed. The optional 326 displaced 336 ci and saw a slight bore reduction in 1964 to get to the correct figure.

It was probably during that episode when someone discovered the loophole in the rule. It stated that standard-equipment engines were not allowed to be larger than 330 ci in intermediate-size cars. Since the GTO was an options package on the LeMans and not a separate series, the larger optional 389 was part of the

*Pontiac's Grand Prix was the Wide Track Division's luxury/performance car and could be ordered with anything from a 303-hp 389 4-barrel engine to a 370-hp 421 Tri-Power H.O. engine. The attractive eight-lug wheels were optional equipment and dissipated heat well from the aluminum brake drums.*

*This particular 1964 2+2 convertible was built with the 330-hp 389 Tri-Power engine that was paired with a floor-shifted 4-speed transmission. Mark Tilson is the current owner.*

*In case the GTO was not a sales success, Pontiac hedged its bet to a certain extent with the introduction of the Catalina-based 2+2, which was a sporty, bucket-seat, two-door car that was available as a hardtop or convertible. In its first year of production, the 2+2 was available with any Catalina powerplant. In 1965, only the larger 421 engine was available.*

GTO package. Adding a larger engine in a midsize car was technically allowed by the letter of the ruling but certainly not in the spirit.

Why not offer the 421 in the GTO? If it was technically acceptable to use the 389 engine, the 421 engine would have been allowed as well. However, there were several reasons why the 421 engine wasn't used, including mechanical reasons, the cost, and marketing considerations.

First, the 421 was substantially torquier than the 389, which itself had to be modified to move the power band higher in the RPM range for the chassis to hook up. That situation was not possible with a 421. It would have required the development of a new cam to move the power band up even further, which would have become a warranty problem. Obviously, adding a set of slicks would change the traction situation, but that wasn't in the realm of a regular production car.

Secondly, the research and development costs for the GTO were minimal, and that helped keep the sticker price low. The beauty of the GTO was that it came to market without the need to develop any new parts. Everything was off the shelf and shuffled into a new combination that provided a tremendous performance value. It relied on the regular-production short-block with two-bolt mains, a cast bottom, and nothing exotic. The 421 engine relied on a more expensive short-block with four-bolt mains and forged connecting rods.

Most importantly, a 421 H.O. GTO would have negated any market demand for a full-size performance car. The 421 H.O. was a premium engine that was intended for top-of-the-line models and was frequently ordered with Grand Prixs and Bonnevilles, but it could also be ordered in stripped-down Catalinas.

In mid-1963, when the GTO was being readied for production, Pontiac was unsure that the idea of a midsize car was going to take off like it eventually did. It hedged its bet with the introduction of the sporty Catalina 2+2. It had an interior trim package that included bucket seats, a console, specific interior door panels, and exterior badging.

Although it was available with any Catalina powertrain in its first year, by 1965, the 2+2 option was available only with the 421 powerplant. This cemented it as the top-level performance car that was marginally quicker than a GTO but at a much higher

*The 2+2 car featured a luxurious bucket-seat interior with an attractive console.*

*The 1964 Royal Bobcat GTO is shown with the original owner, Bill Sherman (left). The car's original driver and Royal Pontiac mechanic Milt Schornack is on the right. This photo was taken in July 1989, just a few months before Sherman died. The pair had been on a summer show and race tour for a few years in the late 1980s.*

*The original 1964 Royal Bobcat GTO is the same car that was featured in the March 1964 issue of Car and Driver magazine. It was the subject of a Royal Pontiac dealership-installed swap from the stock 389 Tri-Power engine to a blueprinted 421 H.O. Tri-Power engine. It set the stage for the GTO sales surge that soon followed.*

*Under the hood of the 1964 Royal Bobcat GTO is a prototype Ram Air system that used a full-size car air cleaner and custom ducting that pulled air in from the base of the windshield. The engine was a 421 H.O. Tri-Power.*

*The 1964 Royal Bobcat GTO is shown during one of its last trips down the quarter mile in the summer of 1990. It posted an 11.18 ET at 122 mph on this run at Englishtown.*

combustion chamber equalizing, a custom-tailored centrifugal advance curve for the distributor with advance limited to 7 degrees, initial advance at an aggressive 20 to 22 degrees, and 34 to 36 degrees of total advance all in at 3,600 rpm. This required the use of high-octane fuel, but the increase in low and midrange power was substantial.

The rest of the package consisted of 0.022-inch-thick head gaskets, blocked heat risers, Champion J-10 spark plugs, 0.069-inch carburetor jetting for all six barrels, and a hydraulic-lifter restrictor kit that diverted oil to the bottom end, where it was more needed. Rocker-arm locknuts were used to increase the RPM range and allowed the hydraulic lifters to operate like solid lifters. In addition, a mechanical progressive carburetor linkage provided more precise control than the production linkage. Special Royal Bobcat metallic badging was included and became a status symbol of the period. The total cost, including labor, was $200, which is just under $2,000 when adjusted for inflation in 2024.

Later, a mail-order version of the Bobcat package was available from Royal Pontiac, although the milling and cc'ing of the heads wasn't included. The decals were included, of course. The kit came with instructions and was available only to members of the Royal Bobcat Club, which one could join by writing to Royal Pontiac. The kit was $80 and could be installed with normal hand tools in about 8 to 10 hours.

price. The GTO and the 2+2 began as options packages but evolved into separate series before reverting back to options packages on their respective parent platforms.

### GTOs Get the Royal Treatment

By the time that the GTO was ready for production, Royal Pontiac had developed a specific tune for the 389-powered GTOs. Based on prior research from the earlier 389 and 421 Tri-Power engines that were used in full-size cars, the Royal Bobcat performance tune was developed by Royal Pontiac's Performance Service Manager Milt Schornack. It consisted of milled heads,

### The GTO Explodes in the Marketplace

The transition from the drag strip to the street proved to be a very lucrative move for Pontiac. The GTO was an instant hit. By putting the larger 389 into the new intermediate A-Body chassis, it was able to offer a car with nearly as much performance as the Super Duty Catalinas in a much more affordable and street-friendly package.

While the price of a Super Duty Catalina was almost double the Catalina's base price, the total cost of a GTO was roughly the same as a base Catalina. The combination proved to be a wild success. With a sales projection of only 5,000 units, Pontiac sold 32,450 GTOs the first year.

This bigger engine/smaller car combination proved to be a more practical and cost-effective effort for Pontiac than hand-building fewer than 300 Super Duty Catalina, Grand Prix, Tempest, and LeMans race cars over the course of two model years. Without a doubt, Pontiac's stellar reputation as a performance car manufacturer was secured. It was built on the winning record of its factory race car program and was carried forward with a new generation of exciting and affordable performance cars. The GTO was laser-focused on the Baby Boomer generation, which reached driving age at the moment of the GTO's release, and it surpassed everyone's sales expectations. It

ushered in a new market segment, the muscle car, and it wasn't long before all the other Detroit manufacturers came to market with their own version.

It didn't take long for the youth market to flock to the Pontiac GTO. It had more potential than many other cars in the same price range. GTOs ran deep into the 12-second range at more than 105 mph with simple bolt-ons and cheater slicks.

Legendary Pontiac author and drag racer Pete McCarthy immediately saw the incredible performance-per-dollar value that the GTO represented. In the December 1990 issue of *High Performance Pontiac* magazine, McCarthy wrote, "Having spent two years prior to the introduction of the 1964 GTO transforming my 1962 318-hp Grand Prix into a high-13-second, 100-mph record holder, it took little thought to imagine the potential of the GTO. With the right options, I

## Jim Wangers and the *Car and Driver* GTOs

Legendary Advertising Executive Jim Wangers was as much a part of the story of the GTO as those who developed it, and he wasn't even a Pontiac employee. As the account executive for Pontiac's advertising agency (McManus, John and Adams), Wangers spearheaded the print and TV advertising campaigns for Pontiac. He knew that the GTO would be a huge winner in the marketplace.

In late 1963, after *Car and Driver* tested a pair of 1964 GTOs in Florida, the cover blurbs were as dramatic as the artwork that featured a Ferrari GTO just ahead of the Pontiac GTO coming out of a turn. The line boldly stated "Tempest GTO: 0–100 in 11.8 seconds."

Given the performance level of most cars at the time, 11.8 seconds was an average 0-to-60 time. Without a doubt, *Car and Driver* caught the attention of everyone. The story, which compared the Pontiac to its Ferrari namesake, never actually featured one of Enzo's prized machines. Instead, the editors were forced to compare the budget-priced Pontiac to published performance figures for the Ferrari.

In the end, it hardly mattered. The Pontiacs that showed up were both ringers. Their original 389s were replaced with blueprinted 421 H.O.s that produced more than 400 hp. That was the first inconsistency. It wasn't until the 1997 publication of his memoir, *Glory Days*, that Wangers publicly admitted the original engines were swapped out for their larger counterparts.

The second part of the story was the method that was used for the recording the performance. Rather than using

*Jim Wangers poses with the original* Car and Driver *1964 Royal Bobcat GTO at the historic Lime Rock Park in August 1995. The staff of* Pontiac Enthusiast *magazine compared the Pontiac GTO to its Ferrari counterpart, the Ferarri 250 GTO.*

*With then-owner Peter Sachs behind the wheel of the Ferrari 250 GTO and then-owner Joe Conte piloting the Pontiac GTO, the cars make their way around the Lime Rock Park road course. Although the Ferrari had little trouble getting around the Pontiac in the corners, the 421-powered GTO drove past it in the straightaways.*

figured the GTO could be made to run low-13-second ETs at more than 105 mph.

"When I discovered that those sneaky little devils at Pontiac Engineering had slipped on the 421 H.O. (number 9770716) cylinder heads, I realized that my initial estimate may have been a little conservative. Within a year, with modest changes, the GTO was indeed running high 12s at almost 109 mph. No wonder the GTO was such a sensation."

Even back then, McCarthy was no stranger to building fast Pontiacs. He was well aware that the Super Duty–derived 716 heads were substantially better than those that were used on other 389 V-8s, due to larger valves and better port contours. For many, this was a subtle but significant detail that allowed Pontiac to beat everyone to the punch with a groundbreaking new car and maintain its lead for at least a few years. It took until the 1966

model year for the competition to catch up. Chevrolet released the SS 396 Chevelle for regular production in 1966 (not counting the small run of 1965 Z-16 cars), Ford put a 390 in its Fairlane, and Mopar brought its exotic and more expensive Street Hemi to market.

While Ford and Chrysler were still in the factory race car business, the idea of a side-oiler 427 Fairlane or an LO23 Dodge being in the same market segment was an unfair comparison because they were purpose-built cars with the best equipment that the factories had to offer. The GTO was a regular production car with a cast bottom end and a hydraulic camshaft.

The Oldsmobile 442 was the first response in the marketplace to the GTO. It started with a 330-ci engine and didn't receive a larger 400 engine until 1965. By 1966, the W-30 was a formidable performance car and was perhaps the most direct comparison to the GTO.

---

the timing clocks at a drag strip or other equipment, the *Car and Driver* team used stopwatches. The margin for error was substantial. Wangers stated in his book that while the testing was happening, he could see that the times were optimistic and knew the good press that it would generate. The same thing happened a year later with the infamous 0-to-60 time in 3.9 seconds recorded for a 1965 2+2 that was paired with a Ferrari 2+2. Both cars were driven by legendary racing driver Walt Hansgen.

When *Hot Rod* magazine went outside of the regular press pool, got ahold of a base-engine convertible with a 2-speed automatic and an open 3.08 rear end, and recorded a rather anemic 15.80 quarter-mile time, Wangers was furious. *Hot Rod* was the biggest magazine around, and the negative publicity was seen as being problematic to Pontiac's image-building efforts.

Wangers's plan was to run a fleet of press pool cars through Royal Pontiac in Royal Oak, Michigan, for super tuning with the famous Royal Bobcat Package that included thinner head gaskets, blocked heat risers, a distributor recurve kit, fatter jetting, rocker-arm locknuts, and colder spark plugs. Some even had the engines fully blueprinted.

While Wangers didn't sneak larger engines in subsequent vehicles after the GTOs that were tested in *Car and Driver*, he made sure that the cars were optioned for optimal performance. They ran quicker than something off the showroom floor, but nothing was done outside the

realm of tuning that any dealer could do with a Bobcat Package.

In many ways, Jim Wangers created a persona for the GTO that, if objectively scrutinized, even the GTO itself couldn't live up to. However, in the process, he created a legacy for the GTO that continues to this day.

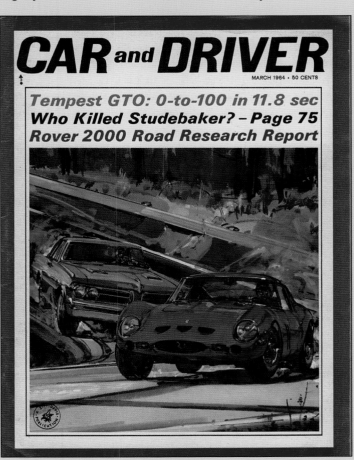

CAR and DRIVER
MARCH 1964 · 50 CENTS

Tempest GTO: 0-to-100 in 11.8 sec
Who Killed Studebaker? – Page 75
Rover 2000 Road Research Report

*The March 1964 issue of* Car and Driver *put the Pontiac GTO and the magazine itself on the map. Under the direction of editor and publisher David E. Davis Jr., the magazine reinvented itself as more than just another sports car magazine.*

# CHAPTER 8

# 1965, 1966, AND 1967: THE GTO DOMINATES MUSCLE CAR SALES AT DEALERSHIPS

Pontiac was riding high on the success of the GTO and, not to rest on its laurels, instituted some improvements to the basic combination. These changes were part of an overall program to modernize and bring a new level of interchangeability to the Pontiac V-8. Since its introduction for the 1955 model year, Pontiac had updated the engine's design and changed coolant routing, intake-manifold bolt patterns, motor mounts, and more.

This time around, the changes standardized the intake-manifold bolt patterns, updated all heads to pushrod oiling, and moved the starter to the block for all models. During the previous two years, these details varied, adding unnecessary cost. By improving the flow potential of the heads at the same time, performance improved.

The new changes increased power production, especially regarding the GTO's 389 V-8 and the B-Body's optional 421 V-8. Although the valve sizes remained constant, the ports were modestly improved, and the Tri-Power intake manifold was raised slightly to give a straighter shot at the valve.

The base GTO's output increased by 10 hp to make 335 hp at 5,000 rpm with 431 ft-lbs of torque at 3,200 rpm. The GTO Tri-Power 389's output increased by 12 hp to make 360 hp at 5,200 rpm with 424 ft-lbs of torque at

*The 1965 GTO returned for its second year with new vertical headlamp styling that mimicked the full-size Pontiacs. Montero Red, which is seen on this hardtop, was a very popular color. This side view shows the trim proportions and angular lines. The roofline was retained from 1964, but all of the sheet metal below it was new that year. A new XS-coded 389 Tri-Power with Ram Air was added to the lineup midyear. (Photo Courtesy Christopher R. Phillip)*

3,600 rpm. With the new stacked-headlamp styling and its relatively light curb weight, the 1965 GTO endures as an enthusiast favorite.

The 421 engine received the same type of upgrades, and three versions were released. All were exclusively available in full-size cars only. They included a 4-barrel, a Tri-Power, and the top-dog 421 Tri-Power H.O. The 4-barrel featured a 10.5:1 compression ratio and used a Carter AFB carburetor and 066 cam. It was rated at 338 hp at 5,200 rpm with 424 ft-lbs of torque at 3,600 rpm.

The 421 Tri-Power engine featured 10.75:1 compression and the 067 camshaft. It was rated at 356 hp at 4,800 rpm with 459 ft-lbs of torque at 3,200 rpm.

The 421 Tri-Power H.O. was the most powerful engine option for Pontiac that year and featured the same 068

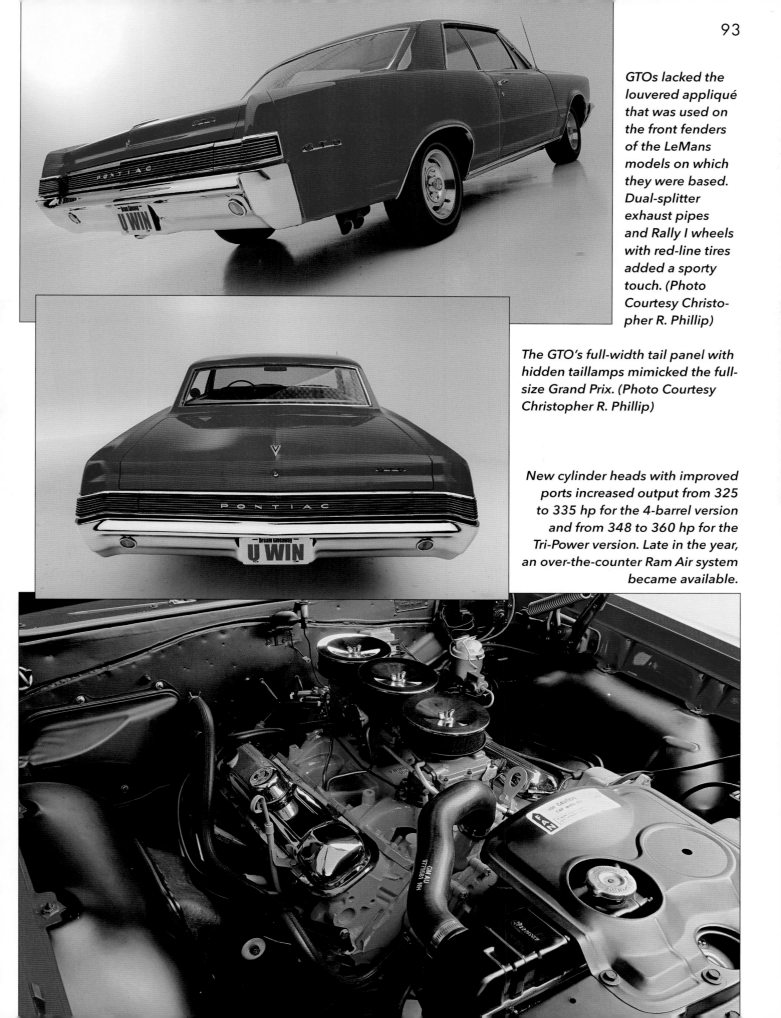

GTOs lacked the louvered appliqué that was used on the front fenders of the LeMans models on which they were based. Dual-splitter exhaust pipes and Rally I wheels with red-line tires added a sporty touch. (Photo Courtesy Christopher R. Phillip)

The GTO's full-width tail panel with hidden taillamps mimicked the full-size Grand Prix. (Photo Courtesy Christopher R. Phillip)

New cylinder heads with improved ports increased output from 325 to 335 hp for the 4-barrel version and from 348 to 360 hp for the Tri-Power version. Late in the year, an over-the-counter Ram Air system became available.

The B-Body Pontiacs returned in 1965 on a completely new platform with a new torque-box-chassis design and updated styling. It featured stacked headlamps and new Coke-bottle body sides that were characterized by a large skeg along the lower bodyside. This 1965 2+2 car is finished in Iris Mist, which was a one-year-only color. (Photo Courtesy Doug Mitchel)

The rear quarter panel sculpting is readily apparent and extends into the bumper contour. A sleek, semi-fastback roofline was used for all B-Body two-door hardtops. (Photo Courtesy Doug Mitchel)

cam used in the GTO Tri-Power 389. It benefitted from streamlined cast-iron exhaust manifolds that were similar to those on the earlier 421 Super Duty but were contoured to fit the new-generation B-Body chassis. It was rated at 376 hp at 5,000 rpm with 461 ft-lbs of torque at 3,600 rpm. It was more than capable of moving those heavy B-body cars with urgency. In fact, a modestly-optioned Catalina or 2+2 could easily keep up with their smaller siblings, if not better. Still, from a performance per dollar value, the GTO was the shining star.

The 1966 model year was essentially a carryover from 1965. The only significant change was that the full-size Pontiac version of the 389 Tri-Power that developed 338 hp in 1965 was dropped. It developed the same peak horsepower as the 4-barrel 421, so Pontiac decided to go with the larger and simpler engine to satisfy that power level.

Another change for 1966 was that the smaller center carburetor used

*Under the hood of this gorgeous 1965 2+2 car is the base 421 Pontiac V-8, which was rated at 338 hp. It is connected to a 4-speed transmission with a Hurst shifter. (Photo Courtesy Doug Mitchel)*

Veteran Pontiac racer Dick Jesse was known as "Mr. Unswitchable." He stayed loyal to the Wide Track Division even after the racing ban. Many Pontiac fans still went to drag races, which made for lucrative match-race opportunities for racers who were willing to compete against factory-backed teams. Jesse's 1965 GTO Funny Car featured an altered wheelbase and was powered by an injected 421 Super Duty. (Photo Courtesy Clinton Wright)

The resemblance between the GTO and the Grand Prix is easy to spot, especially in 1966. This gorgeous Montero Red Grand Prix with a Parchment bucket-seat interior is accented with eight-lug wheels. Power comes from a 421 V-8, which was not available in the GTO.

The Pontiac 2+2 returned for 1966 with updated styling and an upgrade to a separate series rather than being an options package on the Catalina. Powertrain offerings were essentially a carryover from 1965, with horsepower ratings up to 376. (Photo Courtesy Doug Mitchel)

The roofline and rear quarter panel shapes were retained in 1966. They were highlighted by a revised tail panel with dual-element taillamps and a new rear bumper. Rear-quarter hashmarks on the rear quarter panels just behind the doors were a 2+2 exclusive. (Photo Courtesy Doug Mitchel)

This particular 2+2 car features the optional 421 Tri-Power V-8, which was rated at 356 hp and mated to a 4-speed manual transmission. (Photos Courtesy Doug Mitchel)

Two 1966 Pontiac LeMans models compete against each other as part of a dealer promotion at Fontana Drag City in Fontana, California. The near LeMans is a Sprint with the innovative OHC 6-cylinder, and the far LeMans features a 326 V-8. The lower cost and higher available power of the 326 made it the primary choice for most buyers, although the 6-cylinder offered substantially better gas mileage and handling. (Photo Courtesy Clinton Wright)

in previous Tri-Power systems was changed to one that matched the larger-end carburetors. Horsepower and torque figures did not change, but it's generally accepted that the engines did increase horsepower in the process.

## Beat the Tiger Program

Jim Wangers was a promoter of the first order. He was like P. T. Barnum with gasoline running through his veins and three 2-barrel carburetors to let out his enthusiasm. In addition to Pontiac's remarkably successful advertising and print magazine campaigns, there were hit songs such as "GeeTO Tiger" by the Tigers and "Little GTO" by Ronnie and the Daytonas.

*Royal Pontiac's "Beat the Tiger" program featuring the GeeTO Tiger! from 1966 was resurrected in the early 2000s when Jim Wangers had a "new" 1966 GTO race car built to promote* Pontiac Enthusiast *magazine. With a gold upper body, the GTO featured a white body side on the driver's side and black on the passenger's side to commemorate the two original cars that were built in 1966. Power came from a Butler Performance Pontiac V-8.*

Wangers made the most of tie-in promotions with other companies, such as the GTO shoes by Thom McAnn, a GTO giveaway with Kellogg's Rice Krispies cereal, *The Monkees* TV show, and GTO cologne with Max Factor. As a result, the GTO brand was everywhere—from America's breakfast tables to their radios, magazines, and department stores. It was genius, and Wangers deserves every bit of credit for his efforts.

Wangers saw the crowds of people in the stands at drag strips as particularly qualified recipients of Pontiac's message, and he appealed to them on a basic and emotional level. Although General Motors was out of racing, Royal Pontiac was not. General Motors executives weren't exactly enthralled with Wangers's exploits, but they couldn't argue with the sales figures for the GTO and Pontiacs in general.

Beginning in 1965, Royal Pontiac prepared two GTOs for drag-strip use. They were identical except for the color. One was Iris Mist with a black Cordova vinyl top, and the other was white. The cars appeared at the drag strip, and all competitors received a tiger tail. There were 200 fans who received the new "GeeTO Tiger" record, and 10 lucky contestants' names were drawn from a barrel for a chance to race the mascot. It was a traveling exhibition that did a decent job of promoting Pontiac, but Wangers knew that the idea needed more sizzle.

During the second year of the program, Royal Pontiac took it to the next level. Milt Schornack and his team took two Tiger Gold 1966 4-speed GTOs, one with black body sides and the other with white body sides, to modified them. They had blueprinted 421 Tri-Power engines and featured large "GeeTO Tiger!" callouts on the doors, a variety of decals, Hurst wheels with cheater slicks out back, and the signature tiger tails. They were eye-catching and promoted heavily in the areas around the tracks wherever the Royal Pontiac team appeared. The Royal Pontiac driver, who was disguised with a tiger suit, was known as the Mystery Tiger and raced selected audience members as part of the exhibition portion of the track's daily program. Two of the many people who drove included Milt Schornack and John Politzer. The identity of the Mystery Tiger was always kept secret to keep the promotion fresh.

Announcements such as this were published weeks in advance of the appearance of the GeeTo Tiger! cars at drag strips.

Each car was outfitted with a switch that took timing out of the distributor and reduced performance instantly. This was done to intentionally lose some races so that the ratio of the Mystery Tiger's wins and losses could be controlled. Other tactics included over-inflating the tires to reduce traction on the opposing car and installing throttle stops that could be quickly engaged. They didn't want the Mystery Tiger to win every time, but if they could keep the win ratio around 70 percent, it would keep the audience interested. Both cars were capable of running 12.7-second ETs at 112 mph, which was well under the B/Stock record that GTOs normally fit under. However, the 421 engine was not legal for competition.

The Beat the Tiger program was such a success that it attracted the attention of the NHRA officials, who invited the Royal Pontiac team to Indianapolis for exhibition runs with the GTOs. The highlight of the program was the finale when the identity of the Mystery Tiger was revealed as Hurst President George Hurst, who was a skilled driver. The crowd was thrilled. Hurst wasn't the driver at every Beat the Tiger event, but he was the guy at Indy, and it rounded out a very successful promotional program.

The Tiger program ended after the 1966 season, as the use of Tigers was essentially outlawed by General Motors Chairman James Roche. He saw it as unprofessional and not a proper way to promote cars. Roche was under an abundance of pressure from safety advocates. General Motors was being labeled as an irresponsible corporation that sold high-powered cars to inexperienced teenagers.

This took place at the height of the fallout from consumer advocate Ralph Nader's controversial book *Unsafe at Any Speed*, which called out the Big Three manufacturers for not paying enough attention to safety. The Chevy Corvair garnered the most attention because it was the subject of the book's first chapter. In addition, GM's harassment of Nader and its efforts to discredit him resulted in Roche appearing in front of a US Senate subcommittee to formally apologize to Nader. Roche was understandably upset by the experience and forced General Motors to tone down its promotional activities, so the tiger went away in all of its forms.

The truth was that the promotions worked well, regardless of one's

perception of the corporate-responsibility concept. Although Wangers was nearly 40 by this time, his understanding of the youth market was uncanny. The effects helped Pontiac record its best sales year in 1966 for the GTO, with a total production run of 96,946 units. It proved to be a number that was never topped. Maybe the loss of the tiger played a part in that.

## XS

Late in the 1966 model year, a new version of the GTO's 389 Tri-Power became available. Featuring the block code XS, the engine was aimed at Sportsman racers. It featured a Ram Air system that opened up the production hood scoop. It was the first to be installed at the factory. The Ram Air system was a follow-up to the over-the-counter Ram Air pan that was available late in the 1965 model year.

In addition to the Ram Air system, the XS option included a new camshaft. Carrying part number 9785744 and stamped (H), the new profile featured 301/313 degrees of advertised duration. It retained the familiar 0.406-inch lift used in other Pontiac profiles and used heavy-duty valve springs. The year-end Pontiac Engine Log, dated July 26, 1966, states that 190 XS-coded engines were built, which means that an estimated 180 to 185 engines were factory-installed in cars. An unknown number of cars were upgraded with the XS engine's package content through dealer installations.

*The XS package was the precursor to the later Ram Air Pontiac V-8 engines and featured the 301/313-degree 744 camshaft and the special Ram Air pan for the Tri-Power carburetors. It was the one and only model year that Ram Air and Tri-Power were offered in the same year.*

The XS engine was Pontiac's first real indication since the close of the Super Duty era that it was serious about supplying upgraded content for privateer racers to compete in the various NHRA and AHRA classes. More would be coming soon.

## Firebirds and Ram Air

GM's response to the popularity of the Mustang was slower than the market demanded. Initially, GM's response was to say that its Corvair, which entered its second generation for the 1965 model year, was a competitor to the new pony car. However, by early 1965, Chevrolet was at work on a suitable response that was code named "Panther."

Pontiac, now under the direction of General Manager John Z. DeLorean, was not interested in a Pontiac variant of the Panther project. He was secretly developing a two-seat sports car that was known as the XP-833, and later called the Banshee. It was a sleek and attractive car with styling similar to the upcoming 1968 Corvette but

smaller. It was powered by either OHC-6 or V-8 engines, the hottest being the 326 H.O. The chassis was based on a shortened A-Body chassis with shorter front A-arms and a beam axle in the back.

The interior used off-the-shelf pieces and looked very finished and production-ready as a result. In early 1965, when it was presented to General Motors upper management, it was disregarded. Being a two-seater, it would never have the sales potential of a Mustang-style car, and it would be a threat to the Corvette. With a curb weight of about 2,500 to 2,600 pounds, it would not be long before 421 H.O.s found their way under the hoods of these little machines to embarrass 427 Corvettes and compete against 427 Cobras in the process. It was a hard pass. GM's upper management ordered Pontiac and DeLorean to join the Panther program knowing that Pontiac could really inject sales volume and spread its development costs over two divisions.

For Pontiac designers and engineers, the delays caused by the XP-833 program meant that they joined the F-Body program late in the process. Many of the developmental points that they were forced to work with were already set in stone. There was little to work with to give the Firebird its own distinct character, but they brilliantly made it happen with a different hood, front bumper, quarter panels with hash marks, and a new rear panel to accept slotted taillamps. Even the front fender stampings were the same as the Camaro.

The integral grille/bumper design gave the Pontiac F-Body car a definite

*DeLorean's XP-833 was a pet project that never had a chance with General Motors upper management. After it was canceled, Pontiac was forced to take on the F-Body project as a sister car to what became the Camaro. The XP-833 Banshee featured a convertible top that was stored under the reverse-opening decklid. The car was designed to use either the decklid (making the car a roadster) or a fastback roof that fit in the same location as the decklid. One of each bodystyle was built. The coupe featured an OHC 6-cylinder engine, and the roadster used a 326 H.O. Pontiac V-8.*

*This is a rare color photo of Don Gay's Infinity 1966 GTO Funny Car. (Photo Courtesy John Bleil)*

had been racing Pontiacs in various classes for years, including a 1962 421 Super Duty Catalina two-door sedan and a 1963 421 Super Duty Tempest wagon. After the ban, they competed with GTOs and Firebirds in the Stock classes as well as the Funny Car class, including an altered-wheelbase steel-bodied 1965 GTO and a 1966 GTO that were both named *Infinity*. The Gay brothers continued to race for the rest of the decade and ceased activities in 1970 to concentrate on the business. Tragically, Roy died in a 1972 motorcycle accident.

design tie to its divisional brethren and visually added some length compared to the Camaro and its simpler front-end design. In retrospect, DeLorean thought that dropping the XP-833 and going with the Firebird was the right decision for Pontiac, although his rebellious nature within the corporation was far from over.

For budget-minded performance enthusiasts, the Firebird was a game-changer in the same way that the GTO was in 1964. Available with all of the same engines as the A-Body Pontiacs, from OHC 6-cylinders to the new 400 V-8s, the Firebird was lighter and cheaper than the GTO. The simple leaf-spring suspension was easy to modify for better traction.

*The 1966 Gay Pontiac* Infinity *Funny Car is shown in the pits. Although the car was based on a production GTO, much work had been done to the chassis, including a shortened wheelbase for traction, a full roll cage, and a netted interior. Power came from a blown and injected 421 Super Duty. (Photo Courtesy Joel Naperstek)*

### Pontiac Funny Cars

Although General Motors was out of drag racing, the rise of the Funny Cars brought Chevy and Pontiac back into the mainstream from 1965 to 1967. A variety of independently-backed entries were being built and raced to compete with the factory-backed cars from Ford and Chrysler. Arnie Beswick was very active during this period. He built the supercharged and injected 421 Super Duty–powered 1964 *Mystery Tornado* GTO and converted his 1963 Super Duty LeMans into a supercharged and injected altered-wheelbase Funny Car that was called the *Tameless Tiger*.

As the evolution of the Funny Car class was very rapid in those years, Beswick took the body off the *Mystery Tornado*, sold it to a circle-track racer, and added a Fiberglass LTD 1966 GTO body named *Star of the Circuit*.

Brothers Don and Roy Gay from Gay Pontiac in Dickinson, Texas,

*Don Gay, driving the* Infinity *1966 GTO Funny Car, blasts past Joe Davis and the* Colt 45 *Mustang. (Photo Courtesy Jack Ravenna)*

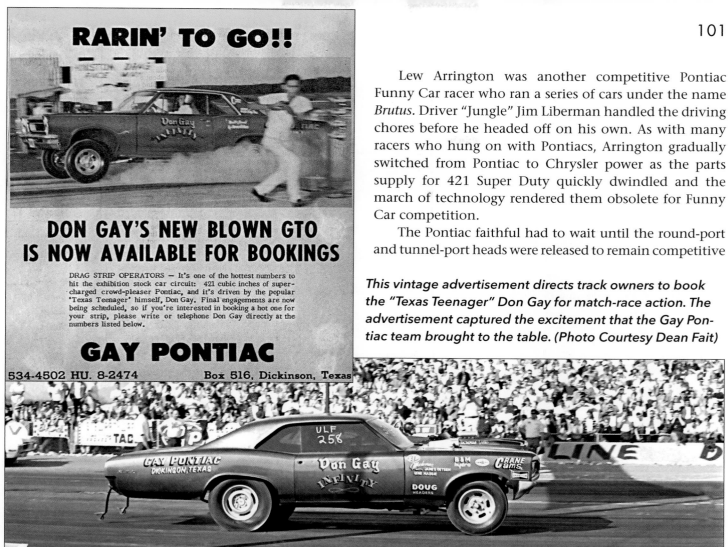

Lew Arrington was another competitive Pontiac Funny Car racer who ran a series of cars under the name *Brutus*. Driver "Jungle" Jim Liberman handled the driving chores before he headed off on his own. As with many racers who hung on with Pontiacs, Arrington gradually switched from Pontiac to Chrysler power as the parts supply for 421 Super Duty quickly dwindled and the march of technology rendered them obsolete for Funny Car competition.

The Pontiac faithful had to wait until the round-port and tunnel-port heads were released to remain competitive

*This vintage advertisement directs track owners to book the "Texas Teenager" Don Gay for match-race action. The advertisement captured the excitement that the Gay Pontiac team brought to the table. (Photo Courtesy Dean Fait)*

*Don Gay and the* Infinity *1966 GTO take on Charlie Wilson's* Vicious Vette *at Bee Line Dragway in Mesa, Arizona. (Photo Courtesy Clinton Wright)*

*This photo collage shows the Gay Pontiac race cars and dealership, circa 1966. (Photo Courtesy Dean Fait)*

The **Infinity** *Funny Car is shown in the pits at Aquasco Speedway in Aquasco, Maryland. (Photo Courtesy Steve Rollins Estate)*

*This is proof that Arnie "the Farmer" Beswick draws a crowd wherever he goes. His* Tameless Tiger *altered-wheelbase Funny Car was a 1963 Super Duty LeMans that was originally sent to Mickey Thompson. After the racing ban, it was sold to Beswick, who campaigned it as* Little B's Runabout *before it was converted in 1966 into its final incarnation as the supercharged, injected, and tiger-striped altered-wheelbase Funny Car. (Photo Courtesy Clinton Wright)*

The Gay's 1967 Firebird Funny Car is shown with the body raised at Cecil County Dragway. It is powered by a blown and injected 421 Super Duty engine. (Photo Courtesy Steve Rollins Estate)

The Star of the Circuit 1966 GTO was actually the 1964 Mystery Tornado with a new body built by Fiber Glass Ltd. of Hillside, Illinois. The original 1964 GTO body was sold to a circle-track racer. It is seen here in February 1967. (Photo Courtesy Clinton Wright)

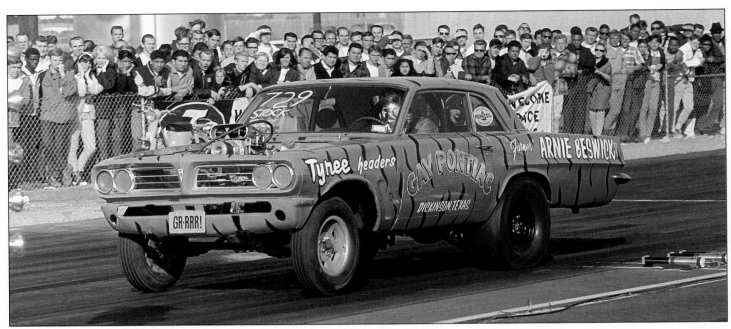

*The* Tameless Tiger *Funny Car is in action at Irwindale Raceway in Irwindale, California. Note the Gay Pontiac livery on the door. (Photo Courtesy Clinton Wright)*

*In February 1967, Arnie Beswick's* Tameless Tiger *Funny Car is in the pits at Famoso Raceway in Bakersfield, California. Jules Meyers Pontiac was the sponsor at that time. (Photo Courtesy Clinton Wright)*

in those classes. However, that window closed pretty quickly, especially when considering that they were up against highly-developed 426 Hemis and the exotic 427 SOHC Fords.

### 1967: Powerplants Updated Again

Without a doubt, General Motors felt pressure from the negative portrayal of the corporation and the American auto industry from Ralph Nader's book *Unsafe at Any Speed*. While the Chevrolet Corvair received the majority of the public's attention in regard to the book, Nader was critical of the entire industry. His perception of a lack of attention to safety had General Motors taking a more safety-oriented stance in light of new Federal safety regulations that

*The rapidly-evolving nature of technology in the FX and Funny Car classes had racers building new cars nearly every year. Dick Jesse built this low-slung fiberglass-bodied 1966 GTO to replace his 1965 altered-wheelbase car. It is shown here at Motor City Raceway. (Photo Courtesy Jim Luikens)*

The 1967 GTO received a mild facelift with a new mesh grille design and revised taillamps. The stacked headlamp design lasted one more year and was updated with a new wire-mesh grille design that replaced the black egg-crate grille that was used in 1966. Grille-mounted turn signals were a GTO exclusive in 1967.

were now in place. All General Motors vehicles featured new collapsible steering columns, safety steering wheels, four-way flashers, dual-chamber master cylinders, and optional front disc brakes.

The new focus on safety also had General Motors eliminate multiple carburetion on all of GM's products except the Corvette (GM's top performance car) and the Corvair, which used a horizontally-opposed 6-cylinder engine and needed at least one carburetor per bank.

Mac McKellar and his team went back to the drawing board to improve their V-8 engines to maintain the performance levels of the Tri-Power engines with one

> **"WITHOUT A DOUBT, GENERAL MOTORS FELT PRESSURE FROM THE NEGATIVE PORTRAYAL OF THE CORPORATION AND THE AMERICAN AUTO INDUSTRY FROM RALPH NADER'S BOOK *UNSAFE AT ANY SPEED.*"**

The 400 engine featured a new block with three freeze plugs per side and new cylinder heads with 2.11 intake valves and 1.77-inch exhaust valves that accounted for a 10-percent increase in flow. Tri-Power was gone due to new corporate mandates, but the cast-iron 4-barrel intake was a near-copy of the 1963 421 Super Duty NASCAR single 4-barrel intake. To this day, it remains one of the best all-around intake manifolds for the Pontiac V-8. Horsepower ranged from 335 to 360 with a new Ram Air option topping the options list.

## The Other *Gray Ghost*

In 1971, Pontiac engineer Herb Adams set the road-racing world on its ear with his 1964 *Gray Ghost* GTO and its 303 Pontiac engine that competed in Sports Car Club of America (SCCA) Trans Am racing. However, five years prior, there was a different GTO that went by the same name and competed in drag racing.

Chicago-based racer Larry Swiatek, who previously ran a 1963 *Gray Ghost* Swiss cheese Catalina in the B/FX category, campaigned a Pontiac-powered 1966 GTO Funny Car for the 1966 and 1967 seasons. It has quite an interesting story behind it.

The *Gray Ghost* was one of six Funny Cars built in 1966 at R&B Automotive Engineering by Dennis Rolain and "Lil' John" Butera in Kenosha, Wisconsin. This car was the only one of that chassis to become a Pontiac. At the time, the state-of-the-art designs utilized scratch-built chromoly chassis and complete fiberglass bodies. There were only three fiberglass 1966 Pontiac Tempest bodies built by Fiberglass LTD in Hillside, Illinois. This car and Arnie Beswick's *Star of the Circuit* are the only two surviving examples.

When the car was completed in the summer of 1966, it featured a Hilborn-injected 421 Super Duty Pontiac engine that was running on an alky-methanol mix. The chromoly chassis featured a seriously altered wheelbase and weighed an ultralight 1,600 pounds.

The *Gray Ghost* is a significant part of Pontiac racing history for a variety of reasons. Its lightweight construction and unique injected powerplant were important, but the most significant aspect about this

Larry Swiatek and the 1966 Gray Ghost *Funny Car lunge off the starting line. This unusual and innovative machine ran with an injected 421 Super Duty and ran in the 9-second range. (Photo Courtesy Todd Holzknecht)*

Scott Repsol, a friend of Larry Swiatek, is seen here in the summer of 1966, which was shortly after the car was finished. Note the dual SW fuel pumps. The engine was pulled from Swiatek's 1963 Swiss cheese Catalina and used for preliminary testing, running a bathtub intake. In 1966, this configuration of the Funny Car was raced at Union Grove and the Indy Nationals in the Gas class. At that point, they were still dialing in the combination and not necessarily looking to compete. It ran 9.90 ETs on gas and 8.80 ETs on nitro. (Photo Courtesy Todd Holzknecht)

The early Funny Cars often had opening doors. The Gray Ghost *and Arnie Beswick's 1966* Star of the Circuit *GTO had this feature, and they were based on Fiber Glass Ltd. replica bodies. (Photo Courtesy Todd Holzknecht)*

*The* Gray Ghost *competes against the* Fugitive, *an altered-wheelbase Dodge Coronet. (Photo Courtesy Todd Holzknecht)*

car was that Pontiac actively supplied parts to Swiatek long after the General Motors racing ban of 1963. In addition to receiving back-door support, Pontiac engineer Tom Nell was responsible for building the Turbo 400 transmission. Nell also designed and built an adapter plate to locate the bellhousing-mounted starter and Crower-Glide clutch.

The *Gray Ghost* ran consistently in the high-8- and low-9-second range at speeds approaching 150 mph on bias-play pie-crust slicks. Swiatek raced in the Midwest United Drag Racer's Association (UDRA) Injected Fuel Funny Car circuit competitively from late 1966 through the 1967 season before he sold the car and built his next car for the 1968 season. Chassis and tire technology was evolving rapidly at the time, and cars often became obsolete after a season or two.

After the car was sold, it was renamed *The Assassin*, which is how it remains today. Chicago-based collector Todd Holzknecht purchased the car and is in the process of restoring it back to its as-built 1966 configuration, including an original 421 Super Duty V-8 and Turbo 400 transmission.

*Larry Swiatek is in his fire suit preparing for a run. Rules required the use of a fire suit and gas mask when running nitromethane. Competing in the fuel classes was (and is) serious business. (Photo Courtesy Todd Holzknecht)*

*This photo shows how short the wheelbase was in this Funny Car. It must have been a handful to keep under control. (Photo Courtesy Todd Holzknecht)*

*Pontiac's 2+2 car was reduced to an options package for the 1967 model year on the Catalina. It was the final year for the nameplate, at least in the US. The restyled sheet metal featured stacked headlamps, and the hash marks were moved from the rear quarter panels to the front fenders. The 2+2 cars exclusively featured 428 engines and were mated to a manual or automatic transmission. The 2+2 car was the rarest Pontiac that was available that year, with just 1,768 units built. (Photos Courtesy Doug Mitchel)*

4-barrel carburetor. New block castings added a third freeze plug per side, and the 389 and 421 engines were bored to a 4.12-inch bore size to enlarge their displacements to 400 and 426.6 ci, which rounded up to 428 for marketing purposes. The 428 engine is not really 428 ci, just as the 350 Pontiac engine is actually 354 ci.

New cylinder heads (casting number 670) featured the familiar port entrance, and exit shapes were substantially recontoured for increased flow. They also featured new 2.11 intake and 1.77-inch exhaust valves, which were substantially larger than the 1.92/1.66-inch valves that were previously used on the top-performing engines. The closed combustion chamber design was largely retained in the new design and modified for larger valves. Overall flow was improved roughly 10 percent in both intake and exhaust flow, but there was more to the equation.

### No More Tri-Power

While the new cylinder heads were a significant improvement, there was more to do to maintain performance levels. While the loss of Tri-Power carburetion seemed like a major setback, McKellar had an ace up his sleeve. After he worked on a few "legal in letter but not in spirit" projects, such as a single 6-barrel carburetor that was a trio of 2GC carburetors on a common baseplate, he resurrected the design of the 1963 421 Super Duty single 4-barrel intake manifold.

*The top option for the 1967 Pontiac line was the 428 H.O. Quadra-Power V-8. This engine was only available in full-size models. It was rated at 376 hp at 5,100 rpm with 462 ft-lbs of torque at 3,400 rpm. It featured the 068 cam, 10.75:1 compression, and the long-branch exhaust manifolds. Aside from the exhaust manifolds, the 428 H.O. is distinguished from the standard 428 in the 2+2 car by the large, open-element, chrome air cleaner. (Photos Courtesy Doug Mitchel)*

*The 1967 Pontiac 2+2 car featured the same updated styling as the rest of the Catalina line, including the dramatic fastback roofline on the two-door hardtop. (Photos Courtesy Doug Mitchel)*

*This 1967 2+2 coupe featured the standard 360-hp 428 4-barrel engine along with air conditioning and a 4-speed transmission. This version of the 428 used the standard exhaust manifolds and a louvered air cleaner. (Photos Courtesy Doug Mitchel)*

*The 1967 Grand Prix was based on the short-wheelbase Catalina but featured a unique nose design with hideaway headlamps, a different tail section with slotted taillamps, and a more formal roof design. It was the only year that the Grand Prix was offered as a convertible. Powertrain offerings were the same as the Bonneville, right up to the 428 H.O. Quadra-Power engine.*

He modified it to work with the revised water-neck layout, flanged it for a Rochester Quadrajet carburetor, cast it in Detroit Wonder Metal (cast iron), and made one of the best all-around intake manifolds in Detroit history.

The result was impressive. Power levels were maintained and even increased in some areas. The 428 engine was available in two versions. The standard 4-barrel used the 067 camshaft and was rated at 360 hp at 4,600 rpm with 472 ft-lbs of torque at 3,200 rpm. This engine replaced the 421 4-barrel and the 421 Tri-Power, and it was more powerful than both. The 428 H.O. Quadra-Power was the top-of-the-line engine for full-size Pontiacs. It was essentially identical to the standard 428 except for the use of the 068 cam and the freer-flowing long-branch exhaust manifolds. That engine was rated at 376 hp at 5,100 rpm with 462 ft-lbs of torque at 3,400 rpm. The power levels were nearly identical to the previous 421 Tri-Power H.O. and was easier to keep in tune. There wasn't the same level of visual impact when the hood was raised, but Pontiac did a good job of promoting the fact that the Tri-Power and the Quadrajet intake systems were similar in power production.

## The 400s and Their Confusing Power Ratings

The 400 and the new base GTO 400 used the 067 camshaft. With a 10.75:1 compression ratio, they were rated at 335 hp at 5,000 rpm with 441 ft-lbs of torque at 3,400 rpm. The optional 400 H.O. featured the 068 cam and was rated at 360 hp at 5,100 rpm with 438 ft-lbs of torque at 3,600 rpm.

The 400 engines were used in Firebirds but rated at 325 hp and 410 ft-lbs of torque. The milder of the two engines used the 067 camshaft and had its horsepower and torque peaks at 4,800 and 3,400 rpm, respectively. The 400 Ram Air's horsepower and torque peaks were at 5,200 and 3,600 rpm using the 744 cam.

What was going on? It must have been very confusing for would-be buyers.

*Kerry Klotzman heats the red-line tires on his 1967 Plum Mist Firebird 400 Ram Air at the 2014 Pontiac-Oakland Club International (POCI) Convention Drags in Wichita, Kansas. This car was special-ordered and used for promotional purposes by Pontiac. The 400 Ram Air was available in the 1967 Firebirds and GTOs and featured the 744 camshaft with heavy-duty valve springs, free-flowing cast-iron headers, and a Ram Air pan that sealed off the engine compartment and only allowed cool air through the open hood scoops. Ram Air Firebirds are still competitive machines in Pure Stock and Factory Appearing Stock Tire (FAST) competition.*

There were two factors. The first was that the floor-pan layout of the Firebird required a more restrictive exhaust system that consisted of two muffler-like resonators and a single cross-flow muffler that was tucked behind the rear axle. The second factor was that the Firebird 400 engines used a tab on the accelerator linkage that prevented wide-open throttle. The reason was that GM's corporate powertrain restrictions did not allow a passenger car to have a horsepower-to-weight ratio of less than 10 pounds per 1 hp.

With the shipping weight of a Firebird convertible at generally 3,247 pounds, the maximum power output could only be 325 hp. The peak power RPMs were a subtle indicator of the different performance levels of two seemingly identical power ratings. Bending the tab out of the way or removing it altogether was a common practice that allowed for wide-open throttle and power ratings that were closer to the GTO's numbers. Combined with a significantly lower curb weight, the Firebird quickly became a favorite among performance enthusiasts and took some of the GTO's thunder, just as the Camaro did with the Chevelle.

## Ram Air

For those looking for the ultimate in performance without any consideration for comfort or fuel economy, the 400 Ram Air engines were the top option for GTOs and Firebirds when they were available very late in the model year. The basic engine formula followed the 1966 XS engine and featured functional hood scoops that fed into a Ram Air pan and a 744 camshaft with heavy-duty valve springs.

The 400 Ram Air took it a bit further with a four-bolt main block, special high-chromium-steel, swirl-polished valves, double valve springs, and special free-flowing exhaust manifolds. The manifolds were different for A-Body and F-Body installations, and the Firebird version had a tab to prevent full-throttle opening. The GTO version was rated at the same 360 hp as the 400 H.O. but made closer to 400 hp. The engine was available with manual and automatic transmissions with a standard 3.90 rear-end ratio, and the GTOs had an optional 4.33 gearset. Firebirds and GTOs could have a 4.11 gear installed at the dealership.

*The 1967 Royal Bobcat/ Cars Magazine GTO is parked in front of editor Martyn L. Schorr's home. This car provided a massive amount of publicity for Pontiac, which led to strong sales numbers for GTOs and other Pontiac performance cars. (Photo Courtesy Martyn L. Schorr)*

## Post-Ban Drag Racing for Pontiacs

The overall success for Pontiac racers was not at the level that it had been during the days of the Super Duty program. Some privateers soldiered on with their 1960–1963 Super Duty Catalinas to achieve varying levels of success in the various Stock and Super Stock classes. With the release of the GTO, many found a home in the NHRA B-D/Stock class, depending on the weight and powertrain. The 1964–1966 automatic versions were not competitive due to the sluggish Super Turbine 300, which was essentially like starting out in second gear. If they were used against a Chrysler TorqueFlite or Ford C4 or C6, there was rarely a good outcome.

*The GTO was raced extensively at New York National Speedway in Moriches, Long Island, New York. It is seen here running against a 390-powered Mercury Comet. (Photo Courtesy Martyn L. Schorr)*

*Bill Abraham (top) and Arlen Vanke (bottom) pose with their 1966 LeMans Sprint convertible, which was known as the Mystery Tornado II, as well as the 1966 GTO Tin Indian V, which ran in NASCAR drag-racing classes. (Photo Courtesy Knafel Family Archive)*

AN OFFICIAL TIMED RUN AT

**NEW YORK**
**NATIONAL SPEEDWAY**

CAR NO. 500

CLASS A/S ①

E.T. 13.40

M.P.H. 108

W ⊘    L Rd

*This time slip is proof that the GTO was a strong runner. It was taken during the GTO's second trip to the track. With modern suspension and tire technology, this car ran ETs in the 12s. (Photo Courtesy Martyn L. Schorr)*

In regional competition, Pontiac seemed to perform better, as results from the NHRA Nationals at Indy from 1964–1967 show a dramatic drop in the number of Pontiacs. Many of the most successful teams and racers, such as Mickey Thompson, Hayden Proffitt, and Arlen Vanke, had moved on from the automaker. While they no doubt loved the success that they achieved with Pontiac, they had businesses to run and financial obligations to meet. Loyalty to General Motors wasn't going to pay the bills. Those racers, like others in the same situation, found great success with their newfound factory deals.

In Thompson's case, he enjoyed a long and successful deal with Ford and went on to market tires. With several years of off-road racing experience, he formed the off-road racing sanctioning body Southern California Off Road Enthusiasts (SCORE) and later the Mickey Thompson Entertainment Group, which promoted stadium and indoor truck and motocross racing.

Around this time, more dealers jumped onto the racing bandwagon after seeing the success generated by local and regional race promotions. They were no longer able to buy new 421 Super Duty Catalinas or Tempests, but they could capitalize on Pontiac's performance message. They did this through campaigning cars that customers could readily purchase, namely performance-optioned GTOs and Firebirds, but the occasional Catalinas or 2+2s were rarely used. Royal Pontiac was the most famous dealership that was doing this, but there were countless other dealerships in towns and cities across the country that got in on the action.

"Race on Sunday; sell on Monday" was still the philosophy. With Pontiac's impressive list of performance cars, it was a solid campaign strategy to have a race car on display in the showroom during the week and then race it on the weekends. In addition to Royal Pontiac, Packer Pontiac in Detroit moved onto GTOs. Driver Howard Maseles continued to run his 1962 Catalina for the rest of the decade. Harry Wesch at the Myrtle Motors dealership in Long Island, New York, was a well-known Pontiac

*This 1967 Royal Bobcat GTO Sport Coupe has quite a pedigree. In addition to being delivered to Royal Pontiac, this car received the full treatment, including a full Ram Air system upgrade. (Photos Courtesy David Newhardt)*

racer, and his dealership offered performance upgrade services that were similar to Royal Pontiac. Gay Pontiac in Dickinson, Texas, heavily campaigned a multi-car team in the late 1960s. Knafel Pontiac continued with its highly-successful racing program through the end of the 1960s. Knafel also marketed its limited-edition Magnum 400 Tempests and Golden Sabre Ram Air V GTOs.

It was also at this time that racers in Stock and Super Stock looked for competitive combinations to attack the record books. There were cases where particular engine, transmission, and bodystyle combinations were very competitive in a given class. While it made sense to be running a Hemi-powered lightweight or Ford Thunderbolt in the upper classes, Pontiacs offered competitive advantages in some of the lower classes.

A low-compression 4-barrel 389 engine in a heavy bodystyle or a base 389 or 400 engine in a Catalina or Grand Prix with a manual transmission was an attractive combination, particularly if the national record in a particular class was a bit on the soft side. This meant that it was an overlooked but relatively easy record to top. Those sorts of situations offered racers a strategic opportunity to take a relatively obscure combination with a low factory rating but a lot of power potential and exploit it to achieve the best possible outcome.

*Harry Wesch is shown behind the wheel of the Myrtle Motors 1967 Firebird race car. Myrtle Motors was a dealership that, like Royal Pontiac, was able to turn profits by expertly catering to its customer's high-performance needs. (Photo Courtesy Martyn L. Schorr)*

*This recently uncovered photo of Roy Gay shows him with a female companion while holding a camera and looking at his 1967 SS/DA Firebird 400. (Photo Courtesy Joel Naperstek)*

*Roy Gay's 1967 Firebird ran in the SS/DA class and is seen here with other Gay Pontiac team vehicles at Capitol Raceway in Crofton, Maryland. (Photo Courtesy Clinton Wright)*

# CHAPTER 9

# REACHING THE PINNACLE: PONTIAC'S ROUND-PORT PERFORMANCE ENGINES

The 1968 GTO featured all-new fuselage styling and the new Endura front bumper. When compared to its predecessor, it rode on a 3-inch-shorter wheelbase, was 5.9 inches shorter, and weighed about 50 pounds more. The Firebird and full-size models were essentially carryovers with some updated styling, and the Firebird received a new Flo-Thru Ventilation system that eliminated the wing windows.

In 1968, Pontiac's performance lineup returned largely unchanged, but there were some improvements that increased the power output. A new open-combustion-chamber design was implemented that helped reduce emissions and increase power output. The 428 engines were both more powerful than their predecessors. The milder of the two produced an impressive 375 hp at 4,800 rpm

*Although high-performance engines continued to be offered in full-size cars until 1970, the 1968 model year was the last time that a customer could order a 428 H.O., 4-speed, and 3.90 Safe-T-Track differential. This bare-bones Catalina sedan was ordered to go! (Photo Courtesy Ben Salvador)*

*This 1968 Ram Air I Firebird is the only such vehicle that was exported to Australia, where it was converted to right-hand drive by Holden (GM's Australian division). It has since been changed back to left-hand drive in the United States. Robert Lozins is the current owner.*

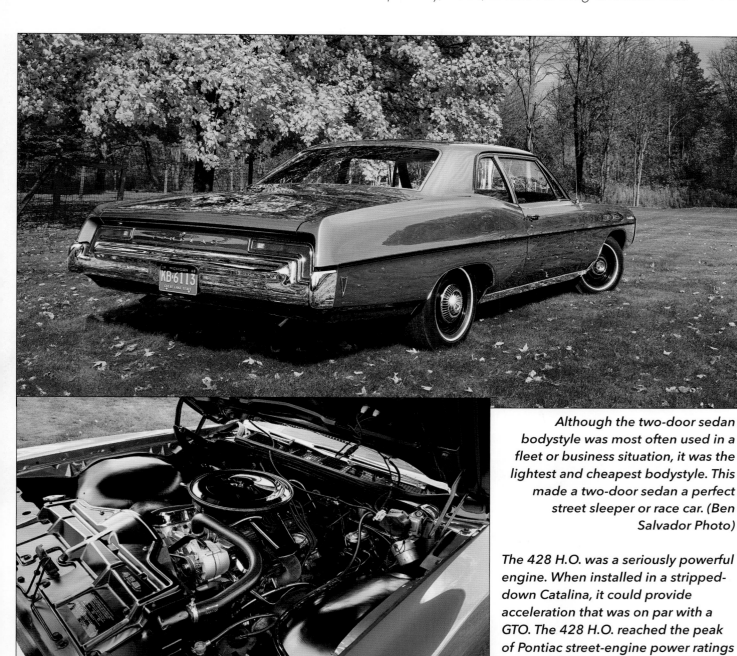

*Although the two-door sedan bodystyle was most often used in a fleet or business situation, it was the lightest and cheapest bodystyle. This made a two-door sedan a perfect street sleeper or race car. (Ben Salvador Photo)*

*The 428 H.O. was a seriously powerful engine. When installed in a stripped-down Catalina, it could provide acceleration that was on par with a GTO. The 428 H.O. reached the peak of Pontiac street-engine power ratings and developed 390 hp at 5,200 rpm with 472 ft-lbs of torque at 3,200 rpm. (Ben Salvador Photo)*

with 472 ft-lbs of torque at 3,200 rpm. The 428 H.O. reached the zenith of Pontiac street engine power ratings and developed 390 hp at 5,200 rpm with 472 ft-lbs of torque at 3,200 rpm.

## Ram Air II

While the 400 Ram Air engines that were available in the first half of 1968 were essentially carryovers from 1967 (aside from the updated combustion chamber), the big news came late in the season when the new Ram Air II was released. This engine was a game-changer, and to this day, it remains one of the best-performing Pontiac engines of all time. The secret to the success of this engine needs to be understood. I refer to this engine as the Goldilocks combination because everything was just right. The cam timing, carburetion, compression, head flow, and exhaust system were masterfully integrated and worked in complete lockstep to provide the 400-ci Pontiac V-8 with exactly what it needed—not too little and not too much.

First, there were two elements to this engine that

*The 400 Ram Air II was a late-season introduction in 1968. It featured new cylinder heads with round exhaust ports, the new 308/320-degree 041 camshaft, streamlined exhaust manifolds, the Ram Air pan, and open hood scoops. The engine was available only in GTOs and Firebirds. While the advertised power rating was the same as the optional 400 H.O., the Ram Air II was the most powerful 400-ci engine that was built at that time.*

separated it from anything that was previously used by Pontiac in a street engine. The cylinder heads (casting number 96) retained their familiar 2.11/1.77-inch valve sizes and slightly enlarged Ram Air I intake port dimensions. The new head featured an improved version of the open chamber design, known as the spherical wedge. The biggest change was a round exhaust port that dramatically improved exhaust flow so that the exhaust ports flowed nearly as much as the intake ports. This is an important factor to remember.

The other new component was the camshaft profile (part number 9794041 [T]). It was a hydraulic-lifter version of the old McKellar #10 camshaft with a little more lift. It featured 308/320 degrees of advertised duration and 0.469-inch lift with 1.5:1 rockers. As with the earlier Ram Air engines, the Ram Air II used double

*Jim Mino's Autumn Bronze 1968 Firebird drives at full throttle at the 2011 Ames Performance Pontiac Nationals. This particular Ram Air II ran a best ET of 11.75 at 118.90 mph.*

Racers such as Truman Fields and Mike McKinney quickly determined that Ram Air Firebirds were competitive in the upper Stock classes. Here, Fields competes with his Hard Times B/Stock Ram Air II Firebird.

This 1968 Ram Air II Firebird convertible is incredibly rare, as only eight were built. The short ordering window and mandatory 3.90 rear-end ratio kept all Ram Air II orders low.

Only 246 Ram Air II GTOs were built in 1968, which was the year that the GTO won the coveted *MotorTrend* Car of the Year award. (Photo Courtesy Mecum Auctions)

valve springs to ensure stable high-rpm operation. Automatics received the 068 cam, but the power rating was unchanged.

The engine had the regular production cast-iron intake manifold and Rochester Quadrajet carburetor, while new streamlined round-port exhaust manifolds were used. As with the Ram Air I, the Ram Air II was available with manual and automatic transmissions with a standard 3.90 rear-end ratio. The GTOs had an optional 4.33 gearset. Firebirds and GTOs could have a 4.11 gear installed at the dealership.

The Ram Air II was a stopgap that was designed with components from the upcoming Ram Air IV engine, which was still in development. The 400 engines began to lose their competitive edge at the drag strip, so McKellar quickly implemented the parts from the new design that were available.

In the GTO, the Ram Air II was rated at 366 hp at 5,400 rpm with 445 ft-lbs of torque at 3,800 rpm. In the Firebird, it was rated at 335 hp at 5,000 rpm with 430 ft-lbs of torque at 4,400 rpm. The shipping weight of the Firebird convertible was raised to 3,346 pounds. This allowed for the slight increase in the engine's power rating, which was just 5 hp above the regular 400 4-barrel. Obviously, Pontiac still played games with the power ratings, as did all of the other General Motors divisions that were building performance cars.

The Ram Air II combination was the sweet spot for the performance tuning of the 400, and it was very responsive. While it didn't have the same level of bottom-end power as the regular 400 engines, it was a benefit for the traction-limited cars in which they were installed.

The secret regarding why they ran so well was the exhaust port. The intake and exhaust ports flowed nearly the same. Most engine theorists agree that the ideal intake-to-exhaust flow ratio is 75 percent. One would think that with an intake port flowing around 200 cfm at 28 inches of water, it would be proper to have an exhaust port that would flow about 150 cfm. That sounds reasonable, right? Well, when you bolt on the exhaust system, flow is restricted another 15 or 20 percent, and optimal flow numbers go out the window.

Let's look at the Ram Air II again. With the exhaust system bolted on, it's back down to the ideal 75-percent airflow, which means that even when corked up, the Ram Air II ran as well as a normal cylinder-head combination with the exhaust system off. That is the secret of the Ram Air II.

In terms of real horsepower, it is estimated that the Ram Air II produced about 425 hp. Although no vintage road tests are known to have been published, their performances in Pure Stock Muscle Car Drag Racing indicates that figure. The late Jim Mino ran a best ET of 12.363 seconds at 116.55 mph at the 2011 event in his 3,436-pound 1968 Firebird with 4.11 gears and red-line tires. He subsequently bettered those times elsewhere, running an 11.75 ET at 118.90 mph.

## The Ram Air IV: 1969

In early 1968, John DeLorean wrote a letter to Pontiac Motor Engineer Mac McKellar and asked what it would take to make the 400 Pontiac a true 6,000-rpm engine and whether such an engine could be put into production

*Pontiac built only 116 Firebirds with the Ram Air IV V-8 engine and 4-speed transmission. This spectacular example was restored by Lee Barnes Classic Restorations in Piedmont, South Carolina.*

*The Ram Air IV was built on the foundation of the earlier Ram Air II and added forged pistons; larger intake ports; an aluminum two-plane, high-rise intake manifold with a removable cast-iron crossover; and 1.65:1 rockers that raised the valve lift to 0.516 inch. In the Firebird, it was rated at 345 hp at 5,400 rpm with 430 ft-lbs of torque at 3,700 rpm. In actuality, the peak horsepower of the Ram Air IV was closer to 440 or 450. It used a specific Ram Air pan that was slightly more efficient than the one that was used in Ram Air III Firebirds.*

in a reasonable amount of time. McKellar's reply came in the form of an internal memo that stated that they needed zero-lash hydraulic lifters, a 1.65:1 rocker ratio, a new intake manifold, and heads with larger ports.

DeLorean's response was simple: "Go ahead."

The result came in late 1968 as a 1969 model that became known as the Ram Air IV. It was the high-water mark for the 400 engine in terms of overall horsepower. The name for the engine came not from its line of succession but the innovative prototype four-inlet Ram Air system that was originally proposed for it, which added two air inlets in the grille area in addition to the hood scoops that reached production.

Although some of the Ram Air II's package content came to market first on the Ram Air II as a stopgap measure, it was actually designed for the Ram Air IV engine. When it was released for production, the four-inlet Ram Air system was gone, but the name remained.

*Due to the cost, the limited and mandatory options list, poor low-end torque, and diminished drivability, any Ram Air IV is a rarity. Relatively few people outside of racers ordered it, even though it was the top-performing model. This 1969 Ram Air IV convertible with an automatic transmission, which is 1 of 14 that was built. Add in the special-order paint, which was Carousel Red (a Judge-only color), and it is a spectacular one-off machine.*

*The rear end of the GTO was redesigned for 1969 and featured new taillamps that were sandwiched between the bumper and decklid. Since the model was completely redesigned for the 1968 model year, the annual changes for 1969 were relatively minor.*

*The interior of this one-off machine has power windows but featured the standard steering wheel instead of the Custom Sport wood-grain steering wheel.*

The Ram Air IV built upon the foundation of the Ram Air II, including the four-bolt main block, 041 cam, and free-flowing exhaust manifolds. In addition, the Ram Air IV added forged pistons and new cylinder heads (casting number 722) with taller intake ports for increased airflow. The intake and exhaust valves remained at 2.11/1.77 inches and

*The Ram Air IV engine was easily distinguished by its aluminum two-plane, high-rise intake manifold and streamlined, cast-iron exhaust headers. The foam surround on the top of the pan sealed the cool intake air from the hot engine compartment to increase horsepower.*

*This Carousel Red 1969 Firebird features the Ram Air IV engine with a 4-speed transmission. With red-line tires and 3.90 gears, it has run ETs as fast as 12.28 at 115.41 mph at the Pure Stock Muscle Car Drags.*

were operated by 1.65:1 rocker arms to raise the lift of the camshaft to a total of 0.516-inch lift. Special zero-lash lifters helped with high-RPM operation.

Perhaps the largest visual difference between the Ram Air IV and its predecessors was its unique two-plane, aluminum, high-rise intake manifold. This intake manifold featured a separate, removable cast-iron crossover that could be removed in warm weather. It was topped with a Rochester Quadrajet carburetor that was fed by the hood scoop via a Ram Air pan.

The result of this effort had a cost in terms of drivability, resulting in a substantial loss of the low-end torque and overall drivability for which Pontiacs were known. Although, it did make a lot of power. For the GTO, the factory rated the Ram Air IV at 370 hp at 5,500 rpm with 445 ft-lbs of torque at 3,900 rpm.

The Firebird and the new Firebird Trans Am were available with this powerplant. In the F-Body platform, the engine developed 345 hp at 5,400 with 430 ft-lbs of torque at 3,700 rpm. In reality, the peak horsepower of the Ram Air IV was closer to 440 or 450. Even with the increasing weight of the GTO and Firebird, these were spectacular performers.

Trying to find reliable vintage road tests for a Ram Air IV–equipped Pontiac is a challenge. Everything went through Royal Pontiac, and no showroom-stock tests were conducted at that time for a Ram Air IV–powered car during the 1969 model year. Perhaps the one test that most accurately showed the engine's true potential came from a *Popular Hot Rodding* annual known as *Engine Hop Up Ideas: 1970.*

The car in question was a 1969 Royal Bobcat GTO, which later went on to have a Ram Air V engine installed.

The engine was blueprinted, it was fitted with Doug's headers, and it benefitted from a Schiefer Rev-Lok pressure plate and clutch. The car had a 3.90 Safe-T-Track rear end, and 8.00/8.50 x 14 Goodyear cheater slicks were used at the strip as part of the test.

On street tires and through closed exhaust, the GTO produced a 13.42 ET at 108.42 mph. With open exhaust and slicks, the same car produced a 12.62 ET at 109.52 mph on its best run. Traction was obviously a factor here, with a 0.8-second difference in the ETs. In addition, switching from a closed to an open exhaust only increased the top speed by 1.1 mph, even with better traction. It shows how powerful these engines were, but it also shows how much of a difference tire technology factored into the equation. Those ETs are somewhat reflective of the ETs that are currently being run by Pure Stock Muscle Car Drags cars. Although, the current crop of racers is running quicker and faster using stock tires.

## 1969's Top Performers: Firebird Trans Am and GTO Judge

Although the Firebird Trans Am and GTO Judge had different buyer demographics and purposes and the platforms were very different, there were many similarities regarding hardware and approach. Although the Trans Am and Judge were based on their respective platforms, they both offered only Ram Air–equipped 400 engines. The Ram Air III was the base engine, and the heavy-duty 3-speed manual transmission was standard. Optional equipment included the 4-speed manual transmission, 3-speed automatic transmissions, and the Ram Air IV V-8 engine. In terms of differences, there were many,

*Only eight 1969 Trans Am convertibles were built in 1969. All featured the Ram Air III engine. Half had a 4-speed transmission and the other half had an automatic transmission. All eight are still in existence. This one (serial number 104810) was the second one that was built and was the only one with both a Parchment top and interior. It is one of the 4-speed cars. (Photo Courtesy Mecum Auctions)*

*This shows what is under the hood of a Ram Air III–powered 1969 Trans Am. The difference is evident when comparing the Ram Air pans of the Ram Air III and the Ram Air IV. The reason for this is that the tight engine compartment of the Ram Air III required clearance for the air-conditioning compressor. Since the Ram Air IV was not available with air conditioning, no such clearance was needed, which allowed the larger and slightly more efficient design.*

including their intended performance arena, suspension settings, and basic platforms.

When the Firebird Trans Am and GTO Judge were revealed to the press at Riverside Raceway on March 5, 1969, they effectively cornered both ends of the performance youth market. On one end was Pontiac's ultimate pony car. It was a vehicle that was more than the equal of a Shelby or Boss 302 Mustang with the handling, braking, and acceleration that one expected from an SCCA–inspired

### The Judge can be bought.

For a lot less bread than a lot of those so-called performance cars, we hasten to add.
Surprised? The Judge is full of them.
Like a *standard* 366-horse, 400-cube Ram Air V-8 with Quadra-jet carb. Coupled to a *standard* 3-speed, fully-

synched, manual gearbox. Stirred by a *standard* Hurst T-handle shifter.
Those big, black, fiber-glass belted tires? *Standard* too. Same as the mag-type wheels. The 60" airfoil. The custom black grille. And the blue-red-yellow striping.

True. Money will get you most of the equipment on some other car. But you'd be getting short-changed. Because you'd still have some other car. Not a special GTO from Pontiac. The Judge. It's a steal.

**THE JUDGE**

Four color pictures, specs, book jackets and decals are yours for 30¢ (50¢ outside U.S.A.). Write to: '69 Wide-Tracks, P.O. Box 8881, 196 Wide-Track Blvd., Pontiac, Michigan 48056.

*Pontiac Motor Division*

*The release of the 1969 Judge was promoted with this two-page-spread advertisement that ran in various car magazines. It was also made into a poster that was used at dealerships. One even graced John DeLorean's office at one time. (Image Courtesy General Motors Archives)*

*The first 2,000 1969 Judges were painted Carousel Red with blue, red, and yellow vinyl stripes and callouts. After that, all available GTO colors could be ordered on the Judge. Although many Judges were Carousel Red with a black interior, this one features a Parchment interior with pearlescent Morrokide vinyl upholstery. Contrasted with the available wood steering wheel and wood-grain dash and console accents, it makes for an attractive visual presentation.*

*The rear spoiler was new and exclusive for the 1969 Judge, although many have found their way onto standard GTOs. There were separate designs for the coupe and convertible, as the slope of the decklid is different between the two bodystyles.*

specialty car. Even though the available engines were 95 ci larger than the Trans-Am racing series allowed, it hardly mattered. By the following year, all of Detroit's SCCA Trans Am knockoffs sported larger-than-allowed engines, as the under-5.0-liter V-8s all lacked low-end torque, which hurt overall drivability.

The Judge staked its claim as the ultimate muscle car. It featured a cutting-edge design, outrageous colors, graphics, and straight-line performance that was precisely targeted to satisfy the yearnings that consumed enthusiasts of that time. It was a hip, sophisticated approach to grab the attention of that demographic, and it resonated perfectly. It hit the target right between the eyes and sent the competition back to the drawing board. As with the original GTO, the Judge defined the market at the moment of their respective releases. It set the rules for the others to follow and never disclosed that it had already stacked the deck in its own favor. That was the genius of John DeLorean and the talented team at Pontiac.

*The 400 Ram Air III was the top performing D-port 400 ever, and it proved to be one of Pontiac's all-around best street-performance engines. In the GTO and Judge, the 400 Ram Air III was rated at 366 hp at 5,100 rpm with 445 ft-lbs of torque at 3,600 rpm. Unlike the Ram Air Firebirds, the Ram Air III and Ram Air IV GTOs used the same Ram Air pan because there was enough clearance for the air-conditioning compressor.*

*This vintage photo of the Dick Marson Judge was taken after it was sold to its original owner, David John. He changed the lettering and campaigned it successfully in local competition. (Photo Courtesy Thomas A. DeMauro)*

*The young man in this 1969-vintage photo is Gary Treat. At the time, he was a salesman for Dick Marson Pontiac in Yakima, Washington. He was the original driver of the dealership's Ram Air IV E/Stock Judge. (Photo Courtesy Thomas A. DeMauro)*

## Other Dealers Take Notice

Dealers across the nation took notice of Royal Pontiac's success. They wanted to get in on the action once it showed to be a profit generator. In the early 1960s, Packer Pontiac got into the fray and raced a 1962 Super Duty Catalina that was driven by Howard Masales. The next year, he piloted a Swiss cheese Catalina with great success. After he sold the 1963 lightweight and his 1964 and 1965 GTOs, Masales went back to racing the 1962 Super

*Milt Schornack pilots the 1969 Royal Bobcat. Originally a 350 H.O. car, several engines were tested in the year that it was campaigned. It eventually competed using a 400 Ram Air V engine. (Photo Courtesy Jim Luikens)*

Duty Catalina and set the C/Stock record with a 12.27 ET at 114.64 mph in 1968.

The interest spread in other parts of the country. Myrtle Motors in Brooklyn, New York; Gay Pontiac in Dickinson, Texas; Wilson Pontiac in Silver Springs, Maryland; Rockhill Pontiac in Newark, Delaware; and Union Park Pontiac in Union Park, Ohio, began racing doorslammer Pontiacs in the East and Midwest. In California, Livingston Pontiac in Woodland Hills and Bill Barry Pontiac in Santa Ana sponsored and raced Pontiacs, and Bill Barry Pontiac sponsored West Coast racing legend Jess Tyree.

Several other dealerships raced Pontiacs before and after the racing ban. Collingwood Pontiac in Greybull, Wyoming, ran a series of cars known as *Tonto* that were driven by Alan "Cub" Collingwood. Garber Pontiac in Saginaw, Michigan, and Biener Pontiac in Great Neck, New York, were known to race regionally. Rockhill Pontiac in Newark, Delaware, campaigned a series of GTOs driven by Fred Borcherdt that were known as *Rocky's Goat*.

Myrtle Motors, which was in Maspeth, Long Island, New York, was the Royal Pontiac of the East. It offered engine upgrades, crate engine swaps, and specialty cars right off the show-room floor. Harry Wesch was the force behind the high-performance operation. (Photo Courtesy Martyn L. Schorr)

The Gay Pontiac Infinity 4 1968 GTO Funny Car competed with a blown and injected 421 Super Duty V-8. The Gay Pontiac team ran its last Funny Car, a Firebird, in 1970 before Don Gay closed the racing operation to pay more attention to the dealership. Tragically, Roy Gay (Don's brother) died in a motorcycle accident in 1972. Don died in 2007 at age 60. (Photo Courtesy Clinton Wright)

The team of Don Royston and Bert Fortier continued its association with Pontiac and campaigned a Verdoro Green 1968 Ram Air II GTO hardtop through Wilson Pontiac in Silver Springs, Maryland. The hardtop is shown at Capitol Raceway in Crofton, Maryland. (Photo Courtesy Clinton Wright)

"Mr. Pontiac" Jess Tyree is shown with his 1969 Firebird Funny Car at the 1969 US Nationals in Indy. As with many racers, Tyree compensated for the dwindling supplies of Pontiac Super Duty parts by switching to big-block Chevy power. His association with Pontiac stayed strong for the rest of his life. (Photo Courtesy Clinton Wright)

The Greytak and Dorsey team ran Pontiac GTOs for Rockhill Pontiac in Newark, Delaware. Here is the team's 1968 C/SA GTO at Cecil County Dragway. The car ran mid-12 ETs at the time, which is impressive. (Photo Courtesy Clinton Wright)

The Greytek and Dorety 1969–1970 team car was this 1969 Ram Air IV Judge, which set the fastest ET and top speed NHRA E/Stock automatic records. In May 1970, it had a best ET of 12.10 at 114.79 mph with Fred Borcherdt behind the wheel. This photo was taken at the US Nationals in Indy in 1970, right at the time that the record was set. (Photo Courtesy Clinton Wright)

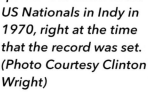

Garber Pontiac returned for the 1970 season with a 1970 Formula 400 Ram Air car. (Photo Courtesy Clinton Wright)

### Knafel Pontiac

Anderson Pontiac, which was later known as Knafel Pontiac, ran one of the most ambitious racing programs in history. Racing from 1959 to 1971, the team usually competed with multiple cars, including a 1962 C/Stock Catalina convertible known as the *Black Whirlwind*, a red 1962 Catalina 421 Super Duty hardtop in Super Stock, and a 1962 Super Duty Catalina two-door sedan in A/Stock. The team later campaigned a 1963 Swiss cheese Catalina; a built-up 1963 Super Duty Tempest called *Running Bear;* a factory Super Duty Tempest wagon known as *Papoose One;* and a string of GTOs and Firebirds, with

a few OHC-6-cylinder-powered Tempests and one Canadian Pontiac Acadian with a 427 Chevy under the hood.

Knafel's traveling road show even took to the air with its own private plane to chauffeur drivers to races. Knafel developed some specialty cars, such as the Magnum 400 Tempest (a competitor to the Plymouth Road Runner) and the *Golden Sabre*, which was a 1969 Ram Air V–powered GTO. Drivers included "Akron" Arlen Vanke, Bill Abraham, Larry "Doc" Dixon, and Norm Tanner. Knafel ended its racing activities after the 1971 season. However, Knafel Pontiac owner Bill Knafel and his son John continued to attend Pontiac events for the rest of their lives.

*The 1970 Knafel Pontiac Tin Indian sits in front of this reunion of Anderson Pontiac and Knafel Pontiac race cars. Behind it (from left to right) is a 1970 Magnum 400 Tempest, the original 1963* Running Bear *421 Super Duty Tempest, the 1966* Tin Indian *GTO, and a replica of Arnie Beswick's* Mrs. B's Grocery Getter, *which was sponsored by Anderson Pontiac. The reunion took place at the 2007 Ames Performance Pontiac Nationals. (Photo Courtesy Thomas A. DeMauro)*

*Norm Tanner in the 1970 Tin Indian Ram Air IV GTO gets the jump on a Plymouth Barracuda at Dragway 42 in West Salem, Ohio. (Photo Courtesy Knafel Family Archive)*

This publicity shot shows the 1970 Knafel Pontiac Ram Air IV GTO with driver Norm Tanner and owner William "Bill" Knafel in front of his Akron, Ohio, dealership showroom. (Photo Courtesy Knafel Family Archive)

## Backdoor Judge Promotion

An interesting sidenote in Pontiac racing history was an unofficial promotion that was instituted to bolster sales of the 1969 GTO Judge. According to accounts from several dealerships that participated, there was behind-the-scenes encouragement by the division to have dealerships compete with the new Judge in local and regional events—even though Pontiac was officially out of racing at the time. The idea was to help generate excitement about the newest GTO and Pontiac. In return, Pontiac would provide warranty coverage for any drivetrain components that were damaged in competition. Approximately 100 minimally-optioned Judges were built in 1969 for this purpose, many of which ran in the D/Stock class.

*The Knafel Pontiac Tin Indian 1970 Ram Air IV GTO is shown in the pits. (Photo Courtesy Jim Luikens)*

Dealerships that participated in this program included Dick Marson Pontiac in Yakima, Washington; Garber Pontiac in Saginaw, Michigan; Weidner Pontiac in Mansfield, Ohio; Lee Pontiac in Jerome, Idaho; Rockhill Pontiac in Newark, Delaware; Terry Shaver Pontiac in Highland, Indiana; Ray Faro Pontiac in Elyria, Ohio; Colonial Pontiac in Miami, Florida; and Schoon Motors in Rochester, Minnesota. In addition, Arnie Beswick's 1969 Ram Air IV Judge Pro Stocker was reportedly part of this program.

> "THERE WAS BEHIND-THE-SCENES ENCOURAGEMENT BY THE DIVISION TO HAVE DEALERSHIPS COMPETE WITH THE NEW JUDGE IN LOCAL AND REGIONAL EVENTS— EVEN THOUGH PONTIAC WAS OFFICIALLY OUT OF RACING AT THE TIME."

*For the 1969 season, Garber Pontiac in Saginaw, Michigan, ran this C/Stock Firebird 400. It is seen here at Tri-City Dragway in Saginaw. It also ran a Judge in E/Stock that year. (Photo Courtesy Clinton Wright)*

Depending on the class in which they desired to race, the Judges could be powered by Ram Air III or Ram Air IV powerplant along with a manual or automatic transmission. At least one car, the Faro car, was raced with an over-the-counter Ram Air V. This was a word-of-mouth promotion that was passed along by zone reps to dealers that they believed would be amenable to the arrangement and keep the details quiet. After the success of the program, the impressive sales figures for a top-level car like the Judge, and its impact on the market, the program was quietly discontinued and did not return for the 1970 model year. It was the end of an era that few people even know about.

While there aren't photos or accounts of all of the Pontiac dealerships that campaigned race cars, this book features a wide array of vehicles.

## The Ram Air III

At the same time that the Ram Air IV was being marketed, the need to fill the gap between the mild base 400 and the barely streetable Ram Air IV was filled by what became one of Pontiacs finest all-around street engines: the engine that is now known as the Ram Air III. However, at the time, the name was not used. It was referred to as the 400 H.O. due to availability questions regarding adding Ram Air to any 400-engine-equipped Firebird. As it turned out, only the L74 400 and the L67 Ram Air IV received the Ram Air hood and air-cleaner package. Regardless, the engine had a solid foundation for all-around performance.

The Ram Air III was the high-point of performance for the 400 engine using D-port heads. Sharing the #48 cylinder-head castings with the 350 H.O., the heads featured the familiar 2.11/1.77-inch valves and open chambers with a smaller 66-cc chamber, which worked out to be close to the advertised compression ratio of 10.75:1. This is in contrast to the compression ratios that were obtained using the 77-cc chambers that were used on other D-port 400 performance heads. The #62 cylinder heads worked out to an actual compression ratio of about 9.8:1, which means that, in most cases, the advertised compression ratios were almost one full point optimistic. The fact that these heads were used on the 428 H.O. engine indicates that the compression ratios were closer to the advertised 10.75:1 ratio than when used on the 400 engine.

Camshaft choices for the Ram Air III depended on the transmission that was used. Manual-transmission installations received the hotter 303/313-degree 744 cam, while the automatic version received the slightly milder 068 cam. This was done to aid low-end torque with a slight penalty at the top end of the RPM range. Regardless of the transmission, the Ram Air III featured the streamlined cast-iron exhaust manifolds, which have proven to flow, and a set of shorty headers.

When installed in the GTO, the Ram Air III was rated at 366 hp at 5,100 rpm with 445 ft-lbs of torque at 3,600 rpm. Firebird installations were rated at 335 hp at 5,000 rpm with 430 ft-lbs of torque at 3,400 rpm. The Ram Air III was optional in all GTOs and Firebirds and was the base engine for the 1969 GTO Judge and Firebird Trans Am.

## Pontiac Special Projects

Considering that General Motors had officially pulled out of racing in 1963, the fact that a Pontiac Special Projects group existed was something of a miracle. Chevrolet, with its huge market share and influence with the General Motors corporate officials, was able to circumvent the corporate edict.

By 1965, Chevrolet worked with several race teams. Most notably, Chevrolet worked with Roger Penske, Jim

*Schoon Motors of Rochester, Minnesota, took advantage of the deal with Pontiac and ordered a Ram Air IV Judge to compete in the D/Stock class. Here, it is competing at the 1969 US Nationals in Indy. (Photo Courtesy Clinton Wright)*

*When Herb Adams was charged with the task of building a Firebird that was superior to the upcoming Chevrolet Camaro Z/28, he formed the Special Projects Group with Pontiac's most talented group of young engineers. Over the course of the group's lifespan, the team included Tom Nell, Jeff Young, Dan Hardin, Joe Brady, Leo Hilke, and others. (Photo Courtesy Rocky Rotella)*

Hall from Chaparral, and Smokey Yunick in various programs and ran the gamut from Can Am to NASCAR, SCCA Trans-Am racing, and drag racing. With its massive influence in the market and unrivaled success with the corporation, General Motors brass was forced to look the other way and allow racing activities, even though it flew in the face of their authority.

Pontiac, on the other hand, did not have the sales or clout with the corporation brass to defy any corporate edict from General Motors—let alone one as large as racing.

Still, Chevrolet developed its F-Body Camaro for various racing classes. With the surge in popularity of SCCA's new Trans-Am series, and classes for under-2.5L and 2.5L-to-5.0L sedans, Pontiac engineers formed the Pontiac Special Projects group headed by Herb Adams.

Adams was one of the young and enthusiastic engineers at Pontiac. He attended General Motors Institute, graduated in 1961, and went to work for Pontiac right after he took off the cap and robe. He was initially assigned to

air conditioning but was promoted to a position as plant liaison. He then headed up the testing group at the Milford Proving Grounds. It was there that he came up with the idea for making the GTO hood scoops functional and designed the first Ram Air pan, initially without authorization from General Motors.

That sort of rebel mindset meshed well with Pontiac General Manager John Z. DeLorean. In 1967, he asked Adams and Engineer Bill Collins, who was instrumental in the earlier Super Duty program, to build a Firebird that was better than the upcoming Camaro Z-28. It was then that the Pontiac Special Projects group was assembled from some of the most talented engineers from Pontiac's ranks. Several came and went over the years, including Tom Nell, Jeff Young, Leo Hilke, and Dan Hardin. They were instrumental in the development of Pontiac's hottest performance engines and cars that were yet to come.

Nell and Young were particularly well-suited to work together. Nell was an old-school hot-rodder who was proficient at building and modifying automatic transmissions for drag racing. Young was a sports-car racer in his younger years. Both graduated from General Motors Institute, and Young went on to receive a master's degree in internal-combustion engines from Massachusetts Institute of Technology (MIT). The hot-rodder and the theorist were huge assets to the cause. They reported to Adams, and they set out to build their better Firebird. It came in the form of the Pontiac Firebird Sprint Turismo (PFST) project, in which a series of Firebirds were upgraded for improved handling, braking, and overall performance.

The first car was a Camaro that was converted to a Firebird and powered by a Weber-carbureted OHC 6-cylinder engine. It was an American approach to a Jaguar XKE. Other versions of the PFST were V-8 powered and used to develop the combination that came to market as the 1969 Trans Am.

The Pontiac Special Projects group had not been formed specifically for drag racing, although that branch of motorsports eventually fell into its list of assignments. Its engine programs, which included the development of the 303 short-deck V-8, was inextricably tied to the larger-displacement Ram Air V program.

## The Ram Air V

The story of how the Ram Air V came about is one of those stories that could only come from Detroit. After the General Motors racing ban, George DeLorean, the younger brother of then-Pontiac General Manager John Z. DeLorean, campaigned a Mercury Comet Cyclone.

*The 400 Ram Air V engine was intended to go to production to be used in the 1969 Firebird, Trans Am, and GTO. However, the program was canceled, and any engines that were built went into the parts network and were offered as crate engines for dealer installation. Although a factory rating was never released, it was rumored to be rated by the factory at 375 hp, which was 5 hp more than the GTO Ram Air IV. The engine actually made 480 to 500 hp. (Photo Courtesy Rocky Rotella)*

According to a taped interview before his death in 2022, George said that he was instrumental in the early development of both round-port and tunnel-port Pontiac cylinder heads. This came by virtue of his association with Ford.

In 1966, George mentioned that Pontiac Engineer Bill Klinger had visited his home shop, and the two began talking about cylinder heads. Drawing upon his Ford experience, he stated that the exhaust ports on a Pontiac were all wrong and that they should be round. Klinger returned a few months later to show George some prototype heads with round ports. The round ports saw production on the 1968 Ram Air II, 1969–1970 Ram Air IV, 1971–1972 455 H.O., and the 1973–1974 455 Super Duty.

They spoke more about cylinder heads, and George talked about opening up the bowls to increase flow and horsepower. He said that the ports needed to be enlarged, but the bowl, the area under the valve, needed to be larger to make big power. George said that Klinger returned about three months later with a set of prototype Ram Air IV heads. Both the bowl and ports were larger than the regular Pontiac heads.

"The 428 Pontiacs were making around 375 hp at the time," George said

*The 1969 Royal Bobcat Ram Air V GTO is on display at the 2009 Pontiac-Oakland Club International (POCI) GTO Association of America convention in Dayton, Ohio.*

during the interview. "With those heads, they were making around 470 [hp]. The head made almost 100 hp more in testing. What they wanted was to be competitive with the 396/375 Chevrolet big-block, which was really big with the street racers. They all loved it. This head put the Pontiac engine in that category. I guess I was instrumental in that stuff."

Several months after that happened, George was at Motor City Dragway and came upon a Ford racer who he knew, Dave Lyall, who raced a Fairlane coupe. It was running really well, and that was enough to capture George's attention. When he went to investigate, he found out that the engine was a new 427 Ford tunnel port. George was impressed by the engine, which had a dual-quad intake with huge intake runners. Shortly after, Lyall blew up the engine. Because it was factory owned, he was told to return the pieces for evaluation.

However, before that happened, DeLorean managed to convince Lyall to bring a head, a piece of the broken camshaft, and the intake to his shop. Lyall left the pieces with DeLorean for a few days. George was very impressed with the large ports and how the pushrods went through the intake ports. Noticing how similar the head layout was to a Pontiac, he set the head on the block of his Funny Car engine, a 428 Pontiac, and discovered that the bore centers and the two bolt holes were identical to the Pontiac V-8. The other eight varied by only about 3/8 inch.

George called his brother John and told him about the engine pieces that he had in his possession. The next

*In hiding for more than 30 years and found on a bank's repossession lot, the original 1969 Ray Faro Pontiac GTO Judge race car has been returned to its Ram Air V race configuration by current owner Chuck Henley. Cragar Super Sport wheels are a nice period touch. The Judge's original race livery was replicated from photos by the talented team at Z&Z Restoration in Pittston Township, Pennsylvania. Unlike many paint schemes from the period, the graphics aren't overdone, and they work well with the Judge stripes. (Photo Courtesy Thomas A. DeMauro)*

day, a Bonneville four-door sedan showed up at his shop. Not knowing what was going on, he was surprised to see that the four men getting out of the car were Chief Engineer Steve Malone, Bill Klinger, Mac McKellar, and Tom Nell. George told them that while they couldn't take the parts with them, they were free to measure and photograph whatever they wanted.

About six months later, DeLorean learned that Pontiac had begun testing its new Ram Air V engine that made 520 hp its first time out with 10:1 compression and a fairly mild cam. The Ford made 10 hp more with a more radical cam and 13:1 compression. There was a lot of potential for more power.

The Ram Air V was developed in four different displacements for various missions. The 303, which was the first engine that the Pontiac Special Projects group tackled, was aimed at the SCCA Trans-Am racing series. It featured a 1-inch-shorter deck height, 2.5-inch mains, and the same bore as a 400 engine. It was 4.12 inches but with a short 2.84-inch stroke and 6.08-inch forged connecting rods. It was designed for continuous high-RPM operation in the 5,000 to 8,000 rpm range. As it turned out, the large tunnel-port head design was too much for the little engine, and it fared better with a set of ported Ram Air IV heads, where it eventually made 470 to 485 hp at 8,000 rpm.

The 366 engine was intended for NASCAR competition and featured a standard deck height, 4.15-inch bore, and 3.375-inch stroke with 7.08-inch rods. Aside from the 3-inch main journal diameter, the block was identical to the later 455 Super Duty. Both concepts were designed with provisions for dry-sump oiling cast into the block. It accepted a Turbo 400 transmission internal/external gear

pump for its operation, which was an ingenious detail that Tom Nell dreamt up from his extensive experience modifying Turbo 400s for racing use. As with the 303 engine, the 366 engine was developed with ported Ram Air IV heads. That version made 575 to 590 hp in full race trim.

The larger two Ram Air V engines were of the most interest to drag racers. The 400 engine was slated for GTO and Firebird models and featured the same bore and stroke dimensions as the production 400: 4.12 x 3.75 inches. The 400 had much more rev potential, and although the low-end power was not as good as Pontiac fans were used to, the midrange and top-end power was something more akin to a 427 L-88 Chevy engine or a 426 Hemi. Some initial planning rated the engine at 375 hp (5 hp more than the severely underrated Ram Air IV), but the actual output is estimated to be closer to 500 hp.

Royal Pontiac's 1969 Royal Bobcat Ram Air V GTO, which had a worn-out Ram Air V that was rebuilt, ran consistent 11.70s in 1970. That ET supports the horsepower estimate.

As for the 428 Ram Air V, it was little more than a racing experiment, as only about a dozen were built. The single 4-barrel, two 4-barrel, and two 4-barrel tunnel-ram intakes were designed and cast, and all were flanged for Holley carburetors. Some of the engines that were built found their way to racers such as Arnie "the Farmer" Beswick, who used one as the basis for a supercharged, nitro-burning engine for his 1969 *Super Judge* Funny Car. Pontiac Special Projects Engineer Tom Nell had a similar 1969 GTO Funny Car powered by a blown and injected 428 Ram Air V. The 428 Ram Air V became the stuff of legends. With the horsepower developed into the 575-plus range, it would have had a huge impact if it were put into limited production.

Although each of the various versions of the Ram Air V were unique, they all featured specific heavy-duty blocks with four-bolt mains and

*The current Ram Air V engine uses a 1970 400 Ram Air V block with the top end from one of the original Faro Pontiac race engines. Built by Don Johnston at DCI Automotive, the tunnel-port Pontiac displaces 451 ci due to a 0.010-inch overbore and a turned-down 455 crankshaft. Horsepower is approximately 575. (Photo Courtesy Thomas A. DeMauro)*

*Arnie Beswick's 1969* Super Judge Funny Car *featured a Logghe chassis and a supercharged and injected Pontiac engine that was based on the prototype 428 Ram Air V powerplant. It is seen here in the pits at Cecil County Dragway. (Photo Courtesy Clinton Wright)*

reinforced lifter galleries, forged pistons, rods, crankshafts, and a tunnel-port head. The 303 engine featured a unique design with rough-cast 56-cc combustion chambers. It also had a high-speed ignition system and used a Holley 4-barrel carburetor. The equally-spaced intake and exhaust ports of the Ram Air V required a specific camshaft with an "EIEIIEIE" (exhaust, intake, exhaust, intake, intake, exhaust, intake, exhaust) layout, as opposed to the production EIIEEIIE layout that paired the intake ports and essentially siamesed the two center exhaust ports.

The intake ports were huge ovals, and the pushrods went through the center of the ports that sealed off from the port with tubes and airfoils to reduce turbulence. The exhaust ports, while evenly spaced, were similar to the Ram Air IV exhaust-port design. The intake valves were 2.19 inches, and exhaust valves were 1.73 inches. Some 303 engines received smaller 1.63-inch exhaust valves to increase exhaust velocity and scavenging. The engines required specific intake and exhaust manifolds to accommodate the revised port layout.

Only the 303 and 400 engines were considered for production. The other two were strictly racing exercises and had little overall effect in racing. Not enough of them were built to homologate for regular competition, as General Motors and Pontiac were still officially out of racing. Their effects were more significant in production engines.

## The First 455 H.O. and Changes for 1970

With the curb weight of many of GM's intermediates approaching two tons, GM's corporate edicts regarding powerplant availability were eased a bit. A-Body cars were approved for the 450-ci-plus powerplants that were being released that year, including the 454 Chevrolet big-block, 455 Buick, 455 Oldsmobile, and the newest and largest Pontiac V-8 ever: the 455. This new version of the Pontiac V-8 replaced the 428, which had been in production from 1967 to 1969.

Even though the Buick, Oldsmobile, and Pontiac 455 engines all had the same displacement, they were from different engine families, and little was shared besides carburetion and some ignition parts. The Pontiac 455 was created by taking the 428, enlarging the bore from 4.12 to 4.15 inches, and lengthening the stroke from 4.0 to 4.21 inches. The engine was undersquare, which means that the bore was smaller than the stroke. This made

*Engine options for the 1970 GTO were essentially a carryover, except for the deletion of the 2-barrel 400 credit option and the introduction of the new 455 H.O. engine. The 455 H.O. engine was essentially a bored and stroked version of the 428, with a 4.15-inch bore and a 4.21-inch stroke. It developed 360 hp at 4,600 rpm with a full 500 ft-lbs of torque at 3,100 rpm. It was a great choice for heavily-optioned GTOs with air conditioning and highway-friendly gearing.*

*The 1970 GTO received all-new body panels except for the roof and hood. A new Endura nose design did away with the hideaway headlamp option. Sales plummeted due to insurance price hikes and a costly United Auto Workers (UAW) strike.*

for an incredibly torquey engine but limited high-RPM breathing.

In 1970, the 455 engine was used in the GTO but not in the Firebird. It was essentially the same engine that could be ordered in a full-size car. It was the only year that the 455 had a high compression ratio. It featured four-bolt mains, big-valve #66 D-port heads with 10.25:1 compression, a 067 cam for automatics, and a 068 cam for manuals. In addition, it was rated at 360 hp at 4,600 rpm with a whopping 500 ft-lbs of torque at 3,100 rpm. Full-size installations with the same engine were rated at 370 hp at 4,600 rpm but with the same torque specifications. There was 10 hp that was lopped off the ratings, but no real changes were made.

The engine was a great choice for a heavily optioned GTO with air conditioning and highway gears. The abundance of low-end torque allowed for quick acceleration in a street performance setting. It was another choice for custom-tailoring a GTO to meet the specific needs of the buyer.

*Car and Driver* road tested a loaded 1970 GTO 455 4-speed. It bemoaned that the GTO wasn't as quick as the other cars that were tested (the Hemi Road Runner, W-31 Cutlass, and 396/325 Chevelle), but the comparison wasn't fair. The GTO was hampered by weight-adding options, such as air conditioning, power windows and door locks, and an open 3.31 rear end. The curb weight was a bloated 4,209 pounds. Despite those setbacks, it managed to post a 0-to-60 time of 6.6 seconds and run the quarter-mile with an ET of 15.0 seconds at 96.5 mph. Considering the combination, it was a respectable number.

*One of the rarest and most desirable combinations for collectors is this 1970 Orbit Orange Ram Air IV GTO Judge convertible. Only seven were built with the automatic transmission, which helped push the bidding to a whopping $1.1 million sale price at the 2023 Mecum Kissimmee Auction. Big-engine, convertible muscle cars were rarely ordered because they weren't the lightest and quickest-accelerating models. In addition, they were the most expensive cars to buy, which makes them very desirable to collectors today. (Photo Courtesy Mecum Auctions)*

The rest of the GTO and Firebird performance engine lineup returned for 1970, except the 350 H.O., which was discontinued due to low sales and upcoming emissions compliance issues. Advertised compression ratios dropped to 10.5:1 for Ram Air III and Ram Air IV engines, but the power ratings did not change. The cylinder-head casting numbers were changed. The Ram Air III was casting number 12, and the Ram Air IV was casting number 614. The Ram Air IV was referred to as the LS1 when ordered in the Firebird line, and it was only available in the Trans Am. Only 59 manuals and 29 automatics were built with that engine.

The 1970½ Firebird line was introduced in February 1970 with all-new styling and front suspension as well as standard front disc brakes. The top-of-the-line Trans Am returned with a new shaker-hood design, spoiler, and air extractor, all of which were functional and aided high-speed stability. (Photos Courtesy Ben Salvador)

The standard powerplant for the Trans Am was the Ram Air III (shown here), which was rated at 366 hp. The Ram Air IV was conservatively rated at 370 hp. A total of 3,196 1970½ Trans Ams were built, and 88 had the LS1 Ram Air IV engine. (Photos Courtesy Ben Salvador)

## The 326 and 350 H.O. Engines

Pontiac released the 326 engine for the Y-Body 1963 Tempest/LeMans, which was essentially a small-bore version of the 389 and available with either 2-barrel or 4-barrel carburetion. The 4-barrel version was referred to as an "H.O." (high output) and featured a Carter AFB carburetor. It was rated at 280 hp at 4,800 rpm with 355 ft-lbs of torque at 3,200 rpm. This engine sported a mild 269/277-degree camshaft with a modest 0.374/0.406-inch lift. The valve sizes measured 1.88 inches for the intake, while the exhausts measured 1.60 inches. The compression ratio was listed at 10.25:1 with a 67-cc combustion chamber.

When the 1964 models arrived, the senior compact Tempest/LeMans was retired. In its place, a completely redesigned and more conventional intermediate-sized option was offered under the same name. The 326 engine was available, but a few changes were made. Along with the bore reduction that is mentioned elsewhere in the chapter, the starter was relocated from the bellhousing to the block. This was done to mate them to the new generation of automatic transmissions. Although the cylinder heads lost two cc's of volume to keep the compression up with the smaller displacement, camshaft, carburetion, and power output, some items remained the same as the previous year.

In 1965, the first major upgrade of the 326 H.O. engine occurred. That year, Pontiac V-8 engines across the board received completely redesigned cylinder heads with superior breathing characteristics. Port shapes were recontoured, and valve sizes were enlarged on the 326 from 1.88 to 1.92 inches on the intake side and from 1.60 to 1.66 inches on the exhaust side. Intake manifolds received reworking to mate to the new heads. Valve timing remained the same, even though the part number of the camshaft was superseded by a new one.

A significant revision in the oiling system was adopted at this time. First used on the 1963–1964 716 cylinder head (used on the 421 H.O. and 389 GTO

With only its hood-mounted tachometer giving a clue regarding its performance potential, this 1969 350 H.O. LeMans was an inexpensive and insurance-friendly performance car that was a viable alternative to the Plymouth Road Runner. George Scott is the owner of this car.

For the final year, the 350 H.O. received new big-valve, small-chamber number-48 heads, which were shared with the 400 Ram Air III. Rated at 325 hp in the Firebird and 330 hp in the A-Body, they used the 067 camshaft with automatic transmissions and 068 with manual transmissions. The NHRA allows the use of the hotter 744 cam in the Stock class because there's evidence that some early manual-transmission engines were assembled with that grind before they were pulled from the lineup due to drivability issues.

*While the 1968 350 H.O. Firebird didn't get the twin-scoop hood that the 400 powered cars had, they had a sporty beltline H.O. stripe in red, white, or black. It was available with the optional hood tachometer and new Rally II wheels.*

Although the changes only raised the horsepower and torque slightly, they represented an elevated standardization of major assemblies and bolt patterns among Pontiac engines. Regarding actual power output, the modernized 326 H.O. produced 285 hp at 5,000 rpm with 359 ft-lbs of torque at 3,200 rpm. It wasn't an earth-shattering improvement, but the added breathing helped in the midrange and top end. Notice that the horsepower peak jumped 200 rpm compared to the previous design. From 1965 to 1967, the 326 H.O. remained almost exactly the same

engines), the rocker-arm lubrication passages were moved from the rocker studs to new-design hollow pushrods that received oil from a rail in the lifter galleries. The rocker studs were now solid and press-fit to the head. Some minor block casting modifications were required for the change.

and differed only in the casting numbers of the major components. In reality, the engines were functionally identical.

The 1968 model year brought a redesigned A-Body—and with it, a revised base V-8. The 326 engine was replaced with an enlarged version. Advertised as a 350, it displaced 354 ci. The move to downplay the size was likely an advertising decision.

The 28-ci enlargement was more than a simple overbore. The engine showcased several other improvements. For starters, the block was recast to accommodate the new bore size of 3.87 inches. The 326 block with its 3.72-inch bore could not be bored out that much. The balance of the basic block assembly stayed the same, including the 6.625-inch connecting rods and 3.75-inch stroke. High-performance piston rings and Moraine 400-A high-performance main and rod bearings were utilized for the H.O. engine.

The valvetrain and top end of the engine received the most revamping. The cylinder heads that were completely redesigned in 1967 for use in the 400 and 428 were used on the 350 engines this year. Intake ports were recontoured for increased flow, and valve centers were moved from 1.82 inches to 1.98 inches to provide room for larger valves.

Although the performance versions of the larger engines sported 2.11-inch intake valves and 1.77-inch exhaust valves, the 350 H.O. used smaller-valved versions of the same head. These heads (number 18) were fitted with 1.96-inch intake and 1.66-inch exhaust valves. They were similar to the heads used on the low-performance 400 engines of that period, except the number 18 heads benefitted from screw-in rocker-arm studs.

New camshafts were implemented in the 350 H.O. that the older 326 H.O. did not enjoy. Depending on the transmission choice, one of two camshafts were used. Manual-transmission cars were recipients of the 9779067 (P) camshaft that had been used in medium-performance 389/400/421 engines of that time. Its specifications were measured at 273/289 degrees of duration with 0.406-inch lift.

Engines hooked to automatic transmissions received the 9779066 camshaft. It featured 273/282 degrees of duration and 0.406-inch lift. This was the same camshaft that was used in high-compression 389/400 2-barrel and 4-barrel engines of this period. While this is an extremely mild camshaft in the larger engines, it was more of a performer in the small-bore engine.

The induction system received an upgrade as well.

The old Carter AFB and restrictive two-plane manifold were gone. In its place was the freer-flowing 400/428 two-plane intake mounting a Rochester Quadrajet carburetor. With 320 hp at 5,100 rpm with 380 ft-lbs of torque at 3,200 rpm, it made for a very responsive package that made a lightweight Tempest or Firebird a real mover. Pontiac really raised the stakes the following year.

In 1969, the 350 H.O. reached its highest level of development, and it was a real screamer. Pontiac engineers elected to not use the same cylinder heads as the previous year and instead used the Ram Air III number 48 heads. It was the only version of the 350 that ever had large 2.11-inch intakes and 1.77-inch exhaust valves at the same time.

The camshaft selection was a little wilder as well. The automatic versions received the 067 camshaft that was used in the manual-transmission 350 H.O. the year before, while the manual-transmission models had two grinds. The first was the famed 9785744 (H) Ram Air III cam. It had 301/313 degrees of duration and 0.406-inch lift.

The 744 cam was only used during the beginning of the 1969 production run because it increased the rev potential of the engine to nearly 6,500 rpm. Pontiac reportedly feared a warranty disaster with the engine, but according to the late Pontiac Engineer John Sawruk, the lighter reciprocating assembly (less piston mass) put less stress on the rods to improve high-RPM reliability in its larger options.

After the 744 cam was phased out for the 350 H.O., the new cam of choice was the 9779068 (S) that was used in the 1965–1966 389 Tri-Power GTO engine. It featured 288/302 degrees of duration and 0.406-inch lift. Carburetion was aptly handled by a Rochester Quadrajet, and standard exhaust manifolds were utilized.

Although the 350 H.O. engines were fantastic performers for their size, they never reached their total potential due to competition from older engines. For instance, power output was listed at 330 hp at 5,100 rpm with 380 ft-lbs of torque at 3,200 rpm. The Firebirds were rated at 5 hp less. This was right up against the power ratings of the 400s and further confused the buyers. Furthermore, John DeLorean was concerned that a 350 H.O.–powered A-Body would cut into GTO sales and hurt its image.

> "IN 1969, THE 350 H.O. REACHED ITS HIGHEST LEVEL OF DEVELOPMENT, AND IT WAS A REAL SCREAMER. PONTIAC ENGINEERS ELECTED TO NOT USE THE SAME CYLINDER HEADS AS THE PREVIOUS YEAR AND INSTEAD USED THE RAM AIR III NUMBER 48 HEADS."

It is too bad Pontiac didn't make more of an effort to promote the smaller-displacement engines such as the Oldsmobile Ram Rod 350/W31 and the free-revving 340 Mopar. With functional Ram Air and long-branch manifolds, the Pontiac 350 H.O. could easily have been the king of the junior muscle cars and would not have incurred the wrath of the insurance companies the way that the bigger-engined Pontiacs did. Pontiac, and DeLorean in particular, didn't want anything stealing the GTO's thunder, so these cars were never given a fair shot in the marketplace. Several stock 350 H.O.–powered machines are running well into the 12s to prove that they had what it took.

## Changing Times and a Changing Market

Although the strategy behind GM's exit from racing likely saved the corporation from being split up by the US Justice Department, it created new problems in the years to come. By the mid-1960s, safety advocates, such as Ralph Nader, vocally criticized General Motors and the rest of the Detroit manufacturers. Nader's 1965 book *Unsafe at Any Speed* was highly critical of the entire auto industry, mostly in an uninformed manner that sensationalized many of the issues.

Topics included a lack of uniformity in the automatic gearshift pattern; occupant safety in the secondary impact regarding the steering column, instrument panel, and windshield; safety belts; pedestrian safety; emissions; etc. The book inspired the formation of the National Highway Safety Bureau, a predecessor of the National Highway Traffic Safety Administration (NHTSA).

In the years that followed, Detroit automakers were loudly decried for building unsafe, overpowered cars, putting them in the hands of inexperienced drivers, and letting them get into high-speed crashes that cost lives and disabled innocent people. The term "corporate irresponsibility" was coined. By the end of the 1960s, the insurance companies had more than their fill of paying for such claims.

By 1970, insurance companies began slapping large surcharges on high-performance cars. Cars with 10 pounds per horsepower or less, or those with 4-speed transmissions were assigned Class 1 status, which meant that they were charged the highest rates possible. Since the GTO was the originator of the muscle-car genre, the insurance companies paid particular attention to it. At the time, it was possible that the insurance costs for muscle cars could exceed the monthly payment for the car itself.

The production figures for the 1969 and 1970 GTOs showed a huge drop in sales—from 72,287 units total to 40,149. Although the 1970 Muskie Clean Air Act was not passed in time to have a significant impact on the 1970

*To counter the high cost of insurance that bit heavily into the sale of high-performance cars, Pontiac introduced the GT-37, which was based on the Tempest/T37 line. The idea was to offer a budget performer similar to what the GTO Judge was originally supposed to be. Powertrain offerings started with a 350 2-barrel engine and went up to the 350-hp 400, which was the base engine in the GTO.*

model-year production cars, the retaliation from the insurance companies bit into sales.

To counter the situation, Pontiac released the GT-37 late in 1970 as an insurance-friendly and budget-friendly (but still sporty) model. It was available in the two-door sedan and hardtop bodystyles. Characterized by its exclusive hood pins, 1969 Judge stripe, and Rally II wheels without trim rings, the GT-37 came standard with a 350 2-barrel V-8 and 3-speed manual transmission. Engine options included the 400 2-barrel and 4-barrel engines, and the manual-transmission version received the same engine as the base 1970 GTO: the 350-hp 400. Ram Air engines were not available in the 1970-1/2 GT-37. A total of 1,419 were made (with no breakdown on bodystyles).

With the tide turning so abruptly, it is easy to see why muscle-car sales decreased. People still wanted them, but the pool of buyers who could afford them and the insurance was significantly smaller. Sadly, for Pontiac, much of its image was centered around the youth market and performance. Sales of the entire line had fallen by about 38 percent, which cost it the coveted third-place position in domestic auto new sales. With Pontiac's youth-oriented General Manager John DeLorean's departure the year before, the division lost its biggest supporter of performance cars. His absence was quickly felt.

There was more bad news. The federal government set its sights on the entire automotive industry. The head of the National Highway Safety Bureau, Dr. William Haddon, Jr., said, "The way the auto industry is pushing muscle cars borders on criminal irresponsibility."

Even GM's upper management felt the pressure and tried to distance themselves from the very products that they so aggressively promoted.

"Too much attention is being directed toward the youthful segment of our population," said General Motors President Ed Cole. "This trend is [based on] two false assumptions. One is an overrated opinion of the sales accounted for by the younger set. The second false assumption is that unless you address yourself in the language of the hip generation, you're not in with the entire population."

Although support for performance cars was waning, and GM's upper management wasn't interested in the negative publicity, there was still a group of performance-minded engineers, designers, and marketers at Pontiac who still fought the good fight. They knew that their time was limited, but there were still many great things to come.

*In late 1969, Royal Pontiac closed. Mechanic Milt Schornack went out on his own and started Royal Automotive in nearby Warren, Michigan. He raced a white 1971 Firebird Formula 455 H.O. automatic in Super Stock. He got out of racing in 1972 and shut down his operation in 1973. (Photo Courtesy Clinton Wright)*

## The Rapidly Changing Face of Racing

Without much in the way of drag race-oriented development by the factory, the end of the 1960s was relatively quiet for Pontiac, at least in the pro ranks. The development of the Ram Air V was a glimmer of hope, but it ultimately never reached fruition. Worse still, it was nearly impossible to run a successful program in the Funny Car or Top Fuel class at this point with Pontiac power.

Funny Cars had become all the rage in drag racing in the late 1960s. With no help from General Motors, it was like bringing a knife to a gunfight at the track. Racers such as Arnie Beswick and Don Gay still ran Pontiac-powered Funny Cars in this period with Ram Air V heads on 428 and 455 blocks. They were supercharged and injected engines with and stiff nitro/methanol fuel blends. They soldiered on with Pontiacs, as they had become synonymous with the brand. As parts dried up, even guys such as Arnie Beswick were forced to use Hemis to compete later in their careers.

It was the same in the new NHRA Pro Stock ranks. While Beswick campaigned the *Righteous Judge* in Pro Stock, it was never a significant player in the class, even with 428 and 455 blocks and Ram Air V heads. The class heavily favored big-block Chevy and Chrysler Hemi cars. Mopar won championships the first two years: 1970's crown went to Ronnie Sox in the Sox & Martin Hemi 'Cuda, and 1971's crown went to Mike Fons in the *Nationwise* Rod Shop Hemi Challenger.

*Arnie Beswick's 1968 GTO Funny Car was a full custom build with a chassis by Romeo Palamides and a one-piece fiberglass body by Fiber Glass Ltd. It suffered some early teething problems with handling, and the front and rear suspension was revised. It is shown at Cecil County Dragway. (Photo Courtesy Clinton Wright)*

*Lew Arrington's* Brutus *Funny Car races against Malcolm Durham's* Strip Blazer *Camaro at the 1968 Super Stock Magazine Nationals at New York National Speedway in Moriches, Long Island, New York. (Photo Courtesy Clinton Wright)*

*Lew Arrington's* Brutus *1968 Firebird Funny Car is shown in the pits with the body raised. It featured a Logghe chassis, and Fiberglass Trends bodywork, and metalwork by Al Bergler. Power came from a blown and injected Chrysler Hemi. (Photo Courtesy Clinton Wright)*

*Lew Arrington's* Brutus *competes at Cecil County Dragway. (Photo Courtesy Clinton Wright)*

By 1972, the rules had been expanded to allow racers to develop smaller-displacement engine combinations in compact-car bodies. This gave rise to cars such as the revolutionary 1972 Vega of Bill "Grumpy" Jenkins. He won the title that year and proved the value of a dual-quad 331 Chevy in a Vega. This virtually neutered Mopar, which joined Pontiac on the "we can't keep up" list.

In 1973, Canadian Bert Straus built a 350-ci Pontiac Astre, which was a badge-engineered Chevy Vega that was not available in the US. It was essentially a de-stroked version of the 400 engine and featured Ram Air V heads with the exhaust-port exits cut off for a less restrictive flow. It was an extremely well-engineered combination, but it was hampered by parts availability and ultimately was never a serious threat. However, it did show a lot of promise. It ran for a few seasons before Straus moved on to more successful options.

*In this rare photo, Lew Arrington's Brutus Funny Car competes against Al Graeber in the Graeber Dodge Tickle Me Pink Funny Car at Cecil County Dragway. (Photo Courtesy Clinton Wright)*

*Gene Conway's 1968 Proud Bird Firebird Funny Car is shown at Lions Drag Strip in Los Angeles, California. It used a Fiberglass Trends body and was powered by a big-block Chevy. Conway competed with C2 Corvette roadster Funny Cars in the 1970s. (Photo Courtesy Clinton Wright)*

*Lew Arrington's Brutus Firebird Funny Car is shown in the pits at York US 30 Drag-O-Way in York, Pennsylvania. (Photo Courtesy Clinton Wright)*

*In the 1960s and 1970, "Flash" Gordon Mineo ran a series of Firebird-bodied Funny Cars that were powered by blown big-block Chevys. He continued racing Funny Cars into the 1990s. This is the 1967 Superbird, which was his first Firebird Funny Car. Sadly, Mineo was killed in a boating accident in 2006. (Photo Courtesy Clinton Wright)*

The final Knafel Pontiac Tin Indian was a 1971 Formula 400 Firebird that was prepped by Arlen Vanke and driven by Norm Tanner. It competed in the AHRA's Grand Touring (GT) class, which was a heads-up class similar to NHRA Super Stock. The team featured Gene Dunlap as crew chief. The wild, multi-colored paint scheme was applied by Greg Pussehl, who was known as "Greg of Akron." Firestone sponsored the team and developed a special 9-inch slick for this car. With more than 525 hp, the Firebird ran a best ET of 11.38 at 119 mph. (Photo Courtesy Knafel Family Archives)

Canadian Bert Straus ran a Pontiac Astre in the early days of Pro Stock. Power came from a de-stroked Pontiac Ram Air V that displaced 350 ci. Parts availability became a problem, and the car was only used to compete for a few seasons. (Photo Courtesy Jim Luikens)

The late Warren Young campaigned his 1971 Quiet Gent 455 H.O. T-37 in the SS/JA class from 1971 to 1978. The car was 1 of only 15 1971 T-37 two-door hardtops that were built with a 455 H.O. engine and Turbo 400 automatic transmission. It was originally delivered to Crown Pontiac in St. Petersburg, Florida. It has been restored to factory-original condition by its current owner, Kevin Guido of Clearwater, Florida. (Photo Courtesy Kevin Guido)

The round-port 455 H.O. was available only for the 1971 and 1972 model years, and it replaced the Ram Air IV. The combination of increased displacement, lower compression, and a milder cam made for a docile-yet-powerful engine that performed well on the street and in the NHRA's Stock and Super Stock classes. Depending on the installation, the 455 H.O. was available with or without Ram Air. The 455 H.O. in this photo, which is in Kevin Guido's 1971 T-37, uses a dual-snorkel air cleaner.

*The* **Quiet Gent** *is shown in its restored condition.*

### The 1971 455 H.O. Debuts

With the impending emissions regulations that were part of the 1970 Clean Air Act, Pontiac engineers knew that the days of high compression and the high-octane fuels that it required were over. Not only that, but also the onslaught of rising insurance premiums and the growing cries of safety advocates who were calling for Detroit to become more corporately responsible meant that if Pontiac was going to keep building high-performance cars, the game plan had to change. The Ram Air IV had to be replaced with something that was more suited for the changing times.

Pontiac released a 455 4-barrel V-8 in 1970 as the top engine option for full-size cars that replaced the previous 428 engine. At the same time, it quietly added it to the GTO lineup. With the weights of the General Motors A-body cars now clearing 2 tons in some cases, GM's corporate office allowed the largest engines that each division built to go into their A-Body lines. This meant that the Chevelle could have the new 454, and Buick and Oldsmobile could join Pontiac and put their own 455s in their intermediates. It made for a good match for a heavily optioned car with highway gearing.

For 1971, Pontiac lowered the compression ratios of all of its engines to below 8.5:1. To compensate for the potential loss of performance, the 400 Ram Air IV was replaced with a high-performance version of the 455, which was known as the 455 H.O. (option code LS5). It borrowed heavily from the Ram Air IV but was more docile and made for a better street-performance engine. It stressed low-end torque over high-end horsepower. When coupled with more sedate gearing in the 3.23–3.55

range, it offered performance that was on par with the Ram Air IV and was able to do so on 87-octane fuel.

Starting with a four-bolt main block, the 455 H.O. used standard cast rods and pistons with a nodular-iron crankshaft with rolled fillets for additional strength. The cylinder heads were a new version of the Ram Air IV castings that used larger 107-cc combustion chambers that worked out to an advertised 8.4:1 compression ratio. Identified by casting number 197, the intake valve sizes remained at 2.11 inches and the exhaust valves remained at 1.77 inches. The valves were actuated by the tried-and-true 9779068 camshaft that was previously used in a variety of Pontiac engines. It featured 288/302 degrees of advertised duration and a 0.407-inch lift when teamed with the standard 1.5:1 rocker arms.

This engine took the Ram Air IV's two-plane, high-rise intake manifold with the removable cast-iron crossover. It was topped off with a special version of the Rochester Quadrajet. This carburetor was a one-year-only version that featured higher-flowing primary barrels that increased the flow from 750 to about 830 cfm. The exhaust system also featured the Ram Air IV's streamlined cast-iron exhaust manifolds.

The 455 H.O. was rated at 335 hp at 4,800 rpm with 480 ft-lbs of torque at 3,600 rpm. It was rated by the Society of Automotive Engineers (SAE) Net system at 305 hp at 4,400 rpm with 410 ft-lbs of torque at 3,200 rpm.

The engine was standard equipment on the 1971 Trans Am and GTO Judge and was available as optional equipment in the Firebird Formula and GTO as well as the entire A-Body line. This wide availability made for some very interesting combinations, from stripped-down drag-oriented T-37s to sleeper chrome-bumpered LeMans

Sports to GT-37s. LeMans Sports and wagons with the T-41 GTO nose option essentially made the car a GTO without the insurance premium that was attached with the GTO nameplate. Although the engine was available with either Ram Air or a dual-snorkel air cleaner (depending on bodystyle and options ordered), the engine's power rating didn't change.

The M-13 3-speed transmission was standard on the 455 H.O. engine only when it was ordered in a Firebird Formula or A-Body car. The Trans Am came with only a Muncie M-22 4-speed or an M40 transmission. The Turbo 400 automatic transmission was available in the other bodystyles and came with a General Motors 12-bolt rear end instead of the normal 10-bolt. The added torque output necessitated the larger rear end.

## Revisions for 1972

The 455 H.O. returned for a second year of production, which was its last. The cylinder head received some subtle changes that were intended to increase low-lift airflow with a very minor decrease in higher-lift airflow to increase bottom-end torque. The heads were casting number 7F6 and retained most of the features that were found in the previous 197s, including the 2.11/1.77-inch valve sizes and 8.3:1 advertised compression ratio. The two-plane aluminum intake was modified a bit with slightly smaller secondary passages that were intended to increase mixture velocity. The Rochester Quadrajet was revised, and overall flow was reduced to 750 cfm. The changes resulted in a 5-hp decrease in the power output, which was rated at an even 300 hp (net) at 4,000 rpm with 5 additional ft-lbs of torque (now 415) at 3,200 rpm. Overall real-world performance was essentially unchanged from 1971.

The availability of the 455 H.O. was revised somewhat. While it was still standard in the Trans Am, the deletion of the GTO Judge midway through the 1971 model year meant that the top-level LS5 engine was optional in the Firebird Formula and the GTO, which itself was now an options package on the LeMans and not a separate series (as it had been from 1966 to 1971). The 455 H.O. required Ram Air, so it was no longer available in chrome-bumpered A-Body cars and required the T-41

nose option, which allowed the Ram Air option.

In many ways, the 455 H.O. was the right engine at the right time, but it proved to be a stopgap. It was the perfect engine to transition the prevailing wisdom away from the idea that performance was only achievable with high-compression, wild cams, and lots of RPM. The brutal torque that was available with the larger but milder 455 proved that the mindset was valid. The success that the 455 H.O. had in NHRA competition was proof that Pontiac was onto something. It was a stopgap because it was a reshuffling of existing parts with a larger combustion chamber version of the Ram Air IV head, which bought some time to finish developing the ultimate street-performance engine. The performance world would be shocked by Pontiac's next move, which was introduced for the 1973 model year.

## The 455 Super Duty

The 455 Super Duty was the final Pontiac Special Projects program. The climate at Pontiac had changed radically since DeLorean left in March 1969. While his successor, F. James McDonald was not the performance-oriented firebrand that DeLorean was, McDonald was more tolerant of the high-performance aspect of Pontiac's identity. He allowed for the release of the 1971–1972 455 H.O. that used a large-chamber version of the Ram Air IV heads along with the aluminum intake. Although it was a four-bolt block, the 455 H.O. used cast rods and a cast crankshaft, which limited the RPM range. Coupled with

*Much of the development work that the Special Projects group performed in the 1971-1972 period for the 1973-1974 455 Super Duty was done to this Herb Adams-built mule car. It featured Motor Wheel Spyder wheels with BFGoodrich Radial T/A tires, fiberglass seats, a roll bar, and many one-off features. Unfortunately, it was scrapped—even though it was intended to be a show car. (Photo Courtesy Rocky Rotella)*

*Only one production 1973 455 Super Duty Grand Am was ever built, although it was never released for retail sale. The 455 Super Duty was intended to be used in A-Body and G-body cars and are NHRA-legal builds. This car was scrapped, but the engine survived. (Photo Courtesy Rocky Rotella)*

*Only 252 LS2 455 Super Duty V-8s were installed in 1973 Trans Ams, which makes it one of the era's most sought-after muscle cars. This Cameo White Trans Am features the iconic hood bird that was designed by Norm Inouye. (Photo Courtesy Rocky Rotella)*

> **"McDONALD ENCOURAGED ADAMS AND HIS TEAM TO ABANDON THE RACE ENGINES AND BUILD A PRODUCTION ENGINE THAT WAS BASED ON THE RACE DESIGNS. THAT WAS THE START OF THE 455 SUPER DUTY PROGRAM."**

the tried-and-true 068 cam, it created a tremendous street performance engine by combining a very docile nature with brutal low- and mid-range torque. In addition, McDonald encouraged Adams and his team to abandon the race engines and build a production engine that was based on the race designs. That was the start of the 455 Super Duty program.

The 455 Super Duty program was a more serious effort than the 455 H.O. As McDonald suggested, it was an outgrowth of the earlier 303 and 366 racing programs. Development of the larger engine was initiated in 1970, which was a month or so after the 366. The idea was to take as much of the experience that they gained from their race programs and bring it to a street engine that privateer and amateur racers could use in competition.

The initial 455 Super Duty prototypes were real fire breathers. They combined Ram Air IV heads, Edelbrock P4B intakes, 800-cfm Holley carburetors, and as much as 12.5:1

*The production 455 Super Duty engine was released late in the 1973 model year after multiple production delays. Only 252 of those engines were installed in Trans Ams that year, including 72 manual-transmission cars. (Photo Courtesy Rocky Rotella)*

compression. Ratings of 600 gross hp and 600 ft-lbs of torque would have annihilated anything on the street or strip at that time, but concessions had to be made for production because no one would have approved putting a warranty on such a beast. Still, that level of power was a great place to start. Even with compression ratios under 9:1, horsepower levels were above 460, so there was still plenty of wiggle room for production.

Aside from the larger 3.25-inch main journal diameter, the 455 Super Duty block was identical to the 366 NASCAR unit. It was a beefy four-bolt main design with a reinforced lifter-gallery area and cast-in provisions for dry-sump oiling. The reason that the larger mains were used is because the request for a forged-steel crankshaft was rejected for cost reasons. A production cast crankshaft was used but featured larger rolled fillets for additional strength and durability. Although it was not optimal, it proved to be more than up to the task.

The rest of the bottom end was forged. Jeff Young worked with TRW on the piston design, which provided 8.4:1 compression when mated with the specified 111-cc combustion chamber. Special forged rods (part number 485225) were used. They were the same 6.625-inch length (center to center) and featured heavier beams than production cast rods along with larger 7/16-inch bolts.

The cylinder heads were the culmination of everything that the Pontiac Special Projects group learned and was directly related to the successful cylinder-head development with the 303 and 366 engine programs. After it moved away from the low-velocity Ram Air V head design, which only worked on larger engines and wasn't optimal, the team worked diligently to improve airflow and velocity with the production Ram Air IV heads as a starting point.

Although they retained the 2.11/1.77-inch valve sizes, the ports were designed to resemble the port design of the latest 366 design but have enough material to compensate for core shift and other production realities. Even with those relatively minor compromises, it was the best all-around performance cylinder head that Pontiac ever released for its V-8s. The intake ports were opened larger than the Ram Air IV design, provided a port area of 2.5 square inches, and necessitated the need for pushrod tubes to be installed, as the port cut into that area. As with the intake port, the exhaust ports were developed from race experience and flow bench testing data. They were complemented by high-flow, streamlined cast-iron exhaust manifolds.

*The 455 Super Duty was available in the Firebird Formula. When equipped, the fiberglass twin-scoop hood was replaced with a Trans Am shaker hood. Only 43 of them were built, including 10 with a manual transmission.*

*The 455 Super Duty returned for 1974 in a restyled F-Body that complied with federal bumper impact standards. Although the final year saw higher production numbers, they were limited. Trans Am installations totaled 943 units with 212 4-speeds.*

The induction system was originally going to be an improved version of the Edelbrock P4B intake with an 800-cfm Holley carburetor, but plans changed when Edelbrock's improvements resulted in smaller ports and reduced performance. This setback resulted in going back to an improved version of the Rochester Quadrajet carburetor and an aluminum Ram Air IV–style intake. Production and cost considerations ditched the aluminum intake. The manifold being cast iron added about 20 hp but didn't hurt performance.

### Reaching Production

The engine that was eventually released for production was compromised by managerial resistance, cost considerations, and emissions compliance. The 455 Super Duty was caught up in a larger scandal involving the US Environmental Protection Agency (EPA) and General Motors.

Initially, the 455 Super Duty was going to have the same camshaft specifications as the Ram Air IV, with 308/320 degrees of advertised dura-

tion and 0.470-inch lift with 1.5:1 rockers. The only difference is that the K cam had a smaller distributor drive gear to control spark scatter. That plan was thwarted after the EPA found out that the exhaust gas recirculation (EGR) valves that Pontiac and Oldsmobile were using

*The 455 Super Duty was often ordered with air conditioning, which was not normally seen on a performance car. However, it was docile enough to tolerate the numerical lower gears that were needed to prevent over-revving the A/C compressor. The A/C option was only available with cars that had an automatic transmission.*

*The 455 Super Duty engines featured this specific instructional decal that outlines Pontiac's recommended oil type.*

new codes and painted a darker shade of blue. This revised design came after the EPA made the threat to shut down the assembly lines until the problem was corrected. Having recently survived a months-long strike, General Motors quickly did what was necessary to avoid that harsh punishment.

To pass emissions standards, the 455 Super Duty was fitted with a version of the Ram Air III camshaft with 301/313 degrees of advertised duration and 0.407-inch lift. It had a smaller distributor drive gear than the previous K grind that it replaced. The big cam passed emissions, but Pontiac wanted a larger margin of error, so the Y cam was installed anyway.

would only work for a short period of time—long enough to pass the EPA testing but no more.

After that, a second-generation design was implemented that stayed operational. Engines were assigned

Although Pontiac initially rated the engine at 310 hp at 4,000 rpm with 390 ft-lbs of torque at 3,600 rpm, that

*The 455 Super Duty was installed in only 58 1974 Formula Firebirds. No breakdown on transmissions was available.*

rating was with the K cam and was never released for production. The engine that finally made it to production was rated at 290 hp at 4,000 rpm with 395 ft-lbs of torque at 3,200 rpm. The 310-hp rating is found in many magazines and other published material, but that has only confused enthusiasts. Some think that the 1973 engine was the 310-hp version and the 1974 was the 290-hp version, but that is not the case. All production 455 Super Duty V-8s were the lower-horsepower version due to the cam specification change before the car's release.

## The Martin J. Caserio Experience

As with DeLorean before him, F. James McDonald was promoted to the general manager position at Chevrolet, and once again replaced DeLorean. McDonald's successor at Pontiac, Martin J. Caserio, came from GMC and was not a performance enthusiast in any sense of the word. In fact, he was opposed to any low-production vehicle or program. He saw it as an unnecessary expense and not worth the effort.

The truth was that Pontiac benefitted greatly from limited-edition vehicles. They drew floor traffic at dealerships. Even if the customers weren't going to buy a specialty Pontiac, they often left with a more pedestrian LeMans or Catalina. Even though Pontiac only built 697 Trans Ams and 6,833 GTO Judges in 1969, they created many promotional opportunities for Pontiac. Magazine and television coverage, advertising, and pace cars for racetracks were just a few ways for Pontiac to work its way into American culture. Although this halo effect was difficult to track from an accounting standpoint, it was a very effective marketing tool, especially for a performance-oriented carmaker such as Pontiac. All of this was lost on Caserio.

In an August 2023 interview, Herb Adams recalled the end of his career as a Pontiac engineer and provided details about that dark time:

"What really happened was that Pontiac's reputation and sales were based on performance," Adams said. "That was the difference between an Olds and a Pontiac. You would get better performance. That was the reason

*Martin J. Caserio replaced F. James McDonald as Pontiac's general manager. He was not interested in performance cars, which was Pontiac's niche in the market. He is seen here when he was GM's vice president, which was about seven years after he was Pontiac's general manager.*

that we were doing the 366 race engine and the 455 Super Duty. It turned out that we had support for that engine from Pontiac Motor Division, the guys in the engine plant. We had Eric Dahlquist, our public relations guy on the West Coast. We had 600 orders for the engine before it was even released because he knew all the magazine guys. He'd show them a demo car, and they got the word out. I even got a guy in the finance department to join our team. It wasn't anything official, but it was a group of people who wanted to do a better job.

"It cost too much to do a Super Duty because we wanted it all hand-assembled. The way that they structure their price, you couldn't do that, so he [the finance guy] got involved. We had this team together and we were all working on the idea of getting a better engine because Pontiac needed one at that point. They were kind of at a shallow point.

"So, we're cooking pretty good. Like I say, we sold 600 engines, and the plant guy let us know he was going to buy the parts, get them together, and get things going.

"Nobody introduced [Caserio] or anything. I got a call on Thursday. They said to show up at the manager's

*In 1975, Alex Mair took over as Pontiac's general manager and was more comfortable with performance cars than Caserio. He helped Pontiac's lagging sales numbers and bolstered the Trans Am into an all-time bestselling performance car. He is seen here with the 1976 Grand Prix that broke the all-time production record for that model.*

*The Clegg family still runs the same 1973 Super Duty Formula that John Clegg bought new. He is seen here with the car at Texas Motorplex in Ennis, Texas. His son J. B. drives it now. (Photo Courtesy John Clegg)*

*One of Pontiac's greatest ideas that never happened was this 1971 Ventura built by the Pontiac Special Projects group. Under the hood was a 455 H.O. V-8 and an automatic transmission. The chassis featured Trans Am componentry, and it handled as well as it accelerated. Although this car would have turned the muscle-car world upside down, it would have seriously threatened the Corvette's "top performer" status. Therefore, it was rejected for production. (Photo Courtesy Martyn L. Schorr)*

office at 4 p.m. tomorrow. Okay. So, I arrived, and there was about seven or eight guys sitting around a table in his office. Big time, okay? No introductions of any kind as to who he is and who they are. Big time, right?

"He goes around the table and asks us, 'What do you know about this engine, this 455 Super Duty?'

"Each guy told him what he knew, and he went around the table. Details came out, including that there were 600 orders for it already. He was standing behind me and I still didn't know who he was—didn't even know what he looked like.

"So, I'm the last guy, and it's my turn to say something, and, of course, I was a smart ass. 'If you got parts for 600 engines and 600 orders, why don't you build them and sell them?'

"He was still standing behind me, so I couldn't see him, and he said, 'We're not going to do that!'

"I said, 'Well, why not?'

"I'm being a smart-ass with the general manager, and I'm the last guy who he wants around.

"'Pontiac is just going to build good cars, and we're not going to do anymore high performance,' he said.

"'Okay, you're the boss,' I replied.

"So, that was Friday at 4 p.m. Monday morning came, and around 9 a.m., my boss Russ Gee called me into his office and said that I have been asked to leave Pontiac. What? It was because of the meeting. [Caserio] didn't want a smart-ass like me to coordinate work in the corporation. I thought that they really couldn't fire me because I didn't do anything wrong.

"But then, I thought, 'What the hell? Why work somewhere where you're not appreciated?' I put in my resignation that day, and Tom Nell put his in the next day. Two other guys in engineering quit, and then I think it was two or three months later that Jeff Young quit. Bill Collins quit, and about seven other guys in engineering quit. They were all very good engineers, and they all came to the same conclusion: Where the hell is Pontiac going with this sort of leadership?

"After things calmed down, Alex Mair took over Pontiac. He was a car guy, and he brought it back. Caserio's sales were a little more than half of what DeLorean's were. Typically, if you look at the history, guys would last four or five years as head of Pontiac: DeLorean, Estes, Knudsen—all of those guys. Caserio lasted just two years before he was taken out. Even the corporation could see

that he was ruining the company. Alex Mair brought things back—not to the sales level that DeLorean did, but he did turn it around."

As it turned out, Pontiac released the 455 Super Duty amid pressure from the media, dealerships that had already taken orders, and some NHRA racers. In one of his trips to Detroit at that time, Truman Fields visited Pontiac headquarters as a guest of the Pontiac Special Projects group in 1972. He managed to strike up a conversation with Caserio while he was there.

"Caserio said to me, 'We're out of racing, and the 455 Super Duty isn't going to reach production.'" Fields said. "I said to him that I personally knew of nine cars that were ordered, and if they weren't produced, there would be lawsuits."

> **"CASERIO SAID TO ME, 'WE'RE OUT OF RACING, AND THE 455 SUPER DUTY ISN'T GOING TO REACH PRODUCTION.'"**

## The 455 Super Duty and Troubles with the NHRA

Truman Fields, who enjoyed a successful tenure in NHRA competition, relayed a fascinating story about what it was like for racers trying to run a 455 Super Duty in NHRA Stock and Super Stock Competition. He passed on purchasing one for himself, as he ran his 1968 Firebirds and the 1972 455 H.O. GTO that he received from Pontiac.

"John Clegg is a friend of mine," Fields said. "He went ahead and ordered a 1973 455 Super Duty Firebird Formula to run in Stock. He had all sorts of problems early on. The engine that reached production was not the same as the initial set of specifications that Pontiac sent to the NHRA. John's car was declared to be illegal because of the discrepancies."

Clegg confirmed the story in a September 2023 phone interview.

"We purchased the car in June, I believe, and had prepped it for Indy in D/Stock," Clegg said. "It was pretty much stock at that point, although we added a set of headers and some other legal modifications. We took it to Indy and won our class and were subject to a teardown. This was the first time that a cylinder head was ever taken off the engine, and we were told that [the car] was illegal because it had an illegal three-angle valve job on it because Pontiacs didn't have that from the factory. Even though we told them the car had never been taken

*The 1974 GTO was one of the most successful platforms for NHRA Stock and Super Stock race cars. Bill Rink's 1974 car was dominant in the M/SA and SS/LA classes, and it was campaigned in several different colors. This is how it looked in the 1990s. Sadly, Bill passed away in 2022.*

*The secret to Bill Rink's success was the 350 Pontiac engine, which was built by Parsons & Myers Racing Engines in Dayton, Ohio. Originally rated at 200 hp, this low-compression 350 engine produced twice that much power and was as reliable as it was consistent.*

apart before, [NHRA Technical Director] Bill 'Farmer' Dismuke threatened to throw us out and cancel our win.

"I'm not sure how we managed to get through to Pontiac Engineering. I think it was a collect call to engineering, and we got Tom Nell on the phone. He confirmed to Dismuke that the engine was new, the three-angle valve job was factory, and he would send supporting data out to confirm everything. They approved the car, and we took the win."

Amazingly, more than 50 years later, the Cleggs are still running that same car in the SS/H class, with John's son J. B. driving. It runs consistent 9.50s in the quarter mile and is one of the fastest original Pontiac Super Stockers in the country.

## The End of the Muscle Car

Pontiac is often considered to be the creator of the muscle car and its last stalwart. These Super Duty Pontiacs are thought of as the bookends for the muscle-car era. The GTO was neutered to 350 ci, but it was available with a 4-speed transmission, 4-barrel carburetor, and Safe-T-Track rear end. The icing on the cake was the first shaker hood to ever be offered on the GTO.

One of the most successful Pontiac combinations of NHRA Stock and Super Stock is the much-maligned 1974 GTO that was campaigned by Bill Rink, which featured a 350 4-barrel rated at 200 hp. The late Rink was able to get his car into the 10s and was competitive into the early 2020s. To be competitive, the general rule is to be making twice the rated horsepower amount. Rink had that more than covered.

The GTO nameplate was gone from 1975 to 2004, and it returned as a two-door midsize car with LS power.

## The End of the Road for Special Projects

The Pontiac Special Projects group was essentially dead after Herb Adams and the others left. It was officially closed down by Chief Engineer Steve Malone in October 1972. The official reason was to concentrate on meeting emissions standards, but Caserio's hand was definitely part of the equation. Pontiac soldiered on and produced a total of 252 Super Duty 455 Trans Ams and 43 Super Duty 455 Firebird Formulas. That number increased up to 943 Trans Ams and 58 Formulas in 1974. Then, the door on round-port Pontiac performance engines closed forever.

From that point forward, the traditional Pontiac V-8 and the cars in which they came were not a major force in drag racing beyond the Sportsman ranks. Although, in that capacity, they found great success in the Stock, Super Stock, and GT classes. That success continues to this day with racers such as Stacy McCarty in his 428-powered 2002 Grand Am, Rick Unterseh in his 301 Turbo–powered Firebird Formula, and J. B. Clegg in the Clegg family's original 1973 Super Duty 455 Formula. They are still carrying the torch for Pontiac at regional and national events and setting records in the process.

# INDEX

**A**

Abraham, Bill, 42, 73, 111, 126
Adams, Herb, 6, 106, 130, 148-149, 153, 157
Alcoa, Kenny, 49
Anderson Pontiac, 48, 59, 64, 70, 72-73, 82, 126-127
Arrington, Lew, 4, 101, 143-145
Autronic Eye, 22

**B**

Benko, Tim, 6, 70
Bennett, Don, 48, 52
Beswick, Arnie, 5-7, 25, 27-28, 33-34, 49, 53, 64-66, 70, 72, 80-82, 100, 102, 104, 106, 127-128, 133-134, 143
Bonner, Phil, 44
Bonneville, 14, 17, 21-23, 25, 31, 85, 109, 133
Brannan, Dick, 44, 58
Broadhead, Ron, 73

**C**

Cadillac, 9-10, 13, 59, 79, 83
*Car and Driver*, 31, 35, 88, 90-91, 135
*Car Life*, 31
Caserio, Martin J., 153, 155, 157
Catalina, 25, 27-43, 46, 48-53, 55, 59-65, 70, 73-75, 78, 80, 82-83, 87-88, 90, 94-95, 100, 106, 108-109, 112-115, 124, 126, 153
Cecil County Dragway, 103, 126, 134, 143-145
Chieftain, 12, 23-25
Clegg, John, 6, 154-155, 157
Collins, Bill, 40, 67, 69, 130, 155
Colson, Milt, 26
Conway, Gene, 145
Cox, Carol, 47, 52-53, 73
Cox, Lloyd, 4, 31, 33, 37, 44, 46-47, 52-53, 73
Critchfield, Robert M., 12, 15, 18-19

**D**

Dartmouth University, 18
Davis, Ken, 31, 42, 91, 100
Davisson, Frank, 49, 73-74
Delaney, George, 14, 20
DeLorean, George, 6, 41, 64-65, 72, 130
DeLorean, John Z., 20, 40, 76, 83, 99, 118, 122-123, 130, 142

DeSoto, 21
Detroit Diesel, 11, 18
Detroit Dragway, 30-31, 43
Dismuke, Bill "Farmer," 34, 157
Durant, William C. "Billy," 9

**E**

Economaki, Chris, 78
Estes, Elliott M. "Pete," 20-21, 24, 40, 76, 83, 155
Exner, Virgil, 26

**F**

Fields, Truman, 6, 117, 155
Firebird, 4, 99-100, 103, 110, 113-114, 116-122, 125, 128-131, 133, 135-137, 139-140, 142, 144-148, 150, 155, 157
Force, Brittany, 47
Fortier, Bert, 37, 125
Forward Look, 26
Foyt, A. J., 28, 55, 78
France, Bill, 22
Frank, Mark, 14

**G**

Garber Pontiac, 124, 126, 128
Gay Pontiac, 41-42, 71-72, 80, 83, 100-101, 104, 113, 124-125
Gay, Don, 49, 71, 73, 100-101, 125, 143
Gee, Russ, 40, 155
General Motors, 7-11, 13, 15-16, 18-20, 26, 28-29, 52, 54, 63, 74-82, 84, 86, 97-100, 104-105, 107, 112, 118, 122, 129-130, 134, 141-143, 147-148, 151-152
Gogola, Vic, 35
Goodwin Pontiac, 49
Goldsmith, Paul, 28, 71-72, 78-79
Grand Prix, 41, 43, 45, 54, 70-74, 86, 90, 93, 95, 109, 113, 153
GTO, 5, 8, 45, 80-95, 97-98, 100-106, 108, 110-112, 114-115, 117-119, 121-123, 125-133, 135-136, 138, 140-143, 147-148, 153, 155-157

**H**

Hardt, Ralph, 32, 48, 53
Hart, C. J. "Pappy," 47, 52
Hershey, Franklin Q., 10, 19
*Hi-Performance Cars*, 80
Hodges Pontiac, 59, 64, 72

*Hot Rod*, 7, 16-17, 31, 46, 52, 91
Howell, Jim, 29, 31
Huffman, Mike, 6, 41, 43, 58-67, 74
Huntington, Roger, 56, 59, 63, 72
Hurst, George, 38-39, 45, 98
Hurst-Campbell, 38, 45
Hutchinson, Roland "Bob," 14
Hydra-matic, 13, 15-17

**I**

Irwindale Raceway, 104

**J**

Jackson Sports Arena, 51
Jenkins, Bill "Grumpy," 43, 69, 144
Jenkins, David Abbot "Ab," 17
Jesse, Dick, 27, 30-31, 38, 44, 46, 48, 69, 81, 95, 104
Johns, Bobby, 28, 55
Judge, 121-124, 126, 128-129, 132-134, 136, 141-143, 147-148

**K**

Kelley, Oliver K., 20, 64
Kennedy, Robert F., 8, 76, 79
Kettering, Charles "Boss," 14, 20
King, Monk, 64
Knafel Pontiac, 42, 113, 126-128, 146
Knox, Frank, 11
Knudsen, Bob, 64
Knudsen, Semon "Bunkie," 5, 7, 18-22, 24-25, 29-30, 36, 40, 42, 64, 76, 83, 155
Knudsen, William "Big Bill," 18

**L**

Lane-Moak Pontiac, 43, 50
LaSalle, 10-11
Leach, Clayton B., 14-15
LeMans, 46, 66-73, 78-80, 82, 84, 86, 90, 93, 96, 100, 102, 111, 138, 147-148, 153
Lenz, Arnold B., 15, 19
Leonard, Larry, 48, 53, 73
Liberman, "Jungle" Jim, 101
Lindamood, Roger, 58
Lions Drag Strip, 47-48, 145
*Los Angeles Times*, 47

**M**

Mair, Alex, 153, 155
Marquette, 10
Mauro, Johnny, 74

Maseles, Howard, 29, 33, 40, 61–63, 65, 82, 112
Massachusetts Institute of Technology, 18, 130
Martin, Buddy, 28, 43
McDonald, F. James, 148, 153
McKellar, Malcolm R. "Mac," 6, 13–14, 20, 26–27, 33–34, 40, 83–86, 105, 108, 116, 118–119, 133
McNamara, Robert S., 75–76
Mattison, Jim, 6, 46
Max Wedge, 44–45, 54, 57–58, 67
Meyer, Louie, 17, 25
Milner Pontiac, 64
Mino, Jim, 6, 116, 118
Morgan, Bruce, 38–39
Motorama, 14, 17, 19
*MotorTrend*, 17, 41, 117
Muldowney, Shirley, 47
Myrtle Motors, 43, 112–113, 124–125

N
Nader, Ralph, 98, 104–105, 141
NASCAR, 7, 17, 22, 24, 26–30, 34, 37, 40–41, 44, 48, 53–55, 74, 76, 83, 105, 111, 130, 133, 150
NHRA, 7, 26–27, 29–32, 34, 37–40, 44–50, 52–54, 56–57, 59, 63–64, 68, 73–74, 78, 83, 98–99, 111–112, 126, 139, 143, 146, 148, 155–157
Nichels, Ray, 25, 28, 46, 48, 50, 53, 62, 68, 70, 72, 78, 80
Nicholson, "Dyno" Don, 34–36, 39, 43, 57, 82

O
Oakland, 9–10, 13
Oldsmobile, 9–10, 12–14, 19–21, 24–25, 79, 83–84, 91, 134, 141, 147, 151
Owens, Cotton, 28

P
Pace, Ray, 73, 153
Packer Pontiac, 6, 31, 33, 40–41, 50, 59–64, 112, 124
Packer Jr., Bill, 6, 31, 33, 40–41, 50, 59–64, 112, 124
Parks, Wally, 7, 39
Pikes Peak, 27, 30, 74
Politzer, John, 97
*Popular Hot Rodding*, 31, 121
Porter, Bob, 46, 76
Powerglide, 16, 69
Proffitt, Hayden, 4, 6, 33–35, 43–44, 46, 49, 52, 57, 112
Pruett, Leah, 47

R
Race Hemi, 7
Racing ban, 25, 30, 36, 40, 52, 56, 61–65, 69, 74–75, 77–78, 81–83, 95, 102, 107, 124, 130
Ramsey, Harold, 49, 64
Rarden, Stan, 6, 56, 72
Ray Faro Pontiac, 128, 132
Repsol, Scott, 106
Rink, Bill, 156–157
*Road & Track*, 31
Roberts, George, 14
Roberts, Dan, 53, 73
Roberts, Glenn "Fireball," 29, 55, 74
Roche, James, 98
Rochester, 17, 22, 24, 41, 109, 118, 121, 128–129, 140, 147–148, 151
Romano, Nunzi, 6, 80
Ronda, Gas, 44
Royal Pontiac, 28, 30–31, 35–36, 38–39, 41–42, 44, 46, 48, 59, 63–66, 68–69, 72–73, 80, 88–89, 91, 97–98, 112–113, 121, 124–125, 133, 142
Royster, Don, 37

S
Safe-T-Track, 25, 38, 46, 114, 121, 157
Sanders, Frank, 43
Sasse, Bill, 48, 53
SCCA, 106, 122–123, 130, 133
Schafer, Ed, 74
Schornack, Milt, 88–89, 97, 124, 142
Schorr, Martyn L., 6, 57, 111–113, 125, 154
Seaton, Louis G., 28–29
Seaton, Pete, 28–31, 33, 64–65
Shahan, Shirley, 47
Sharp, Lewis, 6, 49–52, 80
Shultheis, Jim, 48–49
Sloan, Alfred P., 9
Smith, Jack, 28
Sox, Ronnie, 28, 52, 82, 143
Star Chief, 12, 15, 17
Strato-Streak, 17, 19–20, 30
Strickler, Dave, 36, 43, 57, 64, 69, 73–74
Sturm, Tom, 45
Super Duty, 4–6, 13, 21, 26–35, 37–56, 59–60, 63, 66–78, 80–84, 89–91, 94–95, 99–103, 105–108, 111–112, 124–127, 130–131, 133, 148–155, 157
Super Judge, 133–134
*Super Stock & Drag Illustrated*, 31
Sutton, Len, 28, 55
Swiatek, Larry, 6, 72, 106–107

T
Tanner, Norm, 126–128, 146
Tempest, 4, 24, 26, 31, 37, 44, 46, 52–53, 66, 68–73, 75, 80, 82–84, 90, 100, 106, 126–127, 138, 140–141
Thompson, Mickey, 4, 28, 31, 33–35, 37–38, 41, 44, 46–49, 52, 64, 66, 68–70, 72, 80–82, 102, 112
Transcontinental Safari, 21
Tri-Power, 20–27, 31–33, 41, 45, 56, 85–89, 92–94, 96–98, 105, 108–110, 140
Tyree, Jess, 7, 48–49, 52, 69–70, 81, 124–125

U
Ultramatic, 20
Union Park Pontiac, 28, 64, 68, 72, 75, 124
US 30 Drag-O-Way, 28, 49, 145

V
Vanke, "Akron" Arlen, 48, 53, 59, 64, 70, 72–73, 81, 111–112, 126, 146
Ventura, 7, 32–33, 35, 38, 47, 52–53, 73–74, 154
Voight, Fritz, 46

W
Wangers, Jim, 6, 21, 27–31, 35–36, 38–39, 49, 64, 73–74, 78, 90–91, 97–98
Weatherly, Joe, 28, 55, 74–75
Whipkey, Paul, 49
Wide Track, 5, 26–28, 37, 45, 78, 86, 95
Windeler, Edmund L., 14
Wood, Gary, 6
Wood, Charlene, 4, 6
World War II, 11, 18

X
X-chassis, 24

Y
Young, Warren, 4, 9, 18–20, 61, 124, 130, 146, 150, 155
Yunick, Smokey, 25, 28–29, 35, 76, 130

Z
Zink, John, 25

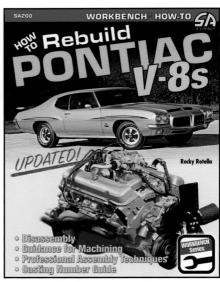
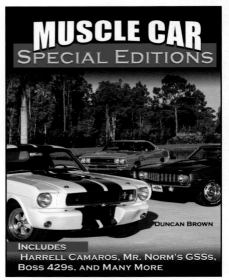
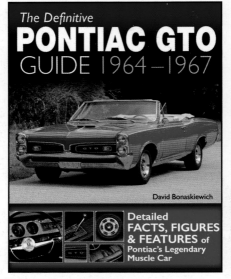

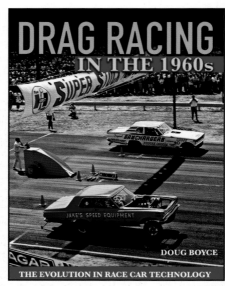